Years of Rage

THE AMERICAN WAYS SERIES
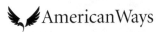
General Editor: John David Smith
Charles H. Stone Distinguished Professor of American History
University of North Carolina at Charlotte

From the long arcs of America's history, to the short time frames that convey larger stories, American Ways provides concise, accessible topical histories informed by the latest scholarship and written by scholars who are both leading experts in their fields and polished writers.

Books in the series provide general readers and students with compelling introductions to America's social, cultural, political, and economic history, underscoring questions of class, gender, racial, and sectional diversity and inclusivity. The titles suggest the multiple ways that the past informs the present and shapes the future in often unforeseen ways.

CURRENT TITLES IN THE SERIES

How America Eats: A Social History of U.S. Food and Culture, by Jennifer Jensen Wallach

Popular Justice: A History of Lynching in America, by Manfred Berg

Bounds of Their Habitation: Race and Religion in American History, by Paul Harvey

National Pastime: U.S. History through Baseball, by Martin C. Babicz and Thomas W. Zeiler

Wartime America: The World War II Home Front, Second Edition, by John W. Jeffries

Enemies of the State: The Radical Right in America from FDR to Trump, by D. J. Mulloy

Hard Times: Economic Depressions in America, by Richard Striner

We the People: The 500-Year Battle Over Who Is American, by Ben Railton

Litigation Nation: How Lawsuits Represent Changing Ideas of Self, Business Practices, and Right and Wrong in American History, by Peter Charles Hoffer

Of Thee I Sing: The Contested History of American Patriotism, by Ben Railton

Years of Rage: White Supremacy in the United States from the Klan to the Alt-Right, by D. J. Mulloy

Germans in America: A Concise History, by Walter D. Kamphoefner

American Agriculture: From Farm Families to Agribusiness, by Mark V. Wetherington

American Exceptionalism, by Volker Depkat

YEARS OF RAGE

*White Supremacy in the United States
from the Klan to the Alt-Right*

D. J. Mulloy

ROWMAN & LITTLEFIELD
Lanham • Boulder • New York • London

Published by Rowman & Littlefield
An imprint of The Rowman & Littlefield Publishing Group, Inc.
4501 Forbes Boulevard, Suite 200, Lanham, Maryland 20706
www.rowman.com

86-90 Paul Street, London EC2A 4NE

British Library Cataloguing in Publication Information Available

Library of Congress Cataloging-in-Publication Data

978-1-5381-2865-7 (cloth)
978-1-5381-9999-2 (paperback)
978-1-5381-2866-4 (electronic)

♾™ The paper used in this publication meets the minimum requirements of
American National Standard for Information Sciences—Permanence of Paper for
Printed Library Materials, ANSI/NISO Z39.48-1992.

To Esme with love

Contents

Look backward on your future and look forward to your past.

—Will Oldham

Acknowledgments

THIS IS MY SECOND BOOK in the American Way series. It has been a privilege once again to work with Jon Sisk, the vice president and senior executive acquisitions editor for American history at Rowman & Littlefield, and John David Smith, the general editor of the series. Thank you both for all your enthusiastic support and for all your expert advice. I would also like to thank the wonderful senior production editor Elaine McGarraugh, Benjamin Knepp, and everyone else at Rowman & Littlefield who has been involved in the production and promotion of this book. The office of the Vice-President: Academic at Wilfrid Laurier University provided me with a much-needed course release so that I could continue to work on the book while also fulfilling my administrative responsibilities as chair of the Department of History. I am grateful for the University's support of my research and for the support of all my friends and colleagues at Laurier, especially my senior administrative assistant Heather Vogel, who has made my working life easier in countless ways. I am also extremely grateful to the many scholars and activists whose work I have utilized in the course of writing *Years of Rage*. (Please see "A Note on Sources" at the book's end for a complete list of these.) I thank Yashin, Caroline, Luca, Maya, and Caitlin for helping to keep me sane during the writing process, and Ryuichi Sakamoto, Christian Fennesz, Jóhann Jóhannsson, Brian Eno, and Miles Davis for providing the musical accompaniment. Last, but certainly not least, I thank my beautiful wife, the novelist Pamela Mulloy, and my marvelous, university-bound daughter Esme for being my first readers and strongest supporters, but also, really, for just being themselves.

Introduction

ON THE NIGHT OF AUGUST 11, 2017, about 200 white supremacists paraded through the normally genteel grounds of the University of
Virginia, in Charlottesville, chanting slogans such as "Blood and Soil!,"
"White lives matter!," and "Hail Trump!," their flaming torches held
proudly aloft. The following day a 20-year-old neo-Nazi named James
Alex Fields Jr. killed 32-year-old Heather Heyer and injured dozens
more, when he drove his Dodge Challenger sports car directly into a
group of anti-racism protestors. Heyer's death was the culmination of a
series of increasingly violent confrontations that had taken place throughout the city that day as over 500 racist activists gathered in what was supposed to be a celebratory rally to "Unite the Right," the largest and most
public gathering of the racist right in the United States for a generation.

The horrific events that took place in Charlottesville in 2017 sparked
a sudden "rediscovery" of the widespread and dangerous presence of
white supremacy in the United States. Yet in truth white supremacy has
been a constant feature of American life since the nation's founding in
1776. Slavery seeded racism into the political, economic, social, and cultural institutions of the United States from the outset, and the imposition
of Jim Crow—legal segregation—in the South, in the aftermath of the
Civil War, ensured that such attitudes would continue on into the modern history of the country, where they remain deeply embedded today. In
September 2020, in a speech at the National Archives Museum in Washington, D.C., President Trump provided a telling illustration of how controversial such a view could be, though, when he took the *New York Times'*
Pulitzer Prize-winning "1619 Project" to task for supposedly attempting
to rewrite "American history to teach our children that we were founded
on the principle of oppression, not freedom." Begun in 2019, the project
was named for the year the first enslaved Africans arrived in the English
colony of Virginia—in August 1619—and was intended, the *Times* said,
to "reframe American history around the consequences of slavery and the
contributions of Black Americans." Because of this, it had become part of

the curriculum of many school boards around the country. The president dismissed it as "left-wing indoctrination."

This book is not about such structural or institutional racism however, and it does not cover the entirety of the history of the United States. Rather, it focuses on the past 100 years or so of America's past, from the rebirth of the Ku Klux Klan in 1915, through to the emergence of the so-called "alt-right"—the organizers of the Unite the Right rally in Charlottesville—in the early 2010s. It is an examination of the many and varied white supremacist groups that have operated in the United States during this time. It explores their underlying beliefs and rationalizations, their propaganda, their composition, their politics, their fears of displacement, their propensity to commit acts of violence, and their deep and unwavering sense of rage.

Many of these white supremacists do not meet the "redneck" stereotype of popular lore. In these pages are many "respectable" racists, from middle-class professionals and college professors to community pastors and decorated military veterans, alongside the seemingly damaged and deranged. In broad terms, three main approaches have been prevalent within the world of the white supremacist right since 1915. The first has emphasized mainstream political activity and has largely taken place in the open, often with significant elements of local community support, especially in the South. The second has been more violent and terroristic, an underground or vanguardist approach built on paramilitary weaponry, race war, and apocalyptic thinking. The third approach has been a separatist one, in which white supremacists have withdrawn into their own compounds, or to remote areas of the United States, in the hope of escaping the "evils" of the modern world, or to prepare for the End Times to come.

Many different groups have adopted these approaches—or variations thereof—over the past 100 years, including the Ku Klux Klan, the Silver Shirt Legion of America, the Citizens' Council movement, the National States' Rights Party, the American Nazi Party, the National Alliance, Liberty Lobby, White Aryan Resistance, the Posse Comitatus, Aryan Nations, The Order, militias, and the many disparate elements of the contemporary alt-right. Yet these racist organizations have been far from unified in their pursuit of white supremacy. On the contrary, the world of the American racist right has frequently been a fractious and divisive one, with much internal conflict and dispute on display. It is also one in which anti-Semitism has frequently been as important as anti-Black prejudice, and where a nativist hostility to immigrants is a recurring and prominent feature, along with a sustained opposition to feminism and gay rights.

I use the term white supremacist to describe the groups and individuals addressed in this book. It is not one that racists often use to describe themselves. They generally prefer less pejorative sounding terms such as "white separatist," "white nationalist," "white power," "racialist," "race realist," or, most recently, the "alt-right." Indeed, since the success of the civil rights movement in the mid-1960s, the search for a more palatable description of the racist politics of the far right has been a key part of its ongoing attempts at mainstream infiltration and rebranding. As the political scientist George Hawley points out, at the theoretical level there is a distinction to be made between white supremacists and white separatists/white nationalists, with the former wanting "the social and legal domination of whites in a multiracial society, as was the case . . . in the South during the Jim Crow era," whereas the latter believe "that races should not live together in the same country at all, even if the prevailing social structure benefits whites." But in my view, white separatists, white nationalists, white power advocates, racialists, race realists, and members of the alt-right are all still fundamentally committed to the so-called "superiority" of the "white race," and the white supremacist label is the one that best captures both this sense of superiority and the desire of hard-core racists to limit and control the lives of others.

Having made this clear, it is important to note, however, that not all white supremacists believe exactly the same thing, or act in exactly the same way. As the chapters that follow will show, whatever commonalities they share—and there are many—there are also significant differences to be found between Klansmen, neo-Nazis, Posse members, militia members, National Alliance members, and so on. Equally, the meaning of "whiteness" has not remained unchanged or uncontested throughout American history. Irish-Americans, Italian-Americans, Polish-Americans, and Jewish-Americans have all been excluded from the category at one point or another, for example. As the historian Nell Irvin Painter has written, this is because "race is an idea, not a fact." It is a social construction, and so too is racism: "the belief that races exist, and that some are better than others," as Painter describes it.

Numerous issues are raised by the long-standing presence of white supremacists in American society. Among them are important constitutional questions about freedom of speech and freedom of association, as well as more practical concerns about how best to monitor and respond to such groups. In 1977, in the case of *National Socialist Party of America v. Village of Skokie*, the U.S. Supreme Court upheld the right of an avowedly neo-Nazi organization to march through the small village of Skokie in Chicago, which was home to a large Jewish population, including many survivors of the Holocaust. Although the march was opposed by numerous Jewish defense groups, the right of the National Socialist Party to parade through the village in their militaristic uniforms emblazoned with the swastika was supported by the American Civil Liberties Union, among other civil liberties' organizations, although in the end it never actually took place. Earlier, during the 1930s and 1940s, the American Jewish Committee (AJC) had argued that rather than any kind of direct confrontation, the best way to deal with white supremacists and other extremists was through a "quarantine strategy," so as to deny them the legitimacy and the publicity they so desperately craved. Expressing its ongoing faith in the classically liberal values of toleration and persuasion, by the 1960s, as the historian Clive Webb reports, the AJC further contended that in "the long run, the most effective defense against unsound ideas is more speech and more ideas, in the certain knowledge that ultimately truth will triumph." In our own "post-truth" age of "fake news," social media, and viral memes, all these issues and questions remain as vital as ever.

The various white supremacists examined in this book also provide important insights into some of the broader developments that have occurred in American history over the past 100 years. After all, these "extremists" are just as much part of American culture and of American society as other more "acceptable" groups and organizations. They too are responding to—and to some extent are reflective of—the times in which they live, and of the major political, social, and economic events of those times: the concerns about mass immigration during the 1920s; the mobilization of the civil rights movement at the end of the Second World War; the impact of the Vietnam War and widespread nuclear anxiety during the late 1970s and early 1980s; the "farm crisis" and globalization in the post-Cold War years; and early twenty-first century issues such as the election of the nation's first African-American president and the rise of Donald Trump, for example. These matters are all considered too.

Six chapters follow this introduction.

Chapter 1 examines the Ku Klux Klan from its sudden reemergence in 1915 to its apparent demise at the end of the 1940s. It focuses especially on the 1920s, a period when the organization had as many as four million members, its politics and its racism shared by a wide swath of the American population. But it also examines several other racist groups of the time, including William Dudley Pelley's Silver Shirt Legion of America, the Black Legion, and the German-American Bund.

Chapter 2 picks up the story in the 1950s, as it considers the furious white backlash that greeted the rise of the civil rights movement in America, particularly following the Supreme Court's decision in the case of *Brown v. Board of Education of Topeka* that declared the whole southern system of racial segregation to be unconstitutional. Among the groups examined in chapter 2 are the various members of the Citizens' Council movement, the fractious and violent elements of the third Klan revival, as well as avowedly National Socialist organizations such as the American Nazi Party, led by the charismatic George Lincoln Rockwell. Other proponents of the "massive resistance" to desegregation such as J. B. Stoner, Asa Carter, and Alabama Governor George C. Wallace are also considered.

Chapters 3 and 4 both explore white supremacy in the United States from the 1970s to the 1990s. Chapter 3 examines the rise of the so-called "new" Klan led by the youthful David Duke, who would go on to have an extensive and highly controversial racist career. But it also examines other important Klan leaders such as Bill Wilkinson and Louis Beam, as well as the enormously influential figures of Willis Carto, the head of Liberty Lobby, and William Pierce, the founder of the National Alliance and author of the white supremacist novel *The Turner Diaries* (1978). The creation of a Nazi-Klan alliance is considered, as is the development of a highly effective Anti-Klan Network, composed of both local activists and national organizations such as the Anti-Defamation League and the Southern Poverty Law Center. Finally, the chapter recounts the increasing appeal of paramilitarism to white supremacists during this period, as well as the "Greensboro massacre" of 1979.

The focus of chapter 4 is on the appearance of the Posse Comitatus movement, the importance of the racist theology of Identity Christianity to many white supremacist groups, the development of several survivalist compounds such as those of the Covenant, the Sword, and the Arm of the Lord; the Christian-Patriots Defense League; and the Aryan Nations; and the so-called "revolutionary turn" of the movement, which began around 1983 and was epitomized by the bank-robbing and murderous operations of The Order, a group also known as Brüder Schweigen, or the Silent Brotherhood. The chapter concludes with a consideration of the federal government's attempts to rein in the activities of these violent racists, including the Fort Smith sedition trial of 1988, and of the important, if circumscribed role, played by women within the white power movement.

Chapter 5 examines the Oklahoma City bombing of 1995 in detail, tracing its roots to the government's raid on the home of a white supremacist and Christian Identity believer named Randy Weaver, in Ruby Ridge, Idaho, in 1992, in which Weaver's son and wife were both killed. It explores the significance of a meeting of 160 far-right activists at Estes Park, Colorado, in the aftermath of the events at Ruby Ridge, as well as the subsequent development of a new citizens' militia movement during the 1990s. It also considers whether there was a wider white supremacist conspiracy behind the bombing—one beyond the former Gulf War veteran Timothy McVeigh and his associates Terry Nichols and Michael Fortier—encompassing members of a Christian Identity compound called Elohim City and the "outlaw" Aryan Republican Army.

Chapter 6 addresses the shift to a politics of "white nationalism" among some members of the American racist right at the start of the twenty-first century, as well as the rise of the so-called "alt-right" from 2009 to the presidential election of 2020. It covers various figures and groups including Reno Wolfe's National Association for the Advancement of White People, Jared Taylor's *American Renaissance*, the neo-Confederate Council of Conservative Citizens, VDare, Identity Evropa, the Traditional Workers Party, and websites and blogs such as *Stormfront, The Daily Stormer, Breitbart News, Occidental Dissent*, and *The Right Stuff*, as well as the anonymous trolls and posters of 4chan and other online locations.

Crucially, the chapter places the rise of the alt-right in the context of three significant developments in mainstream American politics: the election of Barack Obama in 2008, the appearance of the Tea Party movement in early 2009, and the presidency of Donald Trump.

The book's conclusion assesses the significance of the white supremacist right over the past 100 years of American history and considers how best to respond to the challenges such groups pose to the United States.

Finally, a note about language. Many offensive ideas and words appear in this book. I have presented these words and concepts as they were spoken or written because it is important to understand how white supremacists think and how they communicate—how they seek to intimidate and to persuade. Needless to say, the white supremacist views represented in these pages are not mine.

1

The Burning Cross

The Klan, Silver Shirts, Legionnaires, and Bundsmen

ON AUGUST 8, 1925, 50,000 MEMBERS of the Ku Klux Klan marched down Pennsylvania Avenue in Washington, D.C., in a massive and highly coordinated show of strength. They were led by a masked horse and rider who displayed one of the Klan's sacred emblems, a circular red patch containing a white cross with a symbolic drop of blood at its center. Next came the Klan's leader, Imperial Wizard Hiram Wesley Evans, resplendent in flowing purple robes, trimmed with gold, along with a rich array of Klan officials with mysterious and evocative titles such as Grand Dragon, King Kleagle, and Exalted Cyclops. Ordinary members of the Invisible Empire, both men and women, wore their distinctive—and to their enemies, extremely threatening—white robes and pointed hoods, although not their masks, which had been outlawed for the occasion. The marchers were accompanied by bagpipers, a dozen brass bands, and several fife-and-drum corps as they sang patriotic songs and hymns, waved American flags, and carried banners proclaiming the names of their home states or local chapters. The entire march lasted for over three hours and culminated with speeches at the Washington Monument. All in all, it was an impressive and historic sight, the Klan's first ever national parade.

This chapter tells the story of the second Ku Klux Klan from its rebirth in 1915 to the 1940s. It focuses especially on the 1920s, when—as the 1925 march in Washington attests—the Klan was a formidable political force, with over four million members (some estimates put the figure as high as six million, but it is difficult to know for sure), and as many as 18 million supporters spread out across the United States. Indeed, unlike its predecessor, the second Klan was as strong in the North as it was in the South. It was also much more than a night-riding, vigilante organization determined to oppress America's Black citizenry. Racism and white supremacy still remained at the heart of the Ku Klux Klan, but its list of enemies also included Catholics, Jews, and immigrants, as well as those it regarded as moral degenerates such as bootleggers, adulterers, and wife beaters. Nor was it just a political movement. Its social and cultural activities were equally important, as were the business opportunities it provided, especially for its leadership.

Yet although the Ku Klux Klan's impact was significant, it was also relatively short-lived. By the 1930s and the onset of the Great Depression its nativist appeal was much reduced. New white supremacist groups emerged during this time, including William Dudley Pelley's Silver Shirts, a secretive Klan offshoot known as the Black Legion, and the unapologetically pro-Nazi German-American Bund. This chapter examines these organizations too. We begin, though, with the rebirth of the Klan.

The original Klan was formed by a group of Confederate veterans in Pulaski, Tennessee, in 1865, as a secretive, terroristic organization committed to the reinstatement of white supremacy in the American South during the Reconstruction era. The second Klan was formed in 1915 in Atlanta, Georgia, by William Joseph Simmons, a 35-year-old former preacher, fraternity organizer, and veteran of the Spanish-American War. Simmons was a native of Alabama whose father, Calvin Henry Simmons, had been an officer in the "old Klan," or at least so his son claimed. Unable to follow his father into the medical profession, Joe—or "Doc" as he was still nonetheless sometimes called—instead became an itinerant minister for the Methodist Episcopal Church, riding the circuits in Alabama and Florida, where he honed his oratory skills until he was dismissed for "inefficiency" in 1912. Thereafter Simmons had a series of jobs, including as a garter salesman and a teacher, before finding his true calling as a paid organizer for fraternal orders.

The early years of the twentieth century were boom years for fraternal societies, with millions of Americans joining a wide range of organizations including the Masons, the Elks, the Red Men, the Odd Fellows, the Knights of Pythias, and the Ancient Order of United Workmen. Offering mutual support, companionship, community, but also significant

opportunities for networking and personal advancement, fraternal organizations became an integral part of American life. Simmons himself
belonged to 15 different orders—as well as several churches—rising to
the position of "Colonel" in the Woodmen of the World, in command of
five "regiments." He was first and foremost a "fraternalist," he said, and
he had long dreamed of establishing his own fraternal order—the greatest of them all—one he would model on the original Klan. He claimed
that the idea had first come to him in a vision in 1901, when horse-backed
Klansmen in white robes had suddenly appeared riding across the sky
one summer evening.

Fourteen years later Simmons got the opportunity to turn his vision
into reality. Confined to his bed for three months because of a car acci-
dent, he obtained a copy of the Klan's Prescript from 1867 and used both
it and his intimate knowledge of the world of fraternities to create a
revived Ku Klux Klan, with new mystical rituals, a new constitution—
the Kloran—and a new, strict hierarchy of offices. Simmons also had
the considerable foresight to copyright his ideas. Two events in particular made 1915 a good year to attempt a Klan revival. The first was the
appearance of D. W. Griffith's technically groundbreaking, if irremedi-
ably racist film, *The Birth of a Nation*. The second was the lynching of
Leo Frank, a Jewish factory superintendent.

Griffith's film was an adaptation of a best-selling novel by Thomas
Dixon titled *The Clansmen: An Historical Romance of the Ku Klux Klan*
(1905). Both book and film were paeans to the gallantry of the Old South,
the nobility of the Lost Cause, and the heroism of the Klan, with plentiful
depictions of the catastrophic indignities of Reconstruction and the supposed inherent bestiality of African Americans. Dixon, a well-connected,
fiery evangelical minister from North Carolina, who had presided over
New York's Twenty-Third Street Baptist Church for nine years, was
clear about his motivations in writing *The Clansmen* (which he had also
turned into a successful play), telling one interviewer that he wanted "to
create a feeling of abhorrence in white people, especially white women,
against colored men." (Illustrative of this, in one key scene, staged dramatically by Griffith in the film, a white woman commits suicide by
jumping from a rocky precipice when faced with her impending rape at
the hands of a newly freed slave. The Klan eventually tracks down the
perpetrator and lynches him.)

Griffith, whose father had been a colonel in the Confederate Army during the Civil War, had begun his directing career in 1908, but it was *The Birth of a Nation*—which received its world premiere in Los Angeles on February 8, 1915—that established him as the preeminent filmmaker of his generation. The movie not only introduced a range of new filmic techniques, including the close-up and the flashback—what Griffith called "switchbacks"—it was also a runaway box-office success, watched by over 25 million people during its initial run, thereby helping to establish the still relatively new art form of "motion pictures" as a major American industry. Employing his connections to good effect, Dixon also arranged for a special White House screening with his old college friend Woodrow Wilson. "It is like writing history with lightning," the president famously declared in response, "and my only regret is that it is all so terribly true." The film was also controversial. The National Association for the Advancement of Colored People (NAACP) organized a boycott of the movie, for example, and when that failed, tried, albeit with little effect, to pressure local censorship boards to cut the most blatantly racist scenes from the film. There were also significant protests against its showing in major cities such as Pittsburgh, Chicago, Milwaukee, and Atlantic City.

On April 27, 1913, 13-year-old Mary Phagan was found raped and murdered in the cellar of the National Pencil Company in Atlanta, where she worked. Despite considerable doubts about the reliability of the evidence against him, in August that year the Jewish manager of the factory, Leo Frank, was found guilty of the crimes and sentenced to death. Frank's legal appeals went nowhere, but in June 1915 his death sentence was commuted to life imprisonment by the outgoing Georgia Governor John Slaton. The news elicited a furious backlash within the state, not least from the former Populist Party leader and "agrarian rebel" Tom Watson, whose political views by this time had curdled into a toxic mix of racism, paranoia, anti-Semitism, and anti-Catholicism. Through the two magazines he edited, *Watson's Magazine* and *The Jeffersonian*, Watson urged the people of Georgia to "rise up" and avenge Phagan's death. On August 16, a group of 25 men calling themselves the Knights of Mary Phagan responded. They abducted Frank from a prison farm in Milledgeville and drove him 100 miles to Phagan's hometown of Marietta, where he was hanged from an oak tree the following morning; his body turned to face the dead girl's home. A few weeks later the Knights set fire to a giant cross on Stone Mountain, a 1,686-foot-tall granite outcrop 20 miles outside of Atlanta. Writing in the September 2 issue of *The Jeffersonian*, Tom Watson expressed his belief that it might be time for "another Ku Klux Klan" to be organized in order "to restore Home Rule."

Simmons was careful to draw on both the local notoriety of the Knights of Mary Phagan and the enormous nationwide popularity of *The Birth of a Nation* in his re-establishment of the Klan. (Indeed, the congruence of these two events in 1915 provides a much more plausible explanation for its creation at this time than does his 1901 "vision.") He made sure to recruit members of the Knights of Mary Phagan to the organization—alongside other fraternity members and two former members of the original Klan—for example, and on October 26, 1915, he and his 34 new colleagues applied to the state of Georgia for a charter to formally establish the Knights of the Ku Klux Klan as a "purely benevolent" fraternal order, with Simmons its leader and Imperial Wizard. A few weeks later, on Thanksgiving evening, he and 15 others climbed to the top of Stone Mountain to replicate the Knights of Mary Phagan's cross burning. "And thus on the mountain top that night at the midnight hour," as Simmons recalled fondly, "bathed in the sacred glow of the fiery cross, the Invisible Empire was called from its slumber of half a century to take up a new task and fulfil a new mission for humanity's good."

Interestingly, as the historian Wyn Craig Wade has pointed out, cross burning had not actually been a feature of the original Klan. In addition to the influence of the Knights of Mary Phagan, its adoption by Simmons and the generations of racists that came after him really owes more to the imaginations of Thomas Dixon and D. W. Griffith; and behind them to the work of the Scottish novelist, playwright, and poet Sir Walter Scott, whose tales of chivalry had had a major impact on the culture of the slaveholding South during the early part of the nineteenth century.

To coincide with the Atlanta premiere of *The Birth of a Nation*, Simmons took out newspaper advertisements for the Knights of the Ku Klux Klan, describing it as "The World's Greatest, Secret, Social, Political, Fraternal, Beneficiary Order." Simmons also assured potential recruits that his was a "A Classy Order of the Highest Class," with no "'Rough Necks,' 'Rowdies,' nor 'Yellow Streaks'" to be admitted. The ads were illustrated with the image of a robed Klansman on horseback that

Simmons had shamelessly lifted from Griffith, and they ran side by side with promotions for the film itself in the local press. On the day of the film's opening, December 6, Simmons went even further by having a group of Klansmen dress up in uniform and ride up and down in front of the Atlanta Theater firing their rifles in the air. Within two weeks membership of the Invisible Empire had more than tripled.

Yet for all its powerful symbolism and for all Simmons's recruiting gimmicks and deep immersion in the intricacies and allure of fraternal life, the early years of the second Klan were hardly glorious. Although the organization had expanded from Georgia into neighboring Alabama, by 1920 it still only had a few thousand members, its public role was distinctly limited, and its future prospects seemed uncertain. In truth, it was just one more fraternal group among many, albeit one underpinned by deep racism and white supremacy. In need of some professional assistance, Simmons turned to two local publicists, Edward Young Clarke and Elizabeth Tyler. Together, they would transform both the Klan's status and its fortunes.

Clarke and Tyler ran the Southern Publicity Association (SPA), which already counted the prohibitionist Anti-Saloon League, the Salvation Army, the Theodore Roosevelt Memorial, and the Red Cross among its clients. Characterizing Simmons as a "clean living and thinking man," who was "heart and soul for the success of the Ku Klux Klan," in June 1920 they signed a contract with him that gave the SPA an astonishing 80 percent of all initiation fees to be collected from new Klansmen ($8 of every $10 "klecktoken" in Klan terminology), as well as $2 from the membership fees of pre-existing Klan members. The SPA also officially became the Propagation Department of the Klan, with Clarke installed as Imperial Kleagle.

Employing modern business and public relations techniques, Clarke and Tyler raised some much-needed capital by offering bonds in the Klan, began including membership forms with their newspaper advertisements, polished Simmons's public persona and made him available for interviews whenever possible, issued frequent press releases connecting the Klan with the news stories of the day, and offered free memberships to ministers in the hope that they would encourage their congregants to become members too. Crucially, they also trained and financially incentivized a small army of Klan recruiters—effectively traveling salesmen—who would traverse the country in search of new recruits, with each Kleagle receiving a commission for every Klan member he brought in. (King Kleagles oversaw the work of the Kleagles in each state, or "realm" to use the preferred Klan term, while above them, in "domains," or groups of states, stood nine Grand Goblins.) Further funds were generated from the sale of Klan regalia, including hoods and robes, and through the publication of Klan newspapers and magazines courtesy of the newly created Searchlight Publishing Company. Within 15 months of Clarke and Tyler taking over the reins of the Invisible Empire, membership had grown to 100,000. In the process the two of them had earned $200,000 ($2.9 million in today's dollars), while Simmons had pocketed $150,000 and also gained an impressive new $65,000 Imperial Palace in Atlanta.

It was not just improved business practices and a greater degree of professionalism that accounted for the Klan's sudden upturn in fortunes though. Central to its rise was Clarke and Tyler's decision to significantly expand the range of its racist politics. For sure, "keeping the Negro in his place" remained the sine qua non of Klan ideology, but as Linda Gordon has written, Clarke and Tyler also understood that only by "melding racism and ethnic bigotry with evangelical Protestant morality" would the true national potential of the organization be realized, especially at a time when "so few African Americans lived outside the Southeast." It was because of this that the Klan increasingly presented itself as a fervent nativist crusader for "100% Americanism": an organization as hostile to Jews, Catholics, and immigrants—the "hordes of aliens" that were attempting to take over the United States—as it was to Blacks; and one equally determined to face down the myriad forces of degeneracy that were apparently threatening the country, whether in the form of liquor, crime, adultery, prostitution, labor radicalism, or even jazz music. In fact, recruiters were actively encouraged to sell the Klan based on whatever problems seemed most pressing in the localities they were visiting. It was a cynical strategy, perhaps, but in the confidently expressed view of one of Clarke and Tyler's early pamphlets, "If you are a Native Born, White, Gentile, Protestant, American Citizen, eventually you will be a Klansman and proud of that title." The market seemed huge.

The Klan's growth, especially its spreading outside of Alabama and Georgia into other areas of the South, as well as the Midwest and the

Northwest, brought it to the attention of both government authorities and the press. Newspaper editors in particular couldn't seem to get enough Klan stories. In September 1921 the *New York World* ran a two-week exposé of the Invisible Empire, which was syndicated in 18 other major newspapers around the country. (The *World*'s chief rival, William Randolph Hearst's *Journal-American*, ran its own investigation around the same time.) With the help of insider information obtained from disgruntled former Klansmen, the *World* recounted in graphic detail various examples of the financial, moral, and violent misdeeds that it said lay at the heart of the organization, including its involvement in 4 murders, 41 floggings, and 27 tarring and featherings. "Ku Kluxism as conceived, incorporated, propagated, and practiced has become a menace to the peace and security of every section of the United States. Its evil and vicious possibilities are boundless," the paper asserted. Especially embarrassing for the leadership of the Klan was the *World*'s revelation that Clarke and Tyler were apparently more than just business partners, having been arrested together in a state of undress in a brothel in 1919.

Under pressure to pursue matters further, in October the U.S. House of Representatives agreed to hold a formal hearing into the Klan's activities. Simmons traveled to Washington from Atlanta to deliver a tour de force performance, answering questions for two days with a mix of solemnity, good humor, and charm. The Klan was a fraternal and benevolent order like any other, he averred. Its rituals and oaths were standard practice, and anyone wishing to learn more about them should consult the copyrighted copies of the Kloran and other documents that were readily available in the Library of Congress. The acts of violence being ascribed to Klansmen were largely the work of imposters and imitators, he claimed; and, of course, he would be happy to turn over the organization's accounts if it would allay any concerns that might exist about profiteering or tax evasion. As for the Klan's belief in white supremacy, Simmons offered what would become an almost standard rationalization of the racist right in the United States in the years to follow: His members were not motivated by "hatred" of the "Negro race," he said, but only by their "pride" in being white. "If this organization is unworthy, then let me know and I will destroy it, but, if it is not, then let it stand," he concluded his testimony, before falling melodramatically to the caucus room floor in a faint. Seemingly satisfied, Congress determined that no further investigation of the Ku Klux Klan would be required.

Far from damaging the Klan, both Congress's inquiry and the press's investigations actually aided it. Membership increased by 20 percent in the months that followed, providing a revealing illustration of the problems that can be encountered when "extremist" groups are subject to more widespread exposure in this way. (Ironically, some new members simply completed the blank application forms that had been printed in the *New York World* and other newspapers and mailed them in.) Not only was the publicity valuable in itself, but as E. H. Loucks noted in his pioneering study *The Ku Klux Klan in Pennsylvania* (1936), the sense that the Klan was being attacked unfairly by urban elites and intellectuals in the "eastern establishment" also reinforced support for the organization. Indeed, it is important to recognize just how widespread and normative many of the Klan's beliefs were during this period, a point captured particularly well by the prominent journalist and social critic H. L. Mencken in one of his typically acerbic articles for the magazine *The Smart Set*. "Not a single solitary reason has yet been advanced for putting the Ku Klux Klan out of business," he wrote in 1923.

> If the Klan is against the Jews, so are half the good hotels of the Republic and three-quarters of the good clubs. If the Klan is against the foreign-born or the hyphenated citizen, so is the National Institute of Arts and Letters. If the Klan is against the Negro, so are all of the States south of the Mason-Dixon line. . . . If the Klan uses the mails for shaking down suckers, so does the Red Cross. If the Klan constitutes itself a censor of private morals, so does the Congress of the United States. If the Klan lynches a Moor for raping someone's daughter, so would I.

Nonetheless, in the aftermath of the congressional hearings—especially the embarrassing revelations about Clarke and Tyler—a group of Klan leaders led by Hiram Wesley Evans, the former head of the Dallas Klavern and the current Imperial Kligrapp, or national secretary, determined that the time had come for a change in the organization's leadership. Assisted by several Grand Dragons, as well as the leader of the Indiana Klan, David Curtis Stephenson, and Fred Savage, a former New York detective turned Klan chief investigator, the plotters first persuaded Simmons to "temporarily" hand over the role of Imperial Wizard to Evans, with Simmons elevated to the supposedly more exalted position of Emperor, complete with a new $1,000-a-month salary. However, once Evans was installed in office, in November 1922, Simmons quickly realized that he had been had. The Klan's contract with the Southern Publicity Association was canceled, Clarke was dismissed—Tyler had already resigned by this point—and a new constitution was drawn up in which all mention of the awesome powers and responsibilities of the Emperor were strangely absent. A year-long legal battle then ensued with various suits and countersuits being filed, not least over the fate of Simmons's valuable copyrights. Finally, on February 12, 1924, agreement was reached. Simmons would give up his copyrights, his position as Emperor, and would no longer even be allowed to be a member of the order he had founded. In return he would receive a one-time cash payment of $146,500.

As it turned out, Simmons would only get $90,000 of the promised settlement, but the battle was over. Evans had won, and the vanquished Simmons would die in obscurity, in 1945, having failed in his efforts to create two successive rival organizations, the Knights of the Flaming Sword and the White Band.

Like his predecessor, Evans was a native of Alabama, born in the town of Ashland in 1881. His family relocated to Texas when he was a child, and after his education at Vanderbilt University, he became a dentist, running a small-time practice in Dallas (although rumors persisted that his qualifications in the field were more veterinary than human) before rising up through the ranks of the Klan. Confident and ambitious, Evans wanted to continue to grow the Klan while also pushing it in a more overtly political direction. Once in charge, he attempted to centralize its operations, putting the Kleagles on salary rather than commission, providing local Klaverns with greater direction on how to run their meetings and recruitment efforts, and moving the organization's headquarters from Atlanta to Washington, D.C., for example. He also sought to curtail the Klan's acts of violence and lawlessness, even though he himself had run one of its infamous vigilante "black squads" while in Dallas. In addition, Evans doubled down on the militant nativism, hyperpatriotism, and crusading moralism that Clarke and Tyler had first introduced to the Klan. "The Klan is an organization to promote political patriotism," he explained in 1924. "Its ideal is to restore and then preserve and develop the old, fundamental ideas on which the Nation was founded and which have made it great; to provide for the uncontaminated growth of Anglo-Saxon civilization."

"Purity" was a key Klan concept. In numerous publications and pamphlets—*The Fiery Cross, Kourier Magazine, The Imperial Night-Hawk, The Watcher on the Tower*—and in countless speeches, sermons, and orations, Klansmen railed against those who would sully the American nation and its great native-born people: filthy, ignorant immigrants; money-grubbing, unassimilable Jews; disloyal Roman Catholics beholden only to "Popish despotism"; and sexually ravenous Blacks intent on the corruption of white womanhood. And, then, of course, there was the symbolism embedded in the "purity" of its white robes and the cleansing power of its burning crosses.

Yet at the same time as he pushed these explicitly political concerns, Evans also encouraged the development of what he called "vocational Klanishness" or "Klankraft." This was the idea that members of the Invisible Empire should patronize each other's businesses as much as possible, while boycotting those that were owned by "aliens" or opponents of the organization. Lists of "right" stores were drawn up, and Klan-friendly merchants were encouraged to either place advertisements in Klan-owned papers, or to remove them from those that weren't. Businesses could also indicate their support with clearly placed signs such as "100% American," "100%," or "TWK" (which stood for Trade with Klansmen), or even with just an appropriately displayed American flag. Utilizing the Klan's penchant for the letter "k" was another option, with would-be customers hopefully enticed by notices reading "Klan Klothes Kleaned," "Kwik Kar Wash," or "Krippled Kars Kured." Whole ranges of Klan-endorsed products, from cutlery and clothes, to watches, rings, and coffee, were also produced, as Evans monitored the whole enterprise from his newly established Intelligence Bureau.

Nor was the social aspect of Klanishness neglected. On the contrary, there were Klan-sponsored picnics and square dances, baseball games and basketball tournaments, Bible study groups and boating expeditions, circuses and rodeos, firework displays and concerts, alongside the more political marches, rallies, and cross burnings. All in all, it was a heady and successful mix, especially when combined with the Klan's already existing sense of mystique and drama. By 1924 the Invisible Empire had at least four million members. It had become a major cultural and political force.

It was also a national one, with Klansmen active in states such as Michigan, Ohio, Pennsylvania, Colorado, California, and Maine, far from the Southland. Indeed, in terms of per capita membership, the greatest concentration of Klan strength was to be found in Indiana and Oregon. Evans characterized the Klan as "a movement of the plain people, very weak in the matter of culture, intellectual support and trained leadership," who were demanding "a return of power into the hands of the everyday . . . entirely unspoiled and not de-Americanized average citizens of the old stock." There was almost certainly an element of faux naïveté in this though, because far from being a movement of the "everyday plain people"—the country "hicks" and backwoods "rubes" their opponents so often characterized them as—research has shown that the majority of the Klan was actually drawn from the small town and urban middle class: shopkeepers, ministers, physicians, schoolteachers, lawyers, pharmacists, and so on. Robert Alan Goldberg's study of the Colorado Klan, for example, shows that less than 1 percent of the earliest Klansmen in Denver were unskilled workers, and that 71 percent of all Denver Klansmen belonged to what he termed "high nonmanual" or "middle nonmanual" occupations (the first category included architects, bankers, and clergymen; the second, accountants, draftsmen, and embalmers). Similarly, Nancy MacLean's investigation of Klansmen in Athens, Georgia, revealed that the vast majority of them were small-business owners, skilled tradesmen, managers, clerks or salesmen, together with a large number of public employees such as firemen, policemen, and postal workers.

Indeed, the "respectability" of the Ku Klux Klan was a big part of its appeal, which helps explain why many social and political elites also became members, including scores of judges, sheriffs, police chiefs, mayors, city attorneys, and various local and state politicians from both political parties. (In the main, Klansmen tended to be Democrats in the South and Republicans in the North and West.) As Chris Rhomberg has noted with respect to his study of the Klan in Oakland, California—although his point has a much wider application—rather than being some kind of "deviant aberration," the Klan was actually a "significant actor in the urban political arena" throughout the 1920s. As many as 16 senators, 75 congressmen, and 11 governors were Klansmen, as was the Chief Justice of the United States, Edward Douglass White, as well as future Supreme

Court justice Hugo Black and, at least for a brief time, future president Harry S. Truman.

As with any other political or social movement, Americans joined the Klan for a variety of reasons: because they were racist; because it was good for business or politics; because their friends and neighbors had; because of the sense of community it provided; because its oaths and rituals were attractive; because their minister had encouraged them to; because of its proud "American" values; because they were afraid of Catholics and immigrants; or perhaps for a mix of all these factors. As the historian David Chalmers writes:

> The Klan offered a degree of mystery and thrill of power greater than that of any other fraternal order and far outdistanced such contemporaries, and occasional competitors, as the newly founded American Legion. Whatever anyone else had, the Klan seemed to have it too, only better. With its highly accented sense of mystery, patriotism, communal guardianship, and nocturnal ramblings, the Ku Klux Klan gave to the Klansmen the chance to live a second, more fulfilling life within the Invisible Empire. Where else could anyone get so much for ten dollars?

At a deeper level, though, the Klan was responding to the profound changes that were taking place in American society in the early 1920s: economic restructuring and the growth of a new consumer society; the development of mass media in the form of the radio and film industries; new sexual and social freedoms; increasing urbanization and secularization; the expansion of suffrage to women through the passage of the Nineteenth Amendment; the Great Migration of African Americans to the North (which had begun in 1916); and the ongoing arrival of thousands of immigrants into the United States.

Many Americans found these changes to be disorienting, of course, but this was especially the case for native-born white Protestants who felt their political, social, and economic status as "citizens of the old stock" to be under considerable threat. In Rory McVeigh and Kevin Estep's analysis in *The Politics of Losing* (2019), the key factor in explaining the Klan's core middle-class constituency was the underlying economic transformations of the period, both an agricultural depression caused by the collapse of overseas markets at the end of the First World War and, more particularly, the widespread adoption of methods of mass production that "accelerated the use of unskilled factory labor, making skilled manufactures and artisans uncompetitive if not nearly obsolete" in many parts of the United States. The increasing demand for this unskilled factory labor was met from three main sources: Black Southerners, women, and—most important of all—immigrants. As McVeigh and Estep point out, each of these groups also represented a significant political threat as well: large potential voting blocs that might be employed to thwart the interests of Klansmen and their allies.

With respect to women, the Klan sought to remind them of their traditional roles as wives and mothers, but also to engage them—in the words of Kathleen Blee—as active citizens who would help "preserve white Protestant supremacy." Indeed, it was to this end, in 1923, that Evans established the Women of the Ku Klux Klan. Headquartered in Little Rock, Arkansas, the organization was hugely successful, with membership reaching 500,000. Its creed read: "We believe that under God, the Women of the Ku Klux Klan is a militant body of American free-women by whom these principles shall be maintained, our homes and children protected, our happiness insured, and the prosperity of our community, our state and nation guaranteed against usurpation, disloyalty, and selfish exploitation." As for the threats posed by African Americans and immigrants, the Klan's strategy was one of scapegoating, demonization, and bigotry: the effective exploitation of cultural and ethnic prejudice to explain a world that was rapidly turning in a direction that Klansmen wished to resist.

The 1924 Democratic National Convention provided a vivid illustration of the impact of the Klan on the national political scene. Held at Madison Square Garden in New York City for 16 sweltering days between June 24 and July 9, it was the longest-running political convention in U.S. history, one that witnessed a bitter struggle between pro-Klan and anti-Klan supporters. The Klan's preferred candidate was William Gibbs McAdoo from California, the son-in-law of Woodrow Wilson, as well as his former Treasury Secretary (from 1913 to 1918). McAdoo was actually relatively liberal, but he was also an ardent Prohibitionist, and, more significantly, unlike other contenders, someone who had at least taken no public position on the Invisible Empire. Alabama Senator Oscar Underwood called the Klan a "national menace," for example, arguing, "It is either the Ku Klux Klan or the United States of America. Both cannot survive." Then there was Governor Al Smith from New

York. A product of the New York "political machine," an Irish Catholic, and a fierce critic of Prohibition, as David Bennett has noted, Smith was "everything the Klan abhorred," the very "embodiment of the alien menace" and a "spokesman for the jazz age."

The Klan was determined that Smith—the leading candidate—be denied the Democratic nomination, but first it had to defeat a proposed plank in the party's platform that specifically condemned "the hooded and secret organization known as the Ku Klux Klan." It was a deliberatively provocative proposal on the part of Underwood and Smith supporters, and it produced an extremely ugly spectacle as rival factions literally fought it out in the convention hall. Chants of "Mac! Mac! McAdoo!" were met by counter-chants of "Ku! Ku! McAdoo!" and "Booze! Booze! Booze!" With some delegates splitting their votes, the anti-Klan platform was rejected by 543.15 votes to 542.35. (The Republican Party, which had met in Cleveland, Ohio, two weeks earlier, had been careful to avoid any reference to the Klan in its platform so as not to have to deal with any similarly unpleasant and politically damaging scenes at its convention.) With one issue—barely—resolved, battle then resumed over who the Democratic nominee would be. McAdoo withdrew after 19 ballots. But with Klan supporters implacably opposed to both Underwood and Smith, it took another 94 rounds of voting before a compromise candidate emerged, the almost entirely colorless John W. Davis of West Virginia, a former U.S. ambassador to Great Britain and solicitor general in the Wilson administration.

Davis, like McAdoo, had maintained his silence on the Klan during the convention, but he changed his stance during the general election. Speaking at a campaign rally in New Jersey, he declared that if any organization "no matter what it chooses to be called, whether the Ku Klux Klan or by any other name, raises the standard of racial and religious prejudice or attempts to make racial origins or religious beliefs the test for fitness for public office, it does violence to the spirit of American institutions, and must be condemned." The third-party Progressive Party candidate, Wisconsin Senator Robert La Follette, also vehemently condemned the Klan. In contrast, the Republican nominee, Calvin Coolidge, who had taken over the presidency following the death of Warren Harding in August 1923, largely lived up to his nickname of "Silent Cal" (although his running mate, Charles Dawes, did make one anti-Klan speech). Coolidge won easily, by 15,725,106 votes to Davis's 8,386,503 and La Follette's 4,822,856, and by 382 to 136 and 13 in the Electoral College. Coolidge's victory was probably inevitable, but the Klan nonetheless felt vindicated, especially because of its determined and effective blocking of Smith. Indeed, the organization would renew its campaign against him in 1928 when the New Yorker did finally become the Democratic Party's candidate for president. Smith lost overwhelmingly to Herbert Hoover, a defeat for which the Klan also sought to take credit.

Coolidge had already seemingly justified the Klan's support for him by signing the Immigration Act of 1924 into law the previous May. Also known as the Johnson-Reed Act, after its chief sponsors, Congressman Albert Johnson (R-WA) and Senator David Reed (R-PA), the act represented the Klan's most significant and long-lasting political achievement. The Klan had campaigned vigorously for the new law's passage, utilizing all the means at its disposal, through public speeches and meetings, in its publications, through its network of sympathetic ministers, and by an extensive letter-writing campaign. The act set annual immigration quotas for specific countries at 2 percent of the number of residents from those countries who had settled in the United States in 1890. The choice of year was crucial. Prior to 1890 the vast majority of immigrants to the United States had come from Germany, Britain, and Ireland, while after that date they came primarily from southern and eastern Europe—Italians, Slavs, Poles, and Jews—in a great wave of "new immigration," some 20 million by 1920. It was precisely these "new immigrants" with their "alien" beliefs, religions, and attitudes that Klansmen most objected to: a "Mississippi of inferior foreign elements," as Imperial Wizard Evans put it in an article in the *Imperial Night-Hawk* in January 1924, as opposed to the "kindred, desirable, [and] easily assimilable" "Nordic types" who had come before them. The act would restore the earlier geographic and ethnic flow, while simultaneously reducing the number of immigrants overall. (It also had the effect of virtually eliminating all immigration from Asia. Hence another of its names: the Asian Exclusion Act.) Although modified periodically in the years to follow, this Klan-endorsed quota system would remain in place until 1965.

The Ku Klux Klan was certainly a key driving force behind the Johnson-Reed Act, but it was by no means the only one. Indeed, to a large degree, the Klan was simply representing what David Chalmers calls the "dominant American attitude on immigration" of the period. The best-selling success of books such as Madison Grant's *The Passing of the Great Race: The Racial Basis of European History* (1916) and Lothrop Stoddard's *The Rising Tide of Color: The Threat Against White World Supremacy* (1920), testifies to this, as does Henry Ford's extensive promotion of anti-Semitism in his Michigan-based newspaper, the *Dearborn Independent*. Grant, Stoddard, and Ford were also all enthusiastic advocates of eugenics—the pseudoscientific belief that certain social characteristics are genetically determined and that the birth rates of "inferior races" should be limited, while those of "superior races" boosted—as were many other notable Americans of the day, such as President Coolidge, Supreme Court Justice Oliver Wendell Holmes, birth control advocate Margaret Sanger, African-American scholar W. E. B. Dubois, and novelists Upton Sinclair and Sinclair Lewis. Given that the so-called "superior races" included almost all white, Anglo-Saxon, Protestants, the Klan too was a keen promoter of eugenic laws, including the forced sterilization of those of "defective stock." Thirty states passed such legislation during the 1920s and early 1930s, resulting in the sterilization of over 64,000 people.

The promotion of public education was another pressing Klan concern. Or rather, the promotion of public education as a means to get rid of the "corrupting" influence of private Catholic schools, or even just the presence of Catholic teachers in the school system. In Oregon, for example, the Klan threw its considerable weight behind a ballot initiative for a new Compulsory Education Law that mandated public education for all children between the ages of eight and sixteen. It passed by a 4 percent margin in November 1922. Throughout the United States, the Klan lobbied for the rigorous enforcement of the Volstead Act—the law enacted to implement the Eighteenth Amendment that had established prohibition—whether by legal or extralegal means, and launched a campaign against the insidious "immorality" of Hollywood, even going so far as to establish its own production unit, the Cavalier Moving Picture Company. (It only made two films, *The Toll of Justice* and *The Traitor Within*, both released in 1923.) Not all of the Klan's political endeavors were successful, of course. Hollywood was little impacted by the Klan's efforts. Nor was it able to secure the creation of a federal Department of Education, for example.

Indeed, to a considerable extent 1924 marked the peak of the second Klan's influence in the United States. After all, not only had it helped secure the passage of a new, highly restrictive immigration law, but with Coolidge's election victory it also seemed to have "captured" the White House. (While the new president may have found it politically expedient to hold his counsel on the Invisible Empire, in truth Coolidge was no Klan sympathizer, as evidenced by his backing of a federal antilynching law and—at least rhetorical—support for Black civil rights.) In the February 1925 issue of the *Kourier*, Evans basked in the glory of these developments. "I firmly believe that with the new year, a new era is dawning for America," he wrote. "Our people are returning to the safe paths chartered by our forefathers. America swerved under a mighty burden of foreign thought brought to her by those who do not realize the responsibility of freedom, but, thank God, America has awakened." Yet these very "victories" also sowed the seeds for the Klan's rapid downfall. As with many other social movements, the apparent achievement of its goals meant that much of the sense of urgency that had driven its spectacular growth suddenly disappeared. The real death blow, though, was delivered in Indiana, in a torrid and widely publicized scandal that engulfed its Grand Dragon, David Stephenson.

Following his part in the ouster of Simmons in 1922, Stephenson had been rewarded with the organizing rights for seven northern states, as well as the new title of Imperial Klaliff, which meant that he would succeed Evans as Imperial Wizard should Evans die in office. Charismatic, forceful, and a gifted organizer, "the old man," as he insisted on being called, was a key figure in the Klan's rapid rise in power, especially in the Hoosier state, where Klansmen numbered close to 250,000 by the early 1920s, accounting for approximately 30 percent of the state's entire white male population—"I am the law in Indiana," Stephenson would proclaim proudly. Stephenson's success, which combined vigilantism with skilful recruiting and ruthless politicking in the form of the "Stephenson Machine"—also known as the "Military Machine"—made him a serious rival to Evans for leadership of the Invisible Empire and one of its most well-known national figures.

On January 12, 1925, the Grand Dragon met 28-year-old Madge Oberholtzer at the inauguration ball for Indiana Governor Edward Jackson. Three months later, he brutally raped her in a private compartment of a Chicago-bound night train, leaving bite marks all over her body. The distraught and traumatized Oberholtzer took a fatal overdose of drugs in response to the assault and died in agony on April 14, 1925. Stephenson was found guilty of second-degree murder in November and sentenced to life in prison. Paroled in 1950, he received another ten-year sentence a short time after and would not finally be released from prison until 1956.

The Stephenson scandal fatally undermined the Klan's claims to be a law-abiding, morally upright, and noble organization, and it never recovered from its unmasking. Within a year the number of Klansmen in Indiana was down to 15,000, and this precipitous decline was replicated throughout the rest of the United States. By the end of 1927, total membership in the Knights of the Ku Klux Klan stood at 350,000. There were other contributing factors, of course: other scandals and acts of violence; persistent internecine squabbles and the ongoing exposure of Klan secrets—evident, for example, during another high-profile court case, in 1927, when Evans tried to sue a Pennsylvania Klan for $100,000 after it had seceded from the national organization; as well as the efforts of anti-Klan journalists and activists, including those in the National Vigilance Association. Another sign of the changing fortunes of the Klan came during the 1927 Memorial Day Parade in the New York borough of Queens. First, groups such as the Boy Scouts of America and the Knights of Columbus refused to take part because of the Klan presence, then the hooded marchers found themselves under concerted attack from angry, rock-throwing spectators. (One of the people arrested in the ensuing melee was 21-year-old Fred Trump, the father of the future president, although whether he was a participant in the march or an opponent of it remains unclear.)

Broader developments were also at work. Linda Gordon suggests, for instance, that the "longest-term force behind the Klan's decline was . . . the increasing integration of Catholics and Jews into American politics, culture, and economy." Other historians point to the waning influence of traditional fundamentalist religious beliefs, as exemplified by the Scopes "Monkey" Trial of 1925, in which the former populist hero William Jennings Bryan and famed criminal defense attorney Clarence Darrow fought it out over whether schoolteacher John T. Scopes was in violation of a Tennessee law that made it unlawful to teach human evolution in any state-funded school. (Scopes was found guilty, but in the larger court of public opinion, it was science and modernity that were generally taken to be the victor—if perhaps only temporarily—over ignorance and "religious bigotry.") Economic changes were also important. Once the Great Depression struck, following the stock market crash of October 1929, throwing millions of Americans out of work, the Klan's recurring nativist concerns seemed largely irrelevant. By 1930 membership had plummeted to 100,000. The once mighty Invisible Empire was but a shadow of its former self.

Initially the Klan favored Democratic Party candidate Franklin Delano Roosevelt (FDR) in the 1932 presidential campaign over the incumbent, Republican Herbert Hoover. This changed, however, when it became clearer the extent to which FDR was courting the support of Blacks, Catholics, Jews, immigrants, and the labor movement—groups that would form a crucial part of the Democrats' new electoral coalition throughout the 1930s and beyond—and when the wrenching changes that Roosevelt's New Deal program was unleashing on American life were made more manifest: massive government intervention in the economy, huge public works projects, price and wage controls, the protection of unions, and the establishment of Social Security and a welfare state. By 1934 the Klan had turned decisively against the new president and his "un-American," "unconstitutional," and "Communist-inspired" ideas. "Public-spirited people, Klansmen and nonmembers alike, realize that this nation is in great danger," Evans explained in July that year. "Because of its record of heroic achievement, the Klan has been called upon . . . to mobilize and co-ordinate those who are interested in preserving the Constitutional Government set up by our forefathers." What this "preservation" of American constitutional government meant in practice, however, was a concerted, and at times violent, campaign, conducted largely in the South, to attack union organizers and supress Black voters' rights.

The Klan was far from alone in its opposition to Roosevelt and his New Deal, though. Conservatives in both the Republican and the Democratic Party, along with wealthy businessmen in groups such as the American Liberty League and the National Association of Manufacturers, also opposed the "ravenous madness" of the "unprincipled charlatan" now occupying the White House. On the far right, new racist and white supremacist groups also emerged during the 1930s, many of them attracting former Klan members to their ranks. The most notable of these were William Dudley Pelley's Silver Shirts, the Black Legion, and the German-American Bund.

William Dudley Pelley was born in Lynn, Massachusetts, in 1890. The son of an itinerant Methodist preacher, Pelley had already lived a rich and varied life before he formed the Silver Shirt Legion of America in 1933. He had been a police reporter for the *Boston Globe*, a novelist, a missionary, a war correspondent, a real estate salesman, a magazine publisher, and a Hollywood screenwriter. He was also something of a philosopher and mystic. Indeed, what Pelley described as the "turning point" of his life had occurred in April 1928 in a bungalow in Altadena, California, when he had seemingly died and ascended to heaven for a brief, if illuminating, visit. Pelley's "hyperdimensional" journey was published as "Seven Minutes in Eternity—The Amazing Experience that Made Me Over" in *American Magazine* (circulation 2.2 million) in March the following year, wherein Pelley outlined all the "hidden powers" he believed had been revealed to him, as well as his special role as a "monitor" who could now guide the development of the whole human race.

Pelley claimed to have prophesied Adolf Hitler's appointment as German chancellor four years before it actually took place on January 30, 1933—a prophecy based on his complex measurements of the Great Pyramid at Giza—and he established the Silver Shirts the following day in Asheville, North Carolina, where he was running a Christian college (although its headquarters moved to Oklahoma City shortly thereafter). "Posterity will attest that Chief Pelley of the Silver Shirts was the first man in the United States to step out openly and support Adolf Hitler and his German-Nazi program," the self-styled American führer wrote a year later. Organized along military lines, with Pelley as its national commander, membership of the group was restricted to white Christian males, aged 18 or older, who were either native born or naturalized U.S. citizens: a great "American Aryan Militia" of "Christian Patriots," in Pelley's terms. Its uniform, modeled on Hitler's SS, consisted of a service hat, blue corduroy knickers, long socks, a blue tie, and a silver-gray shirt, with a scarlet "L" denoting Love, Loyalty, and Liberation emblazoned above the heart.

Aiming to bring fascism to the United States, the Silver Shirts were vehemently opposed to Roosevelt and the New Deal, which Pelley denounced as a conspiratorial front for the Bolshevik and Jewish interests working behind it. "Every Silver Shirt must know the full extent of the conspiracy," Pelley contended, and if opposing it "meant using force to hurl a great regime of scoundrels from the country, very well then, it meant force." Blacks, Native Americans, and aliens were regarded as inferior groups—"improvident and shiftless," as he put it in his 1933 manifesto *No More Hunger*—who should be made wards of the government, while his solution to the Depression was for the American economy to be reorganized along corporatist lines in order to create a new "Christian Commonwealth."

At its peak, in 1934, the Silver Shirt Legion had 15,000 members spread across 22 states, but it was strongest in the Pacific Northwest and California, especially in Washington State and around the city of Los Angeles. It also published a weekly magazine, *Liberation*, and a weekly newspaper, *Silver Ranger*, which together reached perhaps 50,000 people. Despite its small size, Pelley felt confident enough to run for the presidency in 1936 as the candidate for his newly formed Christian Party. Together with his running mate and fellow Silver Shirt Willard Kemp, he crisscrossed the country under the slogans "Christ or Chaos?" and "For Christ and Constitution," promising to revive "these prostrate United States" with an "American Hitler and a pogrom." In the end the Christian Party only managed to get on the ballot in the state of Washington, with Pelley receiving a total of 1,598 votes.

Pelley endeavored to launch a new recruitment campaign for the Silver Shirts in 1937, but it was hopeless, and by 1938 membership in the paramilitary organization had fallen to 5,000. Under increasing government pressure, the Silver Shirts were officially disbanded in 1941. The following year Pelley was found guilty of sedition and sentenced to 15 years in the federal penitentiary in Terre Haute, Indiana (he was defended at his trial by the same lawyer who had attempted to defend Klan leader David Stephenson in 1925) serving ten. He died in Noblesville, Indiana, in 1965.

As Peter Amman has written, by 1935 "the most formidable nativist organization around" was the secretive Klan offshoot the Black Legion, which had somewhere between 60,000 and 100,000 "armed and disciplined" members spread across the midwestern states of Ohio, Indiana, Illinois, and Michigan, where it attracted mostly unskilled and semiskilled workers struggling to cope with the enormity of the Depression. The Legion had grown out of an older organization known as the Black Guard, or the Klan Guard, founded in 1925 in the small industrial city of Bellaire, Ohio, by Dr. William Jacob Shephard, the Grand Cyclops of the local Klan. Shephard's innovations had been twofold: first he had replaced the Klan's traditional white robes with black ones (hence the new name); and second, he had instituted a frightening new initiation ceremony, based, he claimed, on the "Black Oath of Quantrill"—a Confederate guerrilla leader responsible for the massacre of antislavery forces in Lawrence, Kansas, during the Civil War—that recruits had to repeat while kneeling down as existing Klan members pointed loaded guns at their backs.

Sometime in late 1931 or early 1932, in an echo of the palace coup that had been instituted against William Simmons ten years before, Virgil H. Effinger, an electrician and Klan Grand Titan from Lima, Ohio, persuaded Shepard to let him become the Major General of what was now called the Black Legion for the entire area "east of the Mississippi"— the only area that the organization actually operated in—with Shepard given the notional position of commander in chief. Effinger had initially planned to transform the Legion into a national political force, but once in charge he pushed the organization even further down the road of violence than his predecessor had, calling for a "holy war against Catholics, Jews, Communists, Negroes and aliens," and describing the Legion as a "guerilla army designed to fight the Republican and Democratic parties." (There were also talks about a possible merger with Pelley's Silver Shirts that never came to fruition.)

Under Effinger's leadership, the Black Legion was involved in numerous acts of arson, kidnapping, flogging, intimidation, and murder, including that of union organizer George Marchuk and Silas Coleman, a Black laborer; although it was never proved, the organization was also suspected as being behind the murder of two Communist Party members who worked for the Hudson Car Company in Detroit, Michigan. It also plotted to assassinate Father Charles Coughlin, the famous "radio priest" of Royal Oak, Michigan (who would go on to create his own militaristic and fascist-like organization, the Christian Front, in November 1938), as well as several local politicians. Within a short time Effinger was speculating about seizing power just "like the 30,000 Bolsheviks who took over in the Russian Revolution," and in 1936 he hatched a hideously elaborate plan to kill one million Jews by planting mustard gas bombs in every synagogue in the United States during Yom Kippur. As one disillusioned former Klansman complained, the Legion had become an almost "revolutionary" organization.

The Black Legion was so secretive that the Federal Bureau of Investigation was unaware of its existence until 1935, but not surprisingly the extent of its violence soon began attracting significant levels of attention. Indeed, it was another murder, that of an unemployed auto worker from Dearborn, Michigan, named Charlie Poole, that proved to be the organization's undoing, finally allowing the authorities to penetrate it. Poole, a Catholic, was accused of beating his Protestant and pregnant wife, who also happened to be related to a member of the Legion. In retaliation, on the evening of May 12, 1936, he was dragged from his home and shot in the head, his body dumped in a ditch. The investigative trail led to Dayton Dean, a particularly violent Legion enforcer, who, in clear violation of his sacred oath, proceeded to tell the police everything he knew. These revelations attracted a huge amount of negative attention for the Legion and also helped secure the conviction of over 50 of its members for a wide range of criminal offenses. Effinger somehow evaded the two indictments that were laid against him, but it was clear that the days of the Black Legion were over. In 1938 the now former Major General tried to re-establish himself with the Patriotic League of America, but his efforts went nowhere.

The demise of the Black Legion was at least good news for Hiram Evans who had attacked it from the outset for bringing the entire Invisible Empire into disrepute. The Imperial Wizard was further outraged in 1937, however, when Warner Bros. released the movie *Black Legion*. Directed by Archie Mayo, the film starred Humphrey Bogart as Frank Taylor, an angry midwestern factory worker who is passed over for promotion in favor of his immigrant Polish colleague Joe Dombrowski (Henry Brandon). Taylor joins a secret white vigilante organization—the titular "Black Legion"—in order to get his revenge. This is achieved when Taylor and his fellow Legionnaires burn down Dombrowski's house, forcing him to leave his job, which Taylor then takes. Taylor is then drawn deeper and deeper into the Legion's racist and criminal activities, alienating him from his family and culminating in the shooting of his best friend Ed Jackson (Dick Foran), who has been falsely accused by the Legion of being a woman beater. Arrested for the murder, Taylor agrees to testify against the secret order, resulting in all its members going to prison.

Remarkably, another film inspired by the Legion and the Poole murder case was released in 1936: Columbia Pictures' *Legion of Terror*, directed by Charles C. Coleman. But Evans only sued the Warner Bros. production, seeking $100,000 in damages for copyright infringement over the use of official Klan insignia on the fictional Black Legion's robes. Although the lawsuit was unsuccessful, it was another indication that the Knights of the Ku Klux Klan was in serious decline. Not only was its membership in freefall, but, beginning in 1936, Evans had also been forced to sell off most of the organization's real estate holdings, including the Imperial Palace in Atlanta—the property was sold first to an insurance company and then, in 1939, as if part of some elaborate cosmic joke, to the Catholic Church as the site for a new cathedral. The same year, on June 10, Evans formally retired. His replacement as Imperial Wizard was a 42-year-old former veterinarian named James A. Colescott.

Colescott was from Indiana and had come up under the "Stephenson machine" before becoming the Grand Dragon of Ohio and then, in 1936, Evan's chief of staff. He endeavored to revive the Klan so that the "fiery cross will again blaze on the hilltops of America" by cutting the cost of its initiation fee to $6 and by reducing the cost of its robes from $6.50 to $3.50. He also spoke out against violence—"anyone who flogs, lynches or intimidates ought to be in the penitentiary," he said—and tried especially hard to recruit new members in the North. Little changed though, and in 1940 the Klan found itself embroiled in yet another high-profile controversy, this time over its involvement with the pro-Nazi German-American Bund.

The Bund had been created out of the remnants of an earlier organization, the Friends of New Germany, by Fritz Julius Kuhn in November 1935. A chemist by training, Kuhn had fought in the German Army during the First World War and been a member of the Nazi Party since the 1920s. He saw the Bund as a means to build up support for Nazi Germany within the United States but also as a broader cultural endeavor that would unite all German-Americans—a population of some 30 million—in "one great, nation-wide, respect-commanding movement."

To help fend off criticism that the Bund was largely acting in the interests of a foreign government—although in actuality Hitler and his cronies had almost nothing to do with it—Kuhn sought to "Americanize" the organization as much as possible. The slogan "Free America!" replaced "Sieg Heil!," for example, and in February 1939 a massive rally to celebrate George Washington's birthday was organized at Madison Square Garden, with 22,000 people in attendance. As part of this process Kuhn also wanted to form an alliance with an obviously homegrown American group. Discussions with several Native American tribes and with the Silver Shirts came to nought, so the self-styled Bundsführer turned to the Klan.

Negotiations with Klan leaders from Michigan and New Jersey were still ongoing in May 1939 when Kuhn was arrested for stealing over $14,000 of Bund funds. (Found guilty, he was sentenced to two-and-a-half years in New York's Sing Sing prison before being deported back to Germany in 1945.) Kuhn's replacement was G. William Kunze, and it was Kunze who finally came to an agreement with the Grand Dragon of New Jersey, Arthur H. Bell, for a joint Bund-Klan rally to be held on August 18, 1940, at the Bund's 200-acre Camp Norland, near Andover, New Jersey. Attended by some 200 Klansmen and 800 Bundsmen, both in full regalia, the event included some mutually admiring speeches— "The principles of the Bund and the principles of the Klan are the same," proclaimed Deputy Bundsführer August Klapprott, for example— dinner in the camp's restaurant, music, and a Klan wedding performed beneath a burning cross.

Colescott had not attended the rally, instead sending a supportive letter that was read aloud by Arthur Bell. Such was the outcry in the press over the meeting however, that the Imperial Wizard was quickly forced to backtrack, publicly condemning the entire enterprise and ejecting both Bell and his secretary, Reverend A. M. Young, from the Invisible Empire. The matter was then taken up in Congress in the form of an investigation by the Dies Committee—the forerunner of the House Committee on Un-American Activities, named after the conservative Texas Democrat Martin Dies—during which everyone involved claimed innocence and all plans for a merger between the Bund and the Klan were denied. On May 31, 1941, the attorney general of New Jersey shut down Camp Norland. Shortly thereafter, the federal government seized all of the Bund's funds as part of a general order freezing the assets of the Axis powers in the United States. On December 11, 1941, four days after Japan's attack on Pearl Harbor and America's entry into the Second World War, the Bund's headquarters were raided by agents of the Treasury Department, all of its records were seized, and the wholesale round-up and imprisonment of its leadership began.

The war years were little kinder to the Klan. In another appearance before the Dies Committee, on January 22, 1942, Colescott was forced to admit that there were only 10,000 Klansmen left in the entire country, and in the spring of 1944 the U.S. Bureau of Internal Revenue issued the organization with a demand for $685,000 in back taxes based on profits it had made during the 1920s. Unable to pay, Colescott instead called a special Klonvokation in Atlanta on April 23, where members voted to revoke the charters of all Klaverns, vacate all offices, and relieve "every Klansman of any obligation whatsoever" to the Knights of the Ku Klux Klan, Inc. "The Klan is dead," Colescott told reporters, "the whole thing is washed up."

This was not quite true. In October 1946 Dr. Samuel Green, a 55-year-old obstetrician, brought the Klan back to life—albeit with limited effect—and a "third Klan" emerged during the 1950s and 1960s in opposition to the civil rights movement and desegregation in the South (discussed in chapter 2). Never again, though, would the Invisible Empire operate on the scale it had during the 1920s, when it was a significant and powerful mainstream organization, its politics and prejudices shared by a wide swath of the American population.

Was the Klan also fascist? Its later involvement with groups such as the Silver Shirts, the Black Legion, and the German-American Bund certainly raises the possibility. But as Linda Gordon, among others, has pointed out, while there are obvious similarities that can be drawn between the Klan's practices and some of the "classic" features of European fascism, including a reliance on demagoguery, heightened emotionalism, and a deeply racialized nationalism, these are common features of many populist movements, and Klansmen never sought to overthrow either the capitalist or the democratic systems of the United States. Indeed, the millions of members of the second Ku Klux Klan regarded themselves first and foremost as patriots and traditionalists, as ordinary people who were concerned about the future direction of their country—nativists in every sense. Be that as it may, however—and despite how much it also functioned as a business, or a social organization—the Klan's virulent and unrelenting crusade against Blacks, Jews, Catholics, and "alien" immigrants nonetheless revealed a deep wellspring of white supremacy in the United States, one that would continue to be drawn from during the remainder of the twentieth century and beyond.

2

Fighting Civil Rights

Citizens' Councils, Guerrillas, and American Nazis

ON MAY 17, 1954, CHIEF JUSTICE EARL WARREN, who had only recently been appointed by President Eisenhower, handed down the Supreme Court's decision in the case of *Brown v. Board of Education of Topeka*. The case had begun back in 1950 as part of a broader assault on the South's system of racial segregation—known as Jim Crow—that had been initiated by the long-established civil rights group the National Association for the Advancement of Colored People (NAACP). Led by its principal legal strategist, Thurgood Marshall, the NAACP had filed a series of lawsuits on behalf of Black parents in Virginia, Delaware, South Carolina, Louisiana, Kansas, and the District of Columbia who were seeking to have their children admitted to white schools. (All the cases were consolidated into *Brown*.) The plaintiffs argued that Black schools were fundamentally unequal to white schools, not just in terms of their physical resources, but also because of the damaging psychological impact segregation had on African-American children. They also contended that the entire doctrine of "separate but equal" that had been established in the 1896 case of *Plessy v. Ferguson*, which provided the legal basis for segregation, was incompatible with the Fourteenth Amendment to the U.S. Constitution. The Court agreed. "We conclude," its verdict read,

> that in the field of public education the doctrine of "separate but equal" has no place. Separate educational facilities are inherently unequal. Therefore, we hold that the plaintiffs and others similarly situated for whom the actions have been brought are, by reason of the segregation

complained of, deprived of the equal protection of the laws guaranteed
by the Fourteenth Amendment.

It was a stunning victory. The whole system of Jim Crow law had seemingly been destroyed.

A furious white backlash against the *Brown* decision swiftly developed, however, encompassing a wide range of organizations and people,
from the new and supposedly "respectable" Citizens' Council movement to a revived, reenergized, and increasingly violent Ku Klux Klan.
In part the Supreme Court itself was to blame for this reaction, because
in order to obtain a unanimous verdict—which Warren considered
essential—the Chief Justice had agreed to delay the decision on how
desegregation would be implemented for a whole year. Even worse,
when what became known as *Brown II* was eventually handed down, on
May 31, 1955, it was vague and indecisive, urging only that the integration of the nation's schools should take place with "all deliberate speed,"
but providing no deadline and leaving it up to the federal courts to determine how this would actually take place. As a result, resistance to integration was widespread, and the NAACP was forced to initiate a whole
new legal campaign to force compliance.

This chapter examines how various white supremacists responded
to the *Brown* decision, as well to the broader civil rights movement that
developed in its aftermath. It encompasses both the Citizens' Council
movement and the Klan but also considers groups such as the National
States' Rights Party and the newly formed American Nazi Party,
together with its publicity-hungry leader George Lincoln Rockwell.
Other notable figures of the extreme right including John Kasper, J. B.
Stoner, and Asa "Ace" Carter are also addressed, as is the considerable
support to "massive resistance" that was provided by various Southern
politicians and institutions, including Alabama Governor George Wallace. We begin with the Citizens' Councils.

Inspiration for the formation of the Citizens' Council movement was
provided by a Mississippi circuit court judge named Tom P. Brady. A
dedicated "son of the South," Brady was a former member of the States'
Rights Democratic Party, the third-party group better known as the
Dixiecrats—led by former South Carolina governor Strom
Thurmond—that had broken with the Democratic Party in 1948 over
its support for Black civil rights. In May 1954, Brady gave a speech to the

Greenwood, Mississippi, chapter of the Sons of the American Revolution vehemently defending segregation and denouncing the *Brown* decision for its upending of legal precedent, as well as its supposedly "communistic" intent. Expanded into a 90-page pamphlet, his address was published under the title *Black Monday*, a pejorative reference to the day the *Brown* decision had been handed down that had been coined by the Democratic Mississippi Congressman—and ardent states' rights advocate John Bell Williams.

Brady had various proposals to help Southern whites respond to the post-*Brown* political landscape, including a youth information program, the popular election of Supreme Court justices, and the creation of a separate state for African Americans to reside in, but the idea that struck the most immediate chord was for the formation of organized resistance groups throughout the South. Brady stressed that these resistance groups should be open and "law-abiding" to clearly distinguish them from what he referred to as the "nefarious Ku Klux Klans." Their primary role should be educational, he said, to disseminate "correct information" about the benefits of racial segregation and the dangerous nature of the *Brown* decision; although if necessary they could also help facilitate the creation of a new political party—a successor to the Dixiecrats—to be called the National Party of Sovereign States of America. Brady also envisaged the establishment of a National Federation of Sovereign States to help coordinate the activities of the resistance movement. Each state would be free to choose its own name for the organization it established, but for his home state Brady suggested that the "Sons of the White Magnolia" might be the most suitable.

The first person to put Brady's ideas into practice was Robert "Tut" Patterson, a Mississippi plantation manager and former World War II paratrooper. Together with several prominent local citizens, including the president of the local bank, Herman Moore, and Harvard-educated lawyer Arthur Clark Jr., Patterson established the inaugural Citizens' Council in Indianola, Mississippi, in July 1954. The "Indianola Plan," in turn, provided the organizational model for the spread of the movement throughout the rest of the South; and it was very successful. Within two years, there were 90 groups in existence, with a total membership close to 250,000. Most organizations referred to themselves as Citizens' Councils, although others, perhaps reflecting Brady's

preference, chose more distinctive titles, such as Louisiana's Southern
Gentlemen, the Paul Revere Associated Yeoman of New Orleans, the
American States Rights Association of Alabama, the Patriots of North
Carolina, the Patrick Henry Group of Richmond, and Virginia's Defend-
ers of State Sovereignty and Individual Liberties.

While the movement went to great lengths to stress its "spontane-
ous" and "grassroots" nature—quite literally, in the name of the Citizens
Grass Roots Crusade of South Carolina, for example—as the historian
Neil McMillen has shown, in actuality the "Indianola Plan" was based
upon a highly coordinated, behind-the-scenes process that left little to
chance and was designed to ensure as much uniformity as possible. Not
unlike the methods of the Klan 30 years earlier, Council organizers often
utilized the preexisting network of fraternal or service clubs such as the
Rotary Club, the Exchange Club, the Kiwanis, the Lions, or Civitans
to get the Council movement off the ground in a new location. Typically, a prominent activist like Patterson or Brady would first secure an
invitation to speak to the members of such groups about the nature and
purpose of the Councils. Thereafter, a second meeting of interested individuals would be organized at which both a steering committee and a
temporary chairperson would be selected. Among the tasks of this steering committee would be the drafting of the nascent Council's charter and
bylaws, together with a list of nominees for its board of directors. The
selection of the directors was crucial, since it was from this group that the
permanent officers of the Council would be drawn, the day-to-day operations of the Council directed, and "peace and good order in the community" assured. As McMillen notes, only when these closed-door sessions
were concluded and everything was in place would the organization be
"revealed to the public . . . lacking only a membership to ratify the pre-
fabricated structure."

Tight control over the formation of the Councils ensured that they
would be staffed and led only by the most "upright" and "solid" members of the community. This had been a key concern of Brady's at the
outset, and it remained central to the vision of the Councils throughout
their existence. Their racism and white supremacy would be nothing if
not "respectable." As a 1956 pamphlet on "How to Organize a Citizens'
Council" emphasized, when it came to the establishment of the Council's
board of directors, every effort should be made to reach out to "major

business, agriculture, labor and industrial interests, as well as representatives of religious and social groups." This stress on "respectability" permeated the Councils completely. They were composed, for the most part, of businessmen, lawyers, doctors, farmers, shopkeepers, schoolteachers, and local politicians: the economic and civic leaders of the communities from which they came. This not only enhanced the Councils' credibility, it also greatly facilitated their ability to police any potential dissent to their politics and approach from within the white community itself, another important consideration.

In keeping with Brady's initial recommendation, most of the Councils' energies were directed toward the "education" of their fellow white citizens. Millions of pieces of racist propaganda were distributed throughout the South in the form of pamphlets, newssheets, broadsides, booklets, posters, cartoons, and reprinted copies of speeches from Southern political figures including John Bell Williams, Senator James O. Eastland (D-MS), Georgia Attorney General Eugene Cook, and former Supreme Court Justice and South Carolinian James F. Byrnes. Titles included *Where is the Reign of Terror?*, *We've Reached Era of Judicial Tyranny*, *The Ugly Truth about the NAACP*, and *The Supreme Court Must Be Curbed*. Various Citizens' Council newspapers were also established, including the *Arkansas Faith*, *The Virginian*, the Alabama-based *States' Rights Advocate*, and, most prominently of all, Mississippi's *The Citizens' Council*, which had a monthly circulation of about 40,000. The Councils did not rely on the printed word alone, however. Mass rallies and speakers bureaus were organized, educational funds—modeled after the NAACP's tax-exempt Legal Defense and Educational Fund—were initiated, and various radio and television programs were created.

The latter began in Jackson, Mississippi, in April 1957, with a 15-minute weekly television show called *Citizens' Council Forum*, produced by the indefatigable William J. Simmons, a wealthy local banker who was also the—unpaid—editor of *The Citizens' Council* newspaper, as well as a prominent Council spokesman. Within a year the *Forum* was being broadcast on 17 stations in nine states, while the Councils' prerecorded radio shows could be heard on more than 50 stations throughout the South. Simmons was aided considerably in his endeavors by the support of Representative Williams and Senator Eastland, who, beginning in the spring of 1958, arranged for the Council movement to have access to the federally subsidized government recording facilities in Washington, D.C. This allowed Simmons to create Council programming at well below market cost, with the result that it could then be offered to interested stations for free. In turn, both Williams and Eastland—as well as scores of their Southern congressional colleagues—would appear regularly on the shows that stemmed from their generosity. As far as Simmons was concerned, there was nothing untoward in any this. The whole operation, he explained, was designed simply "to present the Southern point of view on important issues of the day, and to counteract the propaganda barrage leveled at the South by most national media."

For the most part, the Councils' educational efforts were founded upon a vast—and deeply felt—mélange of racist stereotyping, dubious factual assertion, historical mischaracterization, invented statistics, religious rationalization, and pseudoscientific nonsense. Black Americans were more prone to crime than their white counterparts, it was asserted. They were less intelligent. More childlike. More susceptible to disease. Less moral. Less patriotic. More violent. "The races of man are the handiwork of God, as is everything in nature," explained a publication of the Association of Citizens' Councils of Mississippi called *Racial Facts*, for example. "If He had wanted only one type of man, He would have created only one." Both "the Negro and the white man" had started out in "the land of the Nile," the Council leader Roy V. Harris contended in the pages of the Augusta *Courier*, but whereas "no race of people in antiquity" had made as much progress as the Egyptians, the only two things that "the Negro" had contributed to "the history of mankind" were "1. Human slavery" and "2. Cannibalism."

The supposed "innate" biological differences between Blacks and whites—a key Council belief—were clearly spelled out for the South's fifth- and sixth-grade pupils in the June 1957 issue of *The Citizens' Council* in an article titled "A Manual for Southerners." It stated:

1. The Negro's arm is about two inches longer than the white man's.
2. The jaw is shaped differently.
3. The weight of the brains differ.
4. The eyes are different.
5. The noses are different.
6. The lips are different.

7. The cheek bones are different.
8. The skulls are different.
9. The ears are different.
10. The hair is different.
11. The voices are different.

Judge Brady outlined his views on the inherent backwardness of African Americans in extraordinarily crude terms in *Black Monday*, widely regarded as the first official handbook of the Council movement, writing:

> You can dress a chimpanzee, housebreak him, and teach him to use a knife and fork, but it will take countless generations of evolutionary development, if ever, before you can convince him that a caterpillar or a cockroach is not a delicacy. Likewise, the social, political, economic, and religious preferences of the Negro remain close to the caterpillar and the cockroach. . . . It is merely a matter of taste. A cockroach or a caterpillar remains proper food for a chimpanzee.

The expression of such white supremacist views was often underpinned by a profound sense of sexual anxiety, with the fear of miscegenation especially pronounced. For example, in another section of "A Manual for Southerners," the region's schoolchildren were told that the "Race Mixers . . . want Negroes and whites to date each other," and that to "integrate the races means to have them live with each other and marry each other." Similarly, Brady used *Black Monday* to reflect on his ideal of the "well-bred, cultured Southern white woman"—"the loveliest and purest of God's creatures, the nearest thing to an angelic being that treads this terrestrial ball"—while at the same time issuing the dire warning that "[t]he Negro proposes to breed up his inferior intellect and whiten his skin and 'blow out the light' in the white man's brain and muddy his skin" through miscegenation.

The Councils even went so far as to circulate a manufactured tape recording of an address supposedly given by one "Professor Roosevelt Williams" of Howard University—a historically Black college in Washington, D.C.—to an NAACP meeting in Jackson, in which the professor detailed the widespread sexual dissatisfaction of white women with white men and outlined their not-so-secret cravings for "Negro men." As the *Arkansas Faith* saw it, the tape was proof that the "N.A.A.C.P.

and their insolent agitators are little concerned with an education for the 'ignorant nigger'; but, rather, are 'demanding' integration in the white bedroom." This was also the view of Alabama state senator and Council spokesman Walter C. Givhan, who argued that the whole purpose of the NAACP's campaign for desegregation was "to open the bedroom doors of our white women to Negro men." Confronted with evidence that the Williams tape was clearly faked—there was no Professor Williams on the faculty of Howard, for example—Tut Patterson responded by arguing that the Councils had never actually "claimed it to be authentic," and suggesting that, in any event, it was up to the NAACP to prove that it wasn't.

Jazz music, the predominant form of African-American music of the time, was also dragged into suspicion. In an article titled "From Bawdy Houses to Parlor," in the January 1956 issue of *The Citizen Council*, William Stephenson contended that the music had its origins in Africa, where it had been used as the soundtrack for sexual orgies, and that the very term "jazz" was really a "slang word" for "illicit sexual intercourse." In other words, as far as the Citizens' Councils were concerned, jazz was just one more encouragement to interracial sex.

Seemingly higher-level justifications for the continuation of segregation were also widely employed. These centered on the sanctity of states' rights and the supposed "unconstitutionality" of the *Brown v. Board of Education* decision. It was "high time for all Americans to wake up," William Simmons warned an audience at a Farmers-Merchants banquet in Oakland, Iowa, in February 1958. "If any court can tell the people of Mississippi or Louisiana that they shall run their public schools according to the theories of certain social revolutionaries," he argued, "then the Court can tell the people of Iowa or Nebraska that they shall run *their* schools according to notions equally as radical." After all, Simmons reasoned, as he sought support for the Councils' crusade beyond the Southland, "If our States' Rights are usurped with impunity, are yours safe?"

The spurious pre-Civil War doctrine of state interposition was also revived. This was the "theory" that every state legislature had the right to intercede—or interpose—between its citizens and the federal government if the state determined that the rights of those citizens were being threatened by the federal government. In effect—if accepted—each Southern state would possess a veto over every federal law that a majority of its (presumably white) populace disapproved of. That interposition was "legal nonsense," as its many critics pointed out, did nothing to prevent the Citizens' Councils from enthusiastically promoting the idea, nor did it deter the state legislatures of Virginia, Louisiana, South Carolina, Arkansas, Alabama, Mississippi, Florida, and Georgia from formally adopting the doctrine; other states, such as Texas, Tennessee, and North Carolina did not go quite so far—they merely expressed their "support" for the idea. At root, such constitutional and legal arguments all reflected the underlying belief, as expressed by Councillor Louis W. Hollis in an address in Montgomery, Alabama, as late as 1965, that the United States was "a white man's government, conceived by white men and maintained by them, through every year of its history." And, as Hollis also went on to assert, that the country should continue to "be ruled by the white man until the end of time."

A final set of pro-segregationist arguments blamed Communists for stirring up trouble in the South. The NAACP—either "knowingly or unwittingly"—"has allowed itself to become part and parcel of the Communist conspiracy to overthrow the democratic governments of this nation and its sovereign states," claimed Eugene Clark in the Council-promoted pamphlet *The Ugly Truth About the NAACP*, for example. At the same time, the Oklahoma Citizens' Council maintained that "Our White Christian Civilization is the only barrier between Soviet Dictators and World Conquest." As historian George Lewis has noted, linking the push for civil rights with the widespread fear of Communist subversion that was prevalent during the early years of the Cold War was doubly advantageous for Southern segregationists, since it allowed them both to attempt to transform "a southern sectional problem . . . into an American problem of national security" and also to cast one of their more cherished beliefs in a dramatic new light. This was the myth of the "contented Negro," one of the South's most beloved shibboleths. It posited not just that African Americans were "happy" with segregation—as they had previously been with slavery—but that Blacks had also been making great "progress" under the rule of Jim Crow, and that it was only "outside agitators"—whether communists, liberals, Northern carpetbaggers, or radical abolitionists—who ever sought to overturn such mutually beneficial arrangements.

Various attempts were made to coordinate the activities of the local Councils, such as through the establishment of the Federation of Constitutional Government in July 1955 and the creation of the national Citizens' Councils of America in April the following year, in which William Simmons, almost inevitably, became the driving force. But effective regional unity proved elusive, and to a considerable extent the Citizens' Councils remained a largely decentralized movement. Yet any such weakness was more than offset by the degree to which the Councils were both supported by, and entwined with, the local and state political establishments, especially in Deep South states such as Mississippi, Alabama, and Louisiana. Indeed, in 1960, the longstanding Council member Ross R. Barnett was elected governor of the Magnolia state. ("There is no case in history where the Caucasian race has survived social integration," Barnett argued, adding, "We will not drink from the cup of genocide.") The Councils worked hand in glove with these state legislatures to secure the passage of various laws designed to fight back integration, including so-called "freedom of choice" laws that allowed parents to select their children's schools for themselves, thereby creating a system of "voluntary segregation"; "pupil placement" laws that empowered officials to send children to schools based on supposedly nonracial criteria such as "the general welfare" of the local community; and in some cases, laws that simply made it a criminal offense to comply with the *Brown* decision, or abolished public education all together.

The Councils also played a critical role in the unrelenting campaign against the NAACP. Across the South various legislative committees were established to investigate the organization for evidence of tax evasion, criminal law violations, and communist subversion. At the same time, laws were passed that prevented public employees such as teachers—one of the NAACP's key constituencies—from belonging to the organization, leaving members with the choice of either resigning from the group or risk losing their jobs. Other statutes prohibited the NAACP from actively supporting desegregation lawsuits, while governors were granted "emergency powers" to help deal with the organization. Five states passed laws requiring the NAACP to turn over its membership lists to state authorities. If the organization refused, it risked being found in contempt of court and banned from operating altogether—as happened in Alabama, when the NAACP was effectively put out of action for eight years, between 1956 and 1964—but if it complied—as it did in Louisiana—then it lost most of its membership anyway, since, as Adam Fairclough points out, "the Citizens' Councils immediately published the lists, inviting whites to fire, boycott, and intimidate those whose names appeared."

Economic intimidation as a means to retaliate against Blacks who advocated for integration, or even just attempted to participate in the democratic process by registering to vote, had been seen as an important weapon in the Council arsenal from the outset. As Arthur Clark, one of the founders of the Indianola Citizens' Council saw it, for example, the threat of desegregation could be effectively minimized simply by the removal of those who would "stir up discontent." "We propose to accomplish this," he explained, "through the careful application of economic pressure upon men who cannot be controlled otherwise." The Councils would "make it difficult, if not impossible, for any Negro who advocates integration to find and hold a job, get credit or renew a mortgage," boasted another Council spokesman, Alston Keith, from Selma, Alabama. In *Black Monday*, Brady even suggested waging economic warfare on the African-American community through the wholesale firing of Black maids. As already indicated, the tactic was employed frequently against members and supporters of the NAACP. In Selma, in August 1955, for example, 29 Blacks put their names to a NAACP petition in support of desegregation. By the first week of September, 16 of those signatories found themselves out of a job. In Yazoo City, Mississippi, 53 people signed a similar petition, but as James C. Cobb recounts "[o]ne by one those who signed . . . began to lose their jobs or whatever 'business' or 'trade' they had with whites." Within short order, only two names remained on the petition, and both of those people were quickly forced to leave town.

On the national level, it is true that no member of the powerful Southern Caucus—the largely Democratic congressional voting bloc that had prevented the passage of any meaningful civil rights legislation for decades—was officially a member of the Citizens' Councils. But they didn't really need to be, since it was more than clear where the sympathies of most of the region's senators and congressmen lay. This was well illustrated on March 13, 1956, when the caucus issued a Declaration of Constitutional Principles. It was signed by 82 of the region's 106 representatives and 19 of its 22 senators; the only senators not to sign were Estes Kefauver and Albert Gore Sr., both of Tennessee, and Lyndon Johnson of Texas, all three relatively liberal and all three hoping for a run at the presidency. The Southern Manifesto, as it was better known, was a full-throated endorsement of the Citizens' Councils and of massive resistance more generally. The *Brown* ruling was "a clear abuse of judicial power," it asserted, and "all lawful means" should be used to "bring about a reversal of this decision which is contrary to the Constitution and to prevent the use of force in its implementation." Railing against "outside meddlers" and the "agitators and troublemakers invading our States," the Manifesto even invoked the myth of the "contented Negro," as it denounced the Supreme Court for attempting to "destroy the amicable relations between the white and Negro races that have been created through 90 years of patient effort by the good people of both races."

At first women were excluded from being members of the Councils—although they could certainly support them—but this changed as the movement spread across the South, and as Elizabeth Gillespie McRae shows in her book *Mothers of Massive Resistance* (2018), not only did many middle-class white women join up, but they actually did a great deal of the grassroots work. In South Carolina, for example, Council women "conducted membership drives, served as social chairs, organized recruiting events, and planned meetings," constituting up to a third of the total membership in some local chapters. In Mississippi, a Women's Activities and Youth Work (WAYW) group was created in order to give women a more formal role in the Councils' educational outreach program. Led by a former high school history teacher, Sara McCorkle, WAYW was unabashed about its desire to "indoctrinate the nation's youth" with "patriotism, states' rights and racial integrity," as it distributed handbooks for elementary schoolchildren, censored "undesirable textbooks," and sponsored statewide essay contests on the benefits of racial segregation. Independent organizations such as the Women's States' Rights Association of South Carolina and the Mothers League of Arkansas were also established.

Long-standing activists such as Cornelia Dabney Tucker and Nell Battle Lewis were also attracted to the cause. Tucker launched a letter-writing campaign to change the nomination process for Supreme Court justices employing the same methods and even the same stationery that she had used against the "court-packing scheme" of Franklin Roosevelt in the 1930s. And Lewis, a complicated and prolific white supremacist polemist who had been active in the field since the 1920s—when she had been a vocal critic of the violence of the Ku Klux Klan—joined with the Patriots of North Carolina and the North Carolina Defenders of States' Rights to help oust two of the three North Carolina congressmen who had refused to sign the Southern Manifesto in the subsequent 1956 election. Far from being marginal, McCrae writes, in a range of different ways, all these women "made sure that their white neighbors knew that daily vigilance was the cost of a white supremacist political order."

The involvement of women added to the supposed respectability of the Council movement, as did its formal disavowal of violence. Yet as critics have pointed out, the latter was more than a little disingenuous since the ongoing subjugation of Black Americans remained the goal of the Councils in just the same way as it was for the Klan and other, more violent groups (discussed below). Indeed, in the view of contemporary liberal journalists such as Ralph McGill of the *Atlanta Constitution* and Hodding Carter of Greenville, Mississippi's, *Delta Democrat-Times*, the Councils were nothing more than a "scrubbed up cousin of the Klan," an "uptown Klan," "a white-collar Klan," or a "country club Klan." Moreover, the "economic thuggery" of the Councils, along with their other intimidatory practices, even if not regarded as acts of violence in themselves—which is certainly open to debate—nonetheless clearly contributed to a more generalized climate in which violence against African Americans was deemed acceptable (and some of which was committed by individual Council members). "Make no mistake about it, the Citizens' Councils are following the pattern instituted by the White South during Reconstruction," argued Daniel Byrd of the NAACP. The historian Numan V. Bartley characterized the Councils as little more than highly polished "vigilante committees."

Overall, the fortunes of the Citizens' Councils tended to ebb and flow in response to the events confronting them. Their unyielding commitment to white supremacy notwithstanding, theirs was a largely reactive movement. They were most active after the *Brown* decisions, for example, and again in late 1955 in the wake of the Montgomery bus boycott that had been sparked by the arrest of Rosa Parks that December—the protest that propelled Martin Luther King Jr. to national attention as the leader of the Montgomery Improvement Association. There was another upsurge in activity—with a concomitant increase in membership—in the wake of the riots that accompanied Autherine Lucy's attempt to become the first African American to attend the University of Alabama in 1956; and again, the following year, during the crisis at Central High School in Little Rock, Arkansas, that resulted in President Eisenhower federalizing the Arkansas National Guard and dispatching 1,100 army paratroopers to the city in order to keep the peace. But in between such high-profile events, when Council members had less to feel immediately threatened by, there would often be a sharp downturn in activity, as interest—at least among the rank and file—waned, finances diminished, and recruitment became more difficult.

Two new civil rights laws followed in the wake of the confrontation at Little Rock: the Civil Rights Act of 1957, which created a Civil Rights Commission with powers of subpoena and a new civil rights division within the Justice Department; and the Civil Rights Act of 1960, which authorized federal courts to appoint referees to help Blacks register to vote and introduced penalties for anyone who obstructed their registration. Although modest in scope, the new laws indicated that the federal government was at last willing to rein in at least some of the obstructionism of the Southern states. At the same time—and much more significantly—the activism of the civil rights movement itself broadened and intensified, drawing in groups such as the Student Nonviolent Coordinating Committee (SNCC), the Congress of Racial Equality (CORE), and Martin Luther King's new organization, the Southern Christian Leadership Conference (SCLC). From the student sit-in movement that began in Greensboro, North Carolina, in 1960, to the "freedom riders" who faced down daily acts of violence on the nation's interstate bus system in 1961, through to the massive protests that took place in cities such as Albany, Georgia, and Birmingham, Alabama, between 1962 and 1963, thousands of African Americans and their white allies drove the "freedom struggle" forward relentlessly.

As a result, by the early 1960s, the defiance and determination that had characterized the Citizens' Council movement since its formation began to drain away. For sure, the Councils would continue to fight—not least against the passage of the Civil Rights Act of 1964 and the Voting Rights Act of 1965 (see below)—but even in the Deep South it became increasingly clear that, for all the movement's fury, and for all of its promises and justifications, the rule of Jim Crow was not going to prevail after all. Massive resistance was teetering.

What, then, of the Klan and other more "extremist" white supremacists of the period? It is to these that we now turn.

The *Brown* decision certainly provided fresh impetus to the Ku Klux Klan, which, as we saw in the previous chapter, had fallen on hard times during the 1940s. However, the Klan that emerged in the 1950s and 1960s—the so-called "third Klan"—was much different, both in size and in character, from the one that had preceded it. At most, membership never climbed above 40,000, for example, and these mid-century Klansmen belonged to a dizzying array of fractious and competing organizations with names such as the U.S. Klans, Knights of the Ku Klux Klan (U.S. Klans, for short); the National Knights of the Ku Klux Klan; the Militant Knights of the Ku Klux Klan; the Federated Knights of the Ku Klux Klan; the Independent Knights of the Ku Klux Klan, and many others. Generally speaking, the third Klan was also much more violent than its counterpart in the 1920s and 1930s—closer in spirit to the Reconstruction-era Klan—and composed for the most part of lower-skilled, poorly educated, working-class whites who felt most immediately threatened by the possibility of integration, seeing it as a danger both to their livelihoods and their status.

Initially, the largest and best-organized Klan of this period was the U.S. Klans, which was led by Eldon Lee Edwards, an Atlanta automobile paint sprayer. Revising the original Klan rituals of William Simmons—and recopyrighting them—in 1955 Edwards received a charter from the state of Georgia and called on all Klansmen to recognize his organization as the rightful successor to the Invisible Empire, with himself as the new Imperial Wizard. (In a further attempt to establish his bona fides, Edwards began holding regular cross burnings on Atlanta's Stone Mountain, a practice that other Klans, as well as other white supremacists, would regularly imitate in an attempt to confer legitimacy on their organizations too.) By 1959 there were chapters of the U.S. Klans in nine Southern states, with a total membership close to 15,000. Their purpose, Edwards maintained, was to prevent desegregation "at any and all cost."

Edwards died of a heart attack in August 1960, aged 51. His successor was the Georgia Grand Dragon Robert "Wild Bill" Davidson, his nickname a tribute to the fringed leather jacket he wore in his job as an insurance salesman. However, Davidson soon got into a dispute with Edwards's widow, and he and his second in command, Calvin Craig, split off from the U.S. Klans in February the following year to create their own organization: the impressive sounding, if almost parodically titled, Invisible Empire, United Klans, Knights of the Ku Klux Klan of America, Inc. Davidson and Craig then promptly fell out, with Davidson resigning from the group after a little more than a month in charge— organizational chaos, inept leadership, and almost constant infighting being typical features of the whole Klan movement during this time— and so Craig reached out to the head of the Alabama Knights, Robert Marvin Shelton—who had himself once been a leader in the U.S. Klans—to plot a way forward. At a meeting at Indian Springs, Georgia, on July 8, Shelton and Craig, along with the members of seven other Klans, agreed to merge into a new organization: the United Klans of America (UKA). Shelton was installed as Imperial Wizard, the youngest person, at age 32, to attain the position.

Shelton was born in Tuscaloosa, Alabama, in 1929, where his father was both a grocer and a Klansman. In 1947 Shelton joined the Air Force and was stationed in Germany, where the sight of Black servicemen going out with white women appalled him. Following his discharge from the service, Shelton returned home to Tuscaloosa, finding work at the local B. F. Goodrich plant, first on the factory floor and then as a traveling salesman for the company. He also joined Edwards's U.S. Klans, eventually working his way up to become the Grand Dragon of Alabama, before striking out on his own with the Alabama Knights—he was spending so much time on Klan business that Goodrich fired him in 1961. A formidable organizer, with a reputation as a man of "action"—as well as a devout Methodist and devoted family man—by 1967 Shelton had turned the UKA into the dominant Klan in the country, with 15,000 members spread across 19 states. The next largest Klan was the National Knights of the Ku Klux Klan, based in Tucker, Georgia. It was led by an Atlanta lawyer, James Venable, and its membership was a mere 4,000 in comparison.

Violence was central to the activities of the Klan, both the source of its strength and, for many members, also its appeal, with the result that despite its relatively small size it was able to function as a formidable—

and frightening—force throughout the South. The Southern Regional Council, an Atlanta-based civil rights agency, documented 530 cases of suspected Klan violence in the first four years after the *Brown* decision alone, including various beatings, stonings, floggings, stabbings, shootings, bombings, and burnings. In January 1957, in the aftermath of the success of the Montgomery bus boycott, the Klan bombed four Black churches and several Black homes in the city, for example. Later that year in Birmingham, Alabama, Edward Aaron, a Black handyman, was castrated with razor blades before kerosene and turpentine were poured over his wounds as part of an initiation ceremony carried out by the Asa Carter-led group, the Original Ku Klux Klan of the Confederacy. Whites too were affected. A school teacher in Camden, South Carolina, was flogged because of his support of desegregation, and a doctor's home in Gaffney, also in South Carolina, was dynamited because his wife had written an article against Jim Crow. The use of dynamite became so extensive—at least 138 examples of its use by the Klan between 1956 and 1963 have been documented—that a special police intelligence organization, the Southern Conference on Bombing, was created in 1958 to deal with the problem, and the FBI was compelled to act.

The Klan became even more violent during the 1960s. There are three principal reasons for this. The first is connected to the decline of the Citizens' Council movement. As it became increasingly clear that massive resistance was failing—that the Councils supposedly "lawful" efforts at preventing desegregation weren't going to prevail—so violence became seen as the only effective alternative for those who wanted to continue the fight. Ironically, despite the Councils much trumpeted desire to separate themselves from the "lunatics of the far right," the Klan and other extremists simply stepped into the space that the Citizens' Councils had opened up for them. This, in turn, is related to what the historian Matthew Lassiter has termed the rise of the "pragmatic South" in the aftermath of the New Deal and the Second World War. With specific reference to desegregation, as Clive Webb notes, once it became clear that massive resistance was failing, the region's business and civic leaders were faced with a stark choice. They could push for more violent resistance, which would inevitably "blemish the reputation of their community and discourage northern capital investment," or they could shift to a strategy of "token integration" and thereby continue to receive this investment—

including from the considerable coffers of the federal government—that was vital to the South's ongoing development. For the most part, at least for these elites, "token integration" was deemed the better way to go.

The second factor in pushing the Klan toward greater violence was the increasing activism, visibility, and success of the civil rights movement. Simply put, as groups like SNCC, CORE, and the SCLC ramped up their activities, Klansmen and others felt compelled to act to attempt to knock them down again. Finally, the Klan was responding to the election of the new Democratic government of John F. Kennedy in 1960. Not only was Kennedy a Catholic—another of the Klan's long-standing enemies—but his administration was also formally committed to the successful implementation of integration; although, in truth, it would take the ongoing pressure of the civil rights movement, widespread international bad press, and, ultimately, Kennedy's assassination in 1963, to finally secure the passage of vital legislation in this area.

Notable examples of Klan violence during the 1960s include their attacks on the "freedom riders," the orchestration of armed mobs to counteract the activities of sit-in demonstrators and civil rights' protestors in places such as Oxford, Mississippi; Athens, Georgia; and Bogalusa, Louisiana—often with the compliance of the local police—and a deadly increase in bombings. Robert Shelton's United Klans of America were particularly fervent bombmakers. Indeed, in the summer of 1961 Shelton had begun running an "explosive school" and offering other forms of paramilitary training to select Klansmen in conjunction with the terrorist organization Nacirema, Inc. Nacirema—"American" spelled backward— had been formed in July 1961 and was composed almost exclusively of Klansmen and former Klansmen. The authorities first became aware of its existence in 1963 when an Atlanta prostitute informed the police that her boyfriend belonged to the secretive group. It probably had fewer than 60 members but was believed to be responsible for some 138 bombings across 11 Southern states during this time. The most horrific example of the UKA's own bombing campaign took place on Sunday, September 15, 1963, when a massive explosion ripped through Birmingham's 16th Street Baptist Church, killing four young girls—Addie Mae Collins, Cynthia Wesley, Carole Robertson (all aged 14), and Carol Denise McNair (aged 11)—and seriously injuring 22 others. The bombings in Birmingham were so frequent that residents of the city took to calling it

"Bombingham," while the Black section of town was known as "Dyna-mite Hill."

Remarkably, Shelton and the United Klans of America were not even the most violent of the Klansmen in operation in the 1960s. That dubious accolade more rightly belongs to Samuel Holloway Bowers Jr., and his independently run White Knights of the Ku Klux Klan of Mississippi, which, it is estimated, was responsible for 9 murders, close to 100 bomb-ings—including that of 63 churches—and nearly 300 beatings, drive-by shootings, and various other assaults between 1964 and 1968.

The historian Wyn Craig Wade calls Bowers "the most mysterious and dangerous leader in the history of the Klan." He was born in New Orleans in 1924, the grandson of a Mississippi lawyer who had been a four-term U.S. congressman on one side of the family and a wealthy planter on the other. His parents divorced when he was 14, and the young boy became something of a loner. He enrolled in the Navy after Pearl Harbor and was honorably discharged in 1945. After the war he attended Tulane University in New Orleans before transferring to the School of Engineering at the University of Southern California. His col-lege education made Bowers something of an intellectual in Klan cir-cles, an elevated status he was keen to exploit. "The typical Mississippi redneck doesn't have enough sense to know what he is doing. I have to use him for my own cause and direct his every action to fit my plan," he would point out.

After his graduation, Bowers settled in Laurel, Mississippi, where he established the Sambo Amusement Company with his college friend Robert Larson (the company leased pinball and vending machines). Rumors persisted that Larson and Bowers were more than just "friends," but Bowers' eccentricities went well beyond any closeted homosexuality. He trained his dog to respond to his shout of "Heil Hitler!" for example, and was known to parade around his home wearing a Nazi armband; yet, at the same time, an informant for the FBI reported that Bowers had photographs of Marx, Lenin, and the Pope on his fireplace mantle, and that he may even have been a member of the Communist Party in the 1940s. He was certainly religious, and he used this religious belief to justify his acts of violence, seeing no contradiction between the two positions. "As Christians," Bowers wrote, "we are disposed to kindness, generosity and humility in our dealings with others. As militants we are disposed to the use of physical force against our enemies." He further argued that any "eliminations" that needed to be carried out as part of his "Holy crusade" should be "done in silence, without malice, in the manner of a Christian act."

Bowers was elected Imperial Wizard of the White Knights of Mississippi in April 1964, and by the following year the organization had an impressive 5,000 members, before dropping down to 1,500 in early 1966 as federal arrests began to take their toll. Bowers ran the White Knights along clear authoritarian lines. Every major act of arson, bombing, or murder required his personal approval to be carried out. Its most notorious killings occurred in June 1964, when three civil rights workers, who were taking part in a "Freedom Summer" project organized by CORE and SNCC to increase the number of registered Black voters in Mississippi, were abducted and murdered in Neshoba County (the so-called "Mississippi Burning murders.") The three activists—two white and one Black—were Michael H. Schwerner, aged 23; Andrew Goodman, aged 20; and James E. Chaney, aged 21. Another of the Klan's high-profile murders was that of Vernon Dahmer, president of the Forest County chapter of the NAACP, whose home in Hattiesburg was firebombed in a predawn raid on January 10, 1966. Dahmer's wife and children were all inside at the time.

Bowers and six other members of the Klan were convicted on federal civil rights charges in the murders of Schwerner, Goodman, and Chaney in October 1967; another perpetrator, Edgar Ray Killen, was found guilty of his part in the killings in 2005. Having exhausted his appeals, Bowers was sent to prison on April 3, 1970. He served six years of his ten-year sentence and was paroled in 1976. Needless to say, the White Knights floundered without the "inspiration" of their brutal leader, but it revived again upon his release, albeit with fewer than a dozen hardcore members. Between 1968 and 1969 Bowers was also tried four times for the murder of Vernon Dahmer, but each case ended in a mistrial, and the federal charges against him were finally dropped in 1973. The state of Mississippi reopened the case in 1991. Seven years later Bowers was found guilty and sentenced to life imprisonment. He died in the Mississippi State Penitentiary in 2006, aged 82.

As the activities of the White Knights of Mississippi demonstrate, violence against African Americans did not cease with the passage of the Civil Rights Act of 1964 or even the Voting Rights Act of 1965. On the contrary, it continued through the remainder of the 1960s and into the 1970s and long beyond that. Yet it is also important to recognize that white supremacists did not rely on violence alone to further their cause. Indeed, one of the interesting consequences of the success of the civil rights movement during this time was the extent to which it forced members of the extreme right to adapt to it, and even, in some cases, to attempt to imitate it. Significantly, if tentatively at first—although this was a development that provided an early indication of one of the key ways in which the ideology of white supremacy as a whole would develop in the years ahead—as the civil rights movement marched on, Klansmen and other white racists increasingly began to cast themselves as the "victims" of racial oppression and to make the case for the urgent necessity of the protection of *their* civil and political rights.

As early as 1953, for example, Byrant Bowles, a former Korean War and World War II veteran from Florida, established an organization called the National Association for the Advancement of White People in imitation of the NAACP. (Bowles helped to inspire a successful revolt against the *Brown* decision in the small town of Milford, Delaware, in 1954, but his career as a pro-segregationist activist was cut short by his imprisonment for the murder of his brother-in-law in Texas in 1958.) The idea would be taken up again in Cincinnati by one William Miller in 1964, and much more successfully by the former Klansman David Duke in 1980 (see chapter 3). Throughout the 1960s, Klansmen also staged their own sit-ins, organized petitions and protest marches, delivered leaflets, encouraged voter registration, and gave plenty of media interviews. Extensive recruitment drives were also launched. On March 1, 1960, for example, the Klan confidently announced its plans to recruit 10 million new members, and a similar—and similarly ineffective—recruitment drive was launched in the run-up to the passage of the Civil Rights Act in 1964. Even Dr. King's strategy of nonviolent resistance was apparently up for grabs. According to Calvin Craig, who informed a gathering of the United Klans of America in the summer of 1963: "Let's be nonviolent. We've got to start fighting just like the niggers."

In addition to the various Klansmen we have been considering, there were also a number of more independently minded white supremacist

zealots in operation during the 1950s and 1960s. The three most prominent were John Kasper, Asa "Ace" Carter, and J. B. Stoner.

Frederick John Kasper Jr. was born in New Jersey in October 1929.
His father was an engineer and a graduate of the Massachusetts Institute
of Technology; his mother, a housewife. Deemed physically and men-
tally unfit for service in the Second World War, in 1949 Kasper enrolled
at Columbia University to study English and philosophy, where he fell
in love with both the poetry and the politics of Ezra Pound. At the time,
the notorious anti-Semitic author of "The Cantos" and other major early
modernist works was confined to a mental institution in Washington,
D.C., having been convicted of treason for broadcasting pro-fascist propaganda during World War II. (He was eventually released in 1958 and
spent the rest of life in exile in Italy.) A planned PhD on the poet came
to nothing, and in 1952 Kasper opened the Make-It-New Bookshop in
Greenwich Village in New York. The store sold not just Pound's work,
but also various extremist political tracts such as Adolf Hitler's *Mein
Kampf* and the anti-Semitic forgery the *Protocols of the Learned Elders of
Zion*. In early 1956 Kasper volunteered to work on the unsuccessful Alabama senatorial campaign of retired Navy Rear Admiral John G. Crommelin, a committed segregationist and racist who believed that a "hidden
force" of Jewish conspirators was behind both the civil rights movement
and the imminent decline of the American nation. In the course of the
campaign Kasper also met Asa Carter, and together the two men formed
the Seaboard White Citizens' Council in Washington, D.C., in May 1956.

Carter was the more experienced activist. Born in Oxford, Alabama,
in 1925, he had served in the Navy during the Second World War before
receiving a degree in journalism from the University of Colorado at Boulder. He subsequently settled in Birmingham with his wife and four children, finding work as a radio announcer but was fired in 1955 for making anti-Semitic comments on air. That October Carter formed his first
political organization, the North Alabama Citizens' Council (NACC).
The NACC, unlike other Citizens' Councils, excluded Jews from membership and was composed largely of laborers and other unskilled workers. Indeed, as far as Carter was concerned, the whole Council movement
was too "respectable" and too middle class—too concerned with politics
and its own "law-abiding" reputation—when what was really needed
was much more direct and violent resistance to the impending evils of

"mongrelisation, degradation, atheism, and communist dictatorship." Carter also published a magazine, *The Southerner*, that, among other things, attacked rock 'n' roll as "sensuous Negro music" that was eroding the "entire moral structure of man, of Christianity, of spirituality . . . [and] all the white man has created through his devotion to God." Nor was he fond of jazz, as a sign hanging in his office that read "Be Bop Promotes Communism" made clear.

Combining Carter's distrust of popular music with his belief in the efficacy of violence, one of the first "direct actions" carried out by members of the North Alabama Citizens' Council was their assault on the Black singer and jazz pianist Nat "King" Cole during a concert at Birmingham's Municipal Auditorium in April 1956. Dismissing Cole as "a vicious agitator for integration," Carter, who had not himself been present at the attack—although he clearly directed it—then proceeded to organize a White People's Defense Fund for the six members of his organization who were charged in the incident. Increasingly ostracized by the leadership of the Citizens' Council movement, in November 1956 Carter next established the Original Ku Klux Klan of the Confederacy as a kind of paramilitary auxiliary to the NACC; critics have described it as more closely resembling a "cell of Nazi storm troopers." In addition to the previously mentioned castration of Edward Aaron, the group was involved in numerous acts of violence, including a vicious assault on civil rights leader Fred Shuttlesworth—one of the founders of the Southern Christian Leadership Conference—and his wife in 1957. Perhaps not surprisingly, there was also a great deal of violence within the Klan itself. In January 1957, for example, Carter was charged with the attempted murder of his hooded colleagues J. P. Tillery and Charles Bridges. The two had apparently complained about Ace's dictatorial "one-man rule," and so Carter had shot them in retaliation—although the charges were later dropped for "lack of evidence."

The influence of Carter and Crommelin on John Kasper was significant. Within two months of the formation of the Seaboard White Citizens' Council, the organization was suspected as being behind an outbreak of cross burnings that suddenly appeared at the homes of high-prolife figures such as Chief Justice Warren and liberal New York Democratic Senator Herbert Lehman. It also launched a campaign of intimidation against civil rights activists in Charlottesville, Virginia. In

August 1956 Kasper and Carter turned up in the small town of Clinton, Tennessee, where they fanned the flames of racial resentment to such an extent that U.S. Marshals and the National Guard had to be called in to restore order. (Kasper was charged with inciting a riot and sedition but was found not guilty on both counts on November 20; the jury deliberating for less than an hour before reaching its verdict.) Undeterred, Kasper moved on, attempting to stir up trouble in places such as Clay, Kentucky, and Oak Ridge, Tennessee. In February the following year, the jazz musician Louis Armstrong had a stick of dynamite thrown at him while performing on stage at Chilhowee Park in Knoxville, Tennessee. Kasper—presumably inspired by Carter's musical animus—was again suspected of being behind the attack, although no charges were brought.

Kasper never formally belonged to any Klan group, but he was a much in-demand speaker at many of their gatherings. Indeed, his incendiary rhetoric and unabashed racial populism was as much a part of his appeal as was his commitment to action. Kasper called for "roving bands of patriots" to descend on any town threatened by desegregation. "We want all the rabble rousers we can get," he would explain. "We want trouble and we want it everywhere we can get it." Speaking at a meeting of the Florida Klan in Inverness in 1957, Kasper urged the hanging of the nine members of the U.S. Supreme Court and suggested that God had "stamped ugliness on the face of the Jew for the same reason that he put rattlers on the snake."

Earlier that year Kasper had been indicted at the federal level for his ongoing obstruction of school integration. His trial took place in July, and he and six other defendants were found guilty. It was an unexpected decision, since Southern juries usually refused to convict those accused of similar crimes, although Kasper's status as a Northern "outsider" perhaps provides the explanation for the apparent discrepancy in this case. In any event, a six-month sentence was handed down. In the aftermath of his conviction and subsequent imprisonment, Kasper endeavored to present himself as a righteous martyr to the segregationist cause, but by this time his reputation had suffered an almost irreversible setback because of revelations about his personal life that had resulted from investigations by a Florida state senate committee into bombings in the state. Under relentless cross-examination, Kasper had confessed to dating an African-American woman named Florette Henry during his time in New York and also of having associated with Blacks "socially and without distinction" at his Greenwich Village bookstore. Additional rumors that he had had a homosexual relationship with Ned Williams, a Black male dance instructor, went unconfirmed, but the damage was done. Kasper's earlier bohemian lifestyle had come back to haunt him.

The third part of this ugly triumvirate was Jesse Benjamin Stoner Jr. He was born in Walker County, Georgia, in 1924, and his early years were hard. He contracted polio at age two, which left him with a pronounced limp for the rest of his life—and thus exempted him from service in World War II—his father died when he was five, and a few years later he lost his mother to cancer. He was initially educated at the prestigious all-boys private McCallie School in Chattanooga before going on to study law, gaining entry to the Georgia bar in 1951. (Stoner would put his legal skills to wide use, attempting to defend a range of white supremacists in the years to follow, including the assassin of Martin Luther King, James Earl Ray, in 1969.) Stoner claimed that his virulently racist and anti-Semitic political beliefs had come to him almost fully formed at a young age, the product of his observations growing up in the South, where he was able, he said, to see through the "false front" of African Americans living there. A self-proclaimed fascist, he joined the Chattanooga unit of the Klan in 1942. Three years later he established his own, one-man Stoner Anti-Jewish Party, advocating legislation that would "make being a Jew a crime, punishable by death." His views were so extreme, his rhetoric so outlandish, that Stoner was expelled from the Associated Klans of America in 1950. However, by the late 1950s and early 1960s, in a clear indication of just how much the political climate had changed, these same views and the very same rhetoric had turned him into a kind of "Klansman-at-large"—much like John Kasper—ready to drop into whatever trouble spot presented itself.

In August 1958 Stoner and Ed Fields founded the National States' Rights Party (NSRP) one of the most significant neo-Nazi groups of the period. Headquartered first in Jeffersonville, Indiana, and then in Birmingham, Alabama, the NSRP was organized along quasi-military lines. Its emblem, borrowed from Hitler's SS, was a thunderbolt over a Confederate battle flag, and its members were supposed to dress in a uniform of white shirts and black trousers, with a black tie. Stoner served as the organization's general legal counsel for six years. The party's chairman was a former follower of John Kasper's named Ned Dupes, and a number of women were also prominent in the party's leadership, including Anne Bishop, its vice chair, and Bernice Settle, its treasurer. By 1964 the NSRP claimed to have chapters in 36 states, although its actual membership was probably fewer than 500. The party's influence belied its small numbers, however, both because of its newsletter, *The Thunderbolt*—which had a circulation of about 25,000—and, in the words of Clive Webb, because of its "fanatical determination to resist racial reform by any means necessary."

The Party's long-term solution to the nation's "race problem" was the repatriation of Blacks to Africa—as well as Jews to Madagascar and Asian-Americans to Hawaii—but it had other ideas as well. In 1963, for example, in an echo of the program of economic retaliation pioneered by the Citizens' Councils movement, the NSRP launched a "Fire Your Nigger" campaign aimed at undercutting the momentum of the freedom struggle and ultimately driving Blacks out of the South altogether. Nor did it neglect the political arena, going so far as to launch a quixotic bid for the presidency in 1964, with Stoner as the party's nominee and John Kasper his somewhat reluctant running mate. (Kasper had not sought the position and he did no campaigning in the election.) The pair received a grand total of 6,957 votes. Above all, though, the National States' Rights Party believed in the utility of force and violence, as it enthusiastically joined in with the wider guerrilla war that was being waged against the civil rights movement across the South. In fact, although they could not prove it, journalists of the time regularly accused both Stoner and the National States' Rights Party of being directly involved with the activities of Nacriema Inc., as well as another secretive terror group known as the Confederate Underground. Examples of the NSRP's violence include the 1958 bombings of the Bethel Baptist Church in Birmingham and the Hebrew Benevolent Congregation Temple in Atlanta, Georgia, as well as later attacks on civil rights activists in St. Augustine, Florida, in 1964, which, according to Martin Luther King, helped to turn the city into the "most lawless" he'd ever seen. Stoner was finally convicted for his part in the Bethel church bombing in 1980, serving three-and-a-half years in jail.

The most notorious neo-Nazi of the period, however, was George Lincoln Rockwell, the charismatic leader of the American Nazi Party (ANP). He was born in Bloomington, Illinois, in 1918, the son of a famous vaudeville comedian turned radio entertainer, George "Doc" Rockwell. After graduating from Brown University in Rhode Island, the younger Rockwell enrolled in the Navy, serving in both the Second World War and the Korean War and rising to the rank of lieutenant commander. (Indeed, "Commander Rockwell," or sometimes just "the Commander," was how Rockwell would prefer to be addressed for the rest of his life.) It was during the Korean War, while based in San Diego, that Rockwell had an almost religious conversion to the cause of National Socialism after reading a copy of *Mein Kampf*. The book had delivered "mental sunshine which bathed all the gray world in the clear light of reason and understanding," he would subsequently tell his followers. In 1957, after a series of economic setbacks, including the failure to get a right-wing newspaper called the *Conservative Times* off the ground, Rockwell moved his family to Virginia, where he fell under the patronage of Harold Noel Arrowsmith, a wealthy anti-Semitic publisher. Together they established the National Committee to Free America from Jewish Domination in 1958. Yet by the following year the two men had fallen out, with Arrowsmith now regarding his former partner as a "con man" and a "blackmailer," and it was from the remnants of the National Committee to Free America from Jewish Domination that Rockwell would form his Nazi Party.

Headquartered in Arlington, Virginia, in a complex known as "Hatemonger Hill," the American Nazi Party was never large. At most, the organization had 100 to 150 members, with perhaps a few hundred more people subscribing to its two publications, *The Stormtrooper* and the *Rockwell Report*. But what the ANP lacked in numbers, it more than made up for in its ability to attract publicity and media attention. For example, in 1961, the Party picketed various premieres of the movie *Exodus*, about the founding of the modern state of Israel, in cities such as Boston, Philadelphia, Chicago, and Washington, D.C. That same year Rockwell dispatched his so-called "Hate Bus" to New Orleans, with stops in various Southern cities along the way, as a counter to the "freedom riders" of the civil rights movement, telling reporters that the trip was being made to symbolize "the fact that decent Americans do hate and should hate communism and race mixing." In February 1962, dressed in full Nazi uniform and flanked by two of his stormtrooper bodyguards, Rockwell addressed 12,000 members of the Black separatist Nation of Islam in

Chicago. In 1963 he organized an American Nazi Party counterprotest to the massive March on Washington for Jobs and Freedom. Rockwell also gave high-profile speeches on various university campuses throughout this time, while in 1965 he ran for the governorship of Virginia, garnering a few thousand votes. The following year he appeared in *Playboy* magazine in an extensive interview with the future author of *Roots*, African-American journalist Alex Haley. (Their encounter was recreated for the TV series *Roots: The Next Generation* in 1979, with Marlon Brando somewhat improbably cast in the role of "the Commander.")

Another of Rockwell's strategies was to regularly incite street confrontations with anti-fascist groups such as the Jewish War Veterans of America. Seeking to deny him the publicity he so desperately craved, Rabbi Solomon Andhil Fineberg of the American Jewish Committee and others developed a policy of what became known as "dynamic silence"—encouraging organizations such as the Jewish War Veterans to refrain from responding to the ANP's provocations, while also lobbying the media to stop reporting Rockwell's various stunts. The policy, although controversial, was ultimately successful. Rockwell acknowledged as much during his *Playboy* interview, telling Haley: "So you see, the Jew blackout on us is as real as a hand over my mouth. . . . I could run naked across the White House lawn and they wouldn't report it."

On January 1, 1967, Rockwell announced that the American Nazi Party was changing its name to the National Socialist White People's Party and that it would also be replacing its chants of "Sieg Heil" with a new rallying cry of "White Power!" The decision reflected the increasing difficulties the Party was facing in getting out its message, but it also represented Rockwell's reaction to the rise of the Black power movement in the United States. "The Commander" would not live long enough to see his plans for the application of National Socialism in the United States come any closer to fruition, however. A few months later, on August 25, he was shot to death in an Arlington laundromat parking lot by John Patler, a disgruntled former trooper who had recently been expelled from the National Socialist White People's Party. His legacy, though, would continue on—not least in the form of long-standing acolytes like William Pierce.

The passage of the Civil Rights Act in 1964, followed by the Voting Rights Act in 1965, at least brought a formal end to segregation and the rule of Jim Crow in the South. The Civil Rights Act banned discrimination in employment, federally assisted programs, public accommodations and facilities, including hotels, restaurants, movie theaters, lunch counters, concert halls, and shops. It also empowered the attorney general of the United States to initiate lawsuits to desegregate Southern school districts and set up an Equal Employment Opportunities Commission, as well as a Community Relations Service, to help solve future racial problems. The Voting Rights Act outlawed various devices such as literacy tests, constitutional interpretation tests, and "good character" tests that had been widely used to discriminate against African-American voters in the South and authorized federal officials to register qualified voters directly. Together these new laws also undercut support for more overtly expressed white supremacist beliefs, at least for "respectable" racists, like those who belonged to the Citizens' Council movement, pushing such ideas toward a more coded form of racial articulation that would become known as "dog-whistle" politics.

The members of more extreme white supremacist groups like the Klan and the National States' Rights Party were less impacted by the passage of these new laws—and they certainly were not inclined to tone down their rhetoric—but they too began to decline significantly by the end of the 1960s, with the number of Klansmen reduced to little more than 5,000 by the turn of the decade, for example. The principal reason for this, however, was that the FBI had launched a clandestine campaign against them called COINTELPRO-White Hate Groups. (COINTELPRO was short for counterintelligence program, and the FBI had first deployed it against the American Communist Party during the 1950s and then again against the Socialist Workers Party in the early 1960s. It would also be used much more extensively against various left-wing groups connected with the Black power movement, the New Left, and the anti-Vietnam War movement during the late 1960s, particularly the Black Panther Party.) Under pressure from both the Department of Justice and President Lyndon Johnson to do something about the wave of violence that was engulfing the American South, FBI Director J. Edgar Hoover began the operation in September 1964, specifically targeting 17 Klan groups and nine other "hate organizations," including Shelton's United Klans of America, Bowers's Mississippi White Knights, the National States' Rights Party, and Rockwell's American Nazi Party.

The aim was to disrupt and discredit these groups as much as possible. A wide range of techniques were employed, including anonymous phone calls, faked letters, planted news stories, burglaries, bugs, IRS harassment, and even the creation of fictitious Klan groups and other organizations. The use of informers was crucial, and by 1965 the FBI had over 2,000 of them in operation, many in top leadership positions. They were instructed to gather "compromising" material on their compatriots, but also to supply more general information such as membership lists, which could then be used as the basis for mass postcard mailing programs and other activities. (The United Klans of America was so riddled with informers that by 1967 Robert Shelton was proposing that all members of his Imperial Board be injected with truth serum and undergo lie-detector tests in order to establish their true loyalties.) The FBI further exploited the situation through the creation of so-called "snitch jackets," whereby members of various groups were identified as informants when they were not so as to sow even more confusion and mistrust.

Examples of COINTELPRO operations against the white supremacist right include the sending of postcards with captions such as "KLANS-MAN, trying to hide your identity behind your sheet? You received this. Someone KNOWS who you are!" Form letters were dispatched to the wives of Klansmen claiming that their husbands had committed adultery (the alleged adulteress "Ruby" was said to have "lust-filled eyes and [a] smart aleck figure"). In January 1965 Black community associations around Birmingham received an anonymous tip from the FBI that a local white businessman was not only a member of the National States' Rights Party, but that he also depended "on Negro patronage for a very substantial portion of [his] business." The nonexistent National Committee for Domestic Tranquility fomented disputes within the Klan, while the equally imaginary National Intelligence Committee sought to "expel" an assortment of Imperial Wizards and Grand Dragons from the movement. In addition, members of the American Nazi Party were secretly accused of being gay or Jewish. Such "dirty tricks" could have serious consequences, however, and the FBI did not shrink from violating the law in order to achieve its goals. As the Klan informant Gary Thomas Rowe was told: "You can do anything to get your information . . . we don't want you to get involved in *unnecessary* violence, but the point is to get the information" (emphasis added).

In March 1965 Rowe was traveling in a car with three other UKA Klansmen near Montgomery, Alabama, when they shot and murdered a 44-year-old Detroit housewife named Viola Liuzzo who had gone to the South to help support the civil rights movement. Rowe would testify against the killers of Liuzzo at their subsequent trial, but he himself would not be charged for his part in Liuzzo's death until 1978. (The indictment was thrown out because Rowe had been granted immunity from prosecution before entering the FBI's witness protection program.) Another example of the FBI's apparent willingness to at least tolerate, if not actually incite, acts of violence as part of the COINTELPRO program occurred in June 1968, when the bureau paid $38,500 to two members of the Mississippi White Knights to "set up" two other Klansmen, Thomas Albert Tarrants III and Danny Joe Hawkins, who were suspected of being behind a wave of church bombings in the Meridian-Jackson area. The two informants talked Tarrants into bombing the home of a Jewish businessman named Meyer Davidson. At the appointed time Tarrants showed up not with Hawkins, however, but with Kathy Ainsworth, a Klan-supporting local elementary schoolteacher. In the ensuing gun battle Ainsworth was shot and killed, while Tarrants was seriously wounded, as was a police officer and an innocent bystander.

At a much more public level, between October 1965 and February 1966, the House Committee on Un-American Activities (HUAC) held a series of high-profile hearings into the Klan and other white supremacist organizations. Most of the leaders called to testify, including Robert Shelton and J. B. Stoner, refused to do so, pleading the Fifth Amendment, but the committee and its investigators nonetheless uncovered plenty of examples of their organizations' misdeeds, including the existence of numerous secret "front groups" such as the Davidson County Rescue Service in Lexington, North Carolina; the Morehouse Hunt and Gun Club in Bastrop, Louisiana; and the Clark-Washington Hunting and Fishing Club, in Jackson, Alabama. (Rockwell was not called to testify, but true to form he attended anyway.) The Klan's significant investment in paramilitary training was uncovered, as were serious cases of financial impropriety. Not surprisingly, the FBI swiftly incorporated the revelations into its propaganda campaign, issuing cartoons of bloated Klansmen that asked: "Which Klan leaders are spending your money tonight?" and distributing postcards that attacked those leaders for "hiding behind the fifth amendment" just like the communists always had.

Both the HUAC hearings and the COINTELPRO campaign inflicted significant damage on the white supremacist movement in the United States. Indeed, as far as Robert Shelton was concerned, they set the movement back by "about ten years." COINTELPRO was finally disbanded in 1971, when its existence was at last made public.

In 1968 the former governor of Alabama, George Wallace, ran for the presidency as the leader of the third-party American Independent Party, with retired Air Force General Curtis LeMay as his running mate. Wallace had flown bombing missions over Japan during World War II before returning to Alabama to open a law practice and begin his climb up the political ladder. He had first run to be the governor of the state in 1958 but was defeated by John Paterson, who took a harder line on segregation than Wallace and had the support of the local Ku Klux Klan. In words that would follow him for the rest of life, Wallace responded to his defeat by promising that "no other son-of-a-bitch will ever out-nigger me again." Four years later it was Wallace who was the preferred candidate of the Klan, and Asa Carter had been recruited to be Wallace's speechwriter. (When his political career was over, Carter attempted to reinvent himself as a writer, using the alias Forrest Carter, after the Confederate general and Klan leader Nathan Bedford Forrest. One of his novels, *The Rebel Outlaw: Josey Wales* [1972], was made into a successful film by Clint Eastwood in 1976 as the *The Outlaw Josey Wales*.) It was Carter who penned the words of Wallace's infamous inaugural address, delivered on the steps of the Alabama State Capitol in Montgomery on January 14, 1963, in which he promised, "in the name of the greatest people who have ever trod this earth . . . segregation now, segregation tomorrow, and segregation forever!" Five months later the governor gained even more national attention when he stood in the doorway of the University of Alabama in Tuscaloosa to symbolically block the admittance of two Black students, Vivian Malone and Jimmy Hood.

Wallace was backed by all the forces of the far right in 1968, including the Klan, the National States' Rights Party, Willis Carto's Liberty Lobby, the newly created Conservative Society of America, and the anticommunist John Birch Society. Even George Lincoln Rockwell was on board. (The Commander conceded that Wallace was not actually a Nazi, but he was "close enough that, as president, he would probably preserve our nation and race.") The Citizens' Council movement was also supportive. Indeed, according to Wallace's biographer, Dan T. Carter, the Councils' provided $250,000 in financing for the campaign, although they "managed to conceal the source of the money by having three hundred individuals write checks for contributions of a thousand dollars or less."

Reflecting the realities of the new political climate in the wake of the passage of the Civil Rights Act and Voting Rights Act, Wallace made no explicitly racial appeals during the campaign. In fact—somewhat incredibly—he denied being a racist altogether, claiming that he had never in his "public life in Alabama made a speech that would reflect upon anybody because of race, color, creed, religion, or national origin." Instead, Wallace spoke in euphemism and code, a successful early practitioner of the kind of "dog-whistle" politics that would become increasingly common in the years to follow—similar tactics were employed by his Republican opponent, Richard Nixon—as he skillfully exploited the backlash against the civil rights movement that was taking hold in both the North and the South. Wallace received 9,906,473 votes in 1968, which was 13.5 percent of the total cast. The Democratic Party candidate, Hubert Humphrey, won 30,898,055 votes, and Nixon secured 31,710,470. In the Electoral College the tally was 301 for Nixon, 191 for Humphrey, and 46 for Wallace. In whatever way it was now being expressed, there obviously remained a sizable constituency for white supremacist beliefs throughout the United States.

As this chapter demonstrates, resistance to the racial integration of the American South was fierce and it was widespread, encompassing the region's political leadership as much as its ordinary citizens. From the halls of Congress, through state legislatures, and down to the local level in various Citizens' Councils, Klans, and other organizations, hundreds of thousands of white southerners raged against the demands and activities of the civil rights movement following the Supreme Court's ruling in *Brown v. Board of Education* in 1954. The methods employed to prevent integration were many and varied. They included propaganda and "educational" efforts, legal chicanery, political pressure, economic boycotts, and intimidation, as well as hideous acts of guerrilla violence and terrorism. For the most part, members of the Southern political elite like those in the Citizens' Councils went to great lengths to separate themselves from what they referred to as the "lunatic fringe" of the segregationist movement, such as the Klan and the National States' Rights Party. However, the relationship between the "respectable" right and the "extreme" right was actually much closer than this purported distinction would make it. The white supremacist beliefs of each grouping were essentially the same, for example—resting upon the same pseudoscientific, religious, and "historical" justifications—and each was unabashedly committed to the same goal: that of keeping African Americans in their "proper place." Indeed, to a considerable extent, one could argue that the Klan in particular did a great deal of the "dirty work" of the Citizens' Council movement throughout the South during the 1950s and 1960s.

Ironically, as many historians, including David Chalmers and Clive Webb have pointed out, the vicious and unrestrained violence of the Klan, as well as that of other racial militants such as John Kasper, J. B. Stoner, and Asa Carter, actually hastened the demise of segregation in the South rather than preventing it. Not only did their actions cause national outrage—they actively encouraged greater federal government intervention and helped to push more moderate Southerners toward at least "token integration." But if massive resistance ultimately failed, this does not mean racism and white supremacy were vanquished in the process. Far from it. As we shall see in the chapters that follow, for those like David Duke, William Pierce, and Tom Metzger, it simply meant that the fight for white supremacy in the United States needed to be pursued even harder.

3

The "New" Klan

David Duke, Louis Beam, William Pierce, and the
"Greensboro Massacre"

THE PERIOD FROM 1968 TO 1974 was not a good one for the Ku Klux Klan and other white supremacist groups in the United States. The civil rights movement had seemingly been victorious, the FBI's COIN-TELPRO operations had taken their toll, and George Wallace had been paralyzed in an assassination attempt during the 1972 presidential election. Yet in short order a remarkable turnaround took place, as Klan membership began to rise and neo-Nazi groups became increasingly active. At the forefront of these developments was the young and charismatic Klansman David Duke. The revival he helped to spark had two distinct elements: The first focused on mainstreaming the movement through rebranding, electioneering, and a careful exploitation of the post-civil rights political landscape; the second was more confrontational and violent, with a clear paramilitary component to it. Indeed, by 1983 some parts of the white supremacist right had turned fully in a "revolutionary" direction, a development explored more closely in chapter 4, although its roots are to be found in this one.

Significant social, economic, and political factors played into the resurgence of the white supremacist movement during the 1970s and 1980s. These included the ongoing "white backlash" against the gains of the civil rights movement, especially the busing of students to desegregated schools, as epitomized by the crisis that engulfed the city of Boston between 1974 and 1988; the economic downturn of the 1970s, the worst since the 1930s; the Vietnam War; and the Supreme Court's decision in the case of *Regents of the University of California v. Bakke* (1978) that upheld the legality of affirmative action policies designed to address long-standing inequities in hiring, educational, or housing practices. Not surprisingly, perhaps, there was also considerable growth in the power and influence of conservatism during this time, which culminated with the election of Ronald Reagan to the White House in 1980 and again in 1984. This too had a notable impact on the activities of the American far right.

This chapter examines the rise of the "new" Klan pioneered by David Duke, but it also addresses the role played by other Klan leaders such as Bill Wilkinson and Louis Beam. Various neo-Nazi groups, including the National Socialist White People's Party, the National Socialist Party of America, and the National Alliance, are also considered. Indeed, one of the most interesting developments of the 1970s was the so-called "Nazification of the Klan." This too is examined, as is the establishment of a highly effective Anti-Klan Network. The influence of Willis Carto and William Pierce is also assessed, with Carto being a strong advocate for the attempted mainstreaming of American white supremacy and Pierce more committed to a vanguardist approach. Finally, Tom Metzger's White Aryan Resistance organization and his recruitment of racist skinheads is discussed. Let us begin with Duke.

David Duke was born in Tulsa, Oklahoma, in 1950. His father was an engineer for Shell Oil, who traveled frequently, often overseas, while his mother struggled with alcohol addiction. The family eventually settled in Louisiana, in Gentilly Woods, an affluent, middle-class suburb of New Orleans. Duke's interest in white supremacy began when he was in high school. He started attending meetings of the local Citizens' Council when he was just 14, becoming particularly taken with Carlton Putnam's pro-segregationist book *Race and Reason: A Yankee View* (1961). At the same time, Duke was conducting his own research into the history of Nazism and the Third Reich, as well as the supposed "scientific" underpinnings of racism to be found in the work of right-wing academics such as the anthropologist Carlton Coon and the physicist William Shockley. He also claimed to have joined the Klan when he was 17.

After graduating from high school Duke went on to Louisiana State University (LSU), in Baton Rouge, to study history. There he became a member of the National Socialist Liberation Front, the student arm of the National Socialist White People's Party (NSWPP), which had grown out of the American Nazi Party (ANP). (George Lincoln Rockwell was one of Duke's heroes. According to Tyler Bridges, upon hearing of the Commander's assassination in 1967, Duke broke down in tears because "the greatest American who ever lived" had been shot down and killed.) On the campus's "Free Speech Alley," Duke honed his rhetorical skills in battles with other students over the Vietnam War, civil rights, and the Black power movement, as well as his own white supremacist beliefs. In July 1970 he traveled to Tulane University, in New Orleans, to protest a lecture being given by the controversial left-wing lawyer William Kunstler, who had gained national attention because of his defense of the "Chicago 7," a group of radical activists, including Abbie Hoffman, Jerry Rubin, and Tom Hayden, who had been accused of conspiring to incite a riot at the Democratic National Convention in Chicago in 1968. Duke was attired in a full Nazi stormtrooper uniform, complete with a swastika armband, and he carried signs reading "Gas the Chicago 7" and "Kunstler is a Communist Jew." (Photographs of the protest would come back to haunt Duke many years later.)

In 1971 Duke and his Klan mentor, Jim Lindsay, a wealthy New Orleans realtor who operated under the alias "Ed White," established a group called White Youth Alliance, as well as a successor organization called the National Party, both of which were intended to function as the political youth action wing of the Klan. The following year, on January 18, Duke was arrested for the possession of Molotov cocktails, improvised incendiary devices created by pouring flammable liquid into glass bottles topped with rags, that are frequently used in street fights and guerrilla warfare. Duke claimed that the bottles were just torches intended for use in a forthcoming parade, and the charges were subsequently dropped, although critics have noted that this may have been because he secretly provided details of his group's membership to the FBI, something that Duke has denied. In 1973 Duke became both Grand Dragon and national information officer of Lindsay's—or "White's"—Knights of the Ku Klux Klan (KKKK). The following year Duke graduated from LSU, and in 1975 he formally assumed the leadership of the Knights after Lindsay was murdered, although in truth he had been effectively running the organization for some time before then. The exact origins of the KKKK are a little clouded. In order to enhance its legitimacy, at one point Duke claimed that it had been formed in 1956, so that it seemed older and more long-standing than it really was. But legal documents show that it was legally incorporated in 1975. Duke's assertion that he joined the Klan at 17 served a similar purpose.

It was as head of the Knights of the Ku Klux Klan that Duke, aged 25, would transform not just the fortunes of the Klan, but also those of the broader white supremacist movement in the United States. As already noted, before Duke's ascension the Klan was at a low ebb, with less than 1,500 members scattered around the country in dozens of small, demoralized, and fractious groups. Duke set about to modernize the Klan, to move it, as he told his followers, "out of the cow pasture and into hotel meeting rooms." He did this in a number of ways. Much to the chagrin of older leaders such as Robert Shelton and James Venable, who were both still in operation, Duke deemphasized the importance of ritual and tradition, for example. "If our purpose was fraternal amusement, every possible Province, Dominion and Realm could be filled with corresponding Klan officers," he explained in the *Knights of the Ku Klux Klan Handbook*. "But our cause is serious. . . . Therefore, we will not delude ourselves with high sounding titles, or impressive scrolls of asininity." Accordingly, Duke would be known as the Knights of the Ku Klux Klan's national director rather than its Imperial Wizard. He maintained the white robes, although he himself never wore a hood and more regularly appeared in a suit and tie, and he also kept the cross burnings, although these were now referred to as "illuminations." Rock music and bluegrass replaced renditions of "The Old Rugged Cross" and other traditional hymns and "patriotic" music that usually provided the soundtrack to Klan rallies, while Duke also sought to expand the reach of the Klan, opening it up to women, Catholics, and teenagers.

Women had been able to join the 1920s Klan only through ancillary groups such as Women of the Ku Klux Klan. Duke allowed women to join the organization directly, giving them full membership in the Invisible Empire. By the mid-1970s Duke claimed that 40 percent of all his members were female. Many of these new recruits were the wives or girlfriends of existing Klansmen, and they were often asked to do much of the secretarial work of their local Klaverns, such as collecting dues and processing membership applications. But some were also given leadership roles, such as Sandra Bergeron, who became the area coordinator for New Orleans, and Duke's own wife, Chole, who was named Grand Geni (her title suggesting that not all of the Klan's old habits were easy to abandon). An article in the September 1978 issue of the Knight's *The Crusader* entitled "Aryan Women: Racial Comrades in Arms" made the case that: "Our women must be aware of their unique roles, to be sure. Yet, they must be restored to the even more common roles of our fighting partners, capable of heroism and with a potential for leadership in all areas." There should be "no chains imposed by kitchen duties not shared by all," the article went on. Such seemingly progressive attitudes were largely undercut, however, by the much more frequently expressed view that the key role of female Klan members was simply to produce more white offspring. As Duke himself put it during an interview in 1976, "We need women to breed Klan babies, raise their children to become Klan members and exert their great moral force to make the rest of the nation see our purpose."

As for the admittance of Catholics—one of the second Klan's most hated enemies—Duke reasoned that such attitudes had never been a prominent feature of the original Klan and that to keep propagating anti-Catholicism was to unnecessarily divide white Christians among themselves. More practically, Duke realized that a vast untapped constituency of blue-collar Catholics existed in many Northern cities—where he was looking to expand—many of whom had their own racial resentments that might be exploited. In addition, it is also the case that Duke lived and worked in a heavily Catholic area of southern Louisiana, which may have provided a more personal element to his thinking on the subject. His own experience as a young man growing up with a keen interest in the politics of white supremacy was undoubtedly a critical factor behind his decision to establish a Klan Youth Corps aimed at students between the ages of 12 and 17. It was also a continuation of the practices of his short-lived National Party, which had undertaken major recruitment efforts around the high schools of New Orleans throughout 1972.

Above all, though, Duke sought to fundamentally change the way in which the Klan presented itself and its beliefs. He downplayed the Klan's violence, spoke about "racialism" instead of racism, and constantly emphasized the importance of "white rights" and white "self-determination." In the aftermath of the civil rights movement, whites were becoming "second-class citizens" in their "own" country, Duke contended. "We are losing our rights all the way across the board," he claimed. "White people face massive discrimination in employment opportunities, in scholarship opportunities in school, in promotions in industry, in college entrance admittance," he told supporters. The answer was racial separatism, he argued, and it could be achieved by lawful means and through the electoral system. In effect, Duke, ever the student of history, wanted to emulate the political success of the Klan of the 1920s, believing the organization could once again become an engine of mass mobilization. (His attempted remarketing of the Klan also echoed Clarke and Tyler's similar efforts on behalf of William Simmons in the 1920s, of course.) Indeed, the pursuit of political office was an obsession of Duke's throughout his career, and it began in 1975 when he ran as a Democrat for the state senate in Baton Rouge on a platform of white rights and hard-line conservativism. Although he lost, Duke was far from discouraged. After all, he reasoned, "Over 11,000 people went to the polls and voted for my ideals." "The movement has just started," he went on. "We've just begun. This is not the ignorant redneck from the hills voting from me. The voters are just about ready for us."

Central to Duke's rise was his skillful exploitation of the media. Young, educated, good-looking—"the Klan's answer to Robert Redford," as one journalist described him—articulate, and seemingly reasonable, the press, radio, and television found him almost irresistible. He appeared in *Playboy* and on Tom Snyder's late-night chat show *The Tomorrow Show* on NBC, was interviewed by Barbara Walters, and photographed by the fashion model and actor Candice Bergen. Duke estimated that he was a guest on over 100 television and radio shows by 1977, many of which gave him the invaluable opportunity of presenting himself and his ideas to a national audience. (Duke never tired of his media appearances. In later years he also appeared on *The Today Show*, *The Phil Donahue Show*, and *Larry King Live*, among many others.) Emulating the strategy of George Lincoln Rockwell, Duke also demonstrated an uncanny ability to stage events that generated an enormous amount of publicity for his cause at seemingly minimum effort on his part. He spoke regularly on college campuses and held recruitment events there, for example, and in September 1974—and again in December 1975—he traveled to South Boston to lend the Knights of the Ku Klux Klan's support to the anti-busing demonstrations that were taking place in the city.

For the 1974 protest, Duke informed the press that 300 of his Klansmen would be departing from Baton Rouge to take part in what he called the "Freedom Rides North." Three, counting Duke, actually showed up. Nonetheless, their impact was considerable. Duke addressed a crowd of 2,000 people, and scores of reporters followed his every move. The speech he gave, though, indicated just how much of Duke's "reasonableness" was a performance—as many of his critics have noted, Duke was adept at telling different audiences what he thought they wanted to hear. "Two hundred years ago our ancestors stood up and fought against the tyranny of the British bayonets. Our struggle is much harder," he declared. "The federal government is taking money out of your pockets to finance the production of thousands of little black bastards. The real issue isn't education. The real issue is niggers!"

Duke took a similar approach in 1977, when he announced that 500 to 1,000 armed Klansmen would soon be patrolling the U.S.-Mexico border from Brownsville, Texas, to the Pacific Ocean, as part of a new initiative to curtail illegal immigration known as "Klan Border Watch." As anticipated, the media response was extensive, even though only a dozen or so members of the California KKKK actually turned up—along with a few egg-throwing protestors—at the San Ysidro port of entry between San Diego and Tijuana on Sunday, October 16, to launch the operation. The Klansmen arrived in three battered old sedans, with hand-painted "Klan Border Watch" signs taped to their car doors, citizen-band radios in hand, some wearing "white power" T-shirts, as the police and officers of the Immigration and Naturalization Service watched calmly on. No undocumented immigrants were apprehended, but Duke was unperturbed, gleefully announcing to the gathered reporters that it seemed to him that "Mexicans are afraid to enter the country [now] because of the Klan."

The Klan Border Watch was certainly a very successful publicity stunt, but Duke's stress on immigration and his use of paramilitary-style tactics were also both significant harbingers of how the far right more broadly—as well as the nation as a whole—would develop in the years to come. With respect to immigration, for example, Duke argued: "The Mexican birthrate in this country is five times that of white people. The black birthrate is four times larger. America will become a Third World nation if these trends continue. Unless we slow down and cut off immigration by beefing up border control and encourage welfare recipients to have fewer kids, the white population in America will be swamped." From the activities of Klan and other groups in the 1970s and 1980s, to the militia movement of the 1990s, through the "Minutemen" border patrol project of Chris Simcox and Jim Gilchrist in the early 2000s, and on into the presidency of Donald Trump, the Mexican border in particular was an issue—and a cause—that would continue to have wide and powerful resonance throughout the United States. (Not that the concern was entirely new. As far back as 1926, Klan Imperial Wizard Hiram Wesley Evans had warned that "to the South of us thousands of Mexicans, many of them Communists, are waiting the chance to cross the Rio Grande and glut the labor marts of the Southwest.")

Duke's success in reviving the Klan was impressive. By the end of 1975 there were some 6,500 Klansmen in various groups, and by 1979 the figure had leapt to 10,500. The only Klan leader receiving national attention, Duke was, as Jeffrey Kaplan writes, a "sensation." He held the largest Klan rally in a decade in Walker, Louisiana, in May 1975—with 2,700 Klansmen in attendance—and seemed almost solely responsible for a noticeable improvement in the perception of the Klan among America's wider white population, both in the North and in the South. According to Gallup polls, only 6 percent of whites had a "favorable" view of the group in 1965, with 93 percent of whites regarding the Klan "unfavorably." By 1979, 11 percent of whites said they had a "favorable" or "highly favorable" view of the organization, while 88 percent said they viewed the Klan "unfavorably." Duke's own Knights of the Ku Klux Klan peaked at about 3,500 members—its reach extending as far as Connecticut and New York, as well as the previously mentioned California and Texas—but his influence was felt in other ways too, as once independent Klan leaders began affiliating their organizations with his, or, duly inspired, set out on their own.

Duke worked hard to downplay his neo-Nazi past once he become a notable public figure, but those early experiences had a profound influence on his worldview and they did not simply disappear. On the contrary, they informed his political beliefs—as well as his actions—throughout his career. It was no coincidence, for example, that three of Duke's top lieutenants in the Knights, Don Black, William Grimstad, and James Warner, were all former members of the National Socialist White People's Party. (Black, who, in 1970, was shot and seriously wounded while trying to steal the membership list of J. B. Stoner's rival National States' Rights Party, became Duke's Alabama Grand Dragon. Grimstad, one-time managing editor of the National Socialist White People's Party's official newspaper, *White Power*, became the corresponding editor of *The Crusader*. And Warner, an early member of the American Nazi Party, as well as the National States' Rights Party and the National Socialist White People's Party, became both Louisiana Grand Dragon and national information director for the Knights.) It was also the reason that anti-Semitism was such a prominent feature of Duke's and the Knights of the Ku Klux Klan's ideology. All previous Klans had believed there was "a Jewish problem in the Western world," Duke argued, but the Knights, he said, were the first to see it as "the most important issue of our time."

As Leonard Zeskind has suggested, this stress on the "Jewish problem" also helped solve a fundamental paradox for racists like Duke, which was, if whites were supposed to be "superior" in all ways to Blacks and other minorities, how was it that African Americans had won the civil rights struggle of the 1960s? "To explain this situation," Zeskind argues in his book *Blood and Politics* (2009), "white supremacists invented Jewish control of black people as a way of explaining this supposed white dispossession." (As Zeskind notes, white supremacist claims to the contrary notwithstanding, "the dominant position and privileged status" of white people in the United States remained solidly intact in the aftermath of the civil rights movement and long beyond.) The thinking of Dr. William Pierce—discussed further below—was especially influential on Duke, Zeskind says. It was Pierce's view, for example, that "blacks in America" were not "really independent agents," and were therefore not "fully responsible for their actions." Rather, they were the tools of "the Jews," who manipulated racial conflicts in the United States for their "own ends" and used their control of the media "to condition the White majority to yield without protest to minority demands." Both were positions Duke endorsed enthusiastically. J. B. Stoner expressed similar views, telling an interviewer in 1981 that he regarded Jews as being the "real masterminds" behind the civil rights movement because African Americans lacked the intelligence and enterprise to challenge white supremacy themselves. "Of course, the niggers want it," he stated in typically crude terms, "but they don't have the brains or the power to do it."

The "Nazification of the Klan"—or what others have called the creation of a "Nazi-Klan alliance"—spearheaded by Duke, was one of the most significant developments on the white supremacist right during the 1970s and 1980s, and it is examined in more detail later in the chapter, but it is important to point out here that not all Klans went along with it. It is also important to note that one of the reasons it occurred was that Duke and his cohorts represented a very different generation of activists from those who had preceded them. Many Klan members of the 1950s and 1960s had served in the Second World War, and this experience generally made them extremely wary of associating with Nazis of any variety. The white supremacist "baby boomers" of Duke's generation—and those that came after them—did not always have the same inhibitions.

Duke's general approach and his leadership style also generated considerable amounts of criticism, both within the Knights and from other Klans. In early 1978, for example, Robert Shelton, still the Imperial Wizard of the United Klans of America, published a damning article in *The Fiery Cross* accusing Duke of lying about his Klan origins, financial mismanagement, inveterate womanizing, and election rigging. Much to Duke's embarrassment, it also revealed that he was the secret author of not one but two unlikely books: a sex manual for women called *Finders-Keepers* (1976), which contained detailed and graphic instructions on how to "find, attract, and keep the man you want"; and a street-fighting manual for American Blacks for use in their struggle against "Whitey" called *African Atto* (1973)—or "African Attack"—written under the pseudonym of Mohammed X. Duke defended his authorship of the latter on counterintelligence grounds, explaining to the *New York Times* in February that, because the book was only available through mail order, he had intended to use it "to compile a list of blacks who were involved in racist activities against white people" for use in a future race war; and the former on the basis that he had only really helped with the copyediting.

Concerns about Duke's media-centric and seemingly egocentric approach to Klan matters—"the David Duke Show," as some of his opponents termed it—were further raised in the spring of 1978, when he went on a highly publicized tour of the United Kingdom, with appearances in cities including Brighton, Oxford, and London. Predictably, the attention was significant, with photos of Duke posing outside the Houses of Parliament, an interview on the BBC, and tabloid headlines screaming "Get Him Out of Here!" The British Home Secretary, Merlyn Rees, finally issued a "variation order," curtailing Duke's stay in the UK, but this only resulted in Duke gaining even more publicity as he successfully managed to evade the authorities for a further three weeks, before returning to the States. (Once he had gone, Rees made it clear that he would not be welcome back, informing the House of Commons: "I have given a personal direction under the 1971 Immigration Act that Mr. Duke should be refused leave to enter if he attempts to return on the grounds that his exclusion would be conducive to the public good.") Duke certainly reveled in his celebrity status, but for others within the movement it was far from clear how such activities were really helping the cause of white supremacy in the United States.

One of Duke's fiercest critics was Bill Wilkinson, who had broken from the Knights of the Ku Klux Klan to form his own group, the Invisible Empire, Knights of the Ku Klux Klan, as early as 1975. Wilkinson was a native of Galvez, Louisiana. After graduating from high school, he joined the U.S. Navy, serving as a cryptographer aboard the nuclear submarine USS *Simon Bolivar* for eight years. He and his wife then moved to Denham Springs, Louisiana. Initially impressed by Duke's "new" Klan, he joined up, becoming the state's Grand Dragon, as well as the editor of *The Crusader*. Ostensibly, the reason for Wilkinson's 1975 split with Duke was a dispute between the two men over the disposition of Klan funds, but in actuality, each had a fundamentally different vision for how the organization should progress. For sure, Wilkinson enjoyed the attention of the media as much as Duke did, but what Wilkinson really liked was violence and physical confrontation—and he also understood that the two positions were not mutually exclusive. "We tried the moderate approach in trying to halt the extravagant gains by blacks," he contended, "but it failed. Now we are resorting to other methods." To ram home the point, Wilkinson traveled everywhere with an intimidating posse of bodyguards, armed to the teeth with semiautomatic rifles and other weapons, explaining: "You don't fight wars with words and books. You fight them with bullets and bombs."

True to his word, in August 1978 members of Wilkinson's Invisible Empire shot out the windshield of a Black civil rights leader named Dr. Howard Gunn in Okolona, Mississippi. Wilkinson then held a rally to publicly celebrate the attack. On May 26, 1979, in Decatur, Alabama, a pitched battle took place between the Klan and counterdemonstrators on the city's main street, in which three Black marchers and two Klansmen were shot. Two days later Wilkinson again held a celebratory rally, with 200 armed members of the Invisible Empire in attendance. (Two weeks after that, more than 2,000 civil rights supporters returned to "reclaim" the city from the Klan.) There were other violent confrontations in Hartford, Connecticut; Uniontown, Pennsylvania; and Columbia, Mississippi. And in August 1979, Wilkinson even attempted to mimic the famed Selma to Montgomery civil rights march of 1965. On the first day, the police arrested 11 of the Klansmen on the outskirts of Montgomery for being in possession of firearms within 1,000 feet of a demonstration. On the next day all 164 Klansmen, including Wilkinson, were arrested for parading without a permit.

All the "action" and all the violent rhetoric paid off, however, and by the end of 1979, Wilkinson's Invisible Empire was the largest Klan in the country. In 1980 Duke decided to cut his losses, forming a new organization called the National Association for the Advancement of White People (NAAWP) and turning the leadership of the Knights of the Ku Klux Klan over to Don Black. He also tried to sell his Klan membership list to Wilkinson for $35,000, but the plan backfired spectacularly when Wilkinson secretly recorded the meeting and then released the tapes to the press. (Nor was Wilkinson willing to buy the list.) For many white supremacists it was the final confirmation of Duke's untrustworthiness, and he struggled to recover from the blow. Duke blamed Wilkinson for his abandonment of the Klan.

> I'm resigning [he explained in a public statement] because I don't think the Klan can succeed at this point, because of its violent image and because of people like Bill Wilkinson. He's low and dishonorable. And people see Wilkinson and believe all Klansmen are like that—bad and violent. All the good in the world I have done and could do doesn't make any difference because most people don't differentiate between Klans. They think we're all like that, and that's disgusting.

Remarkably, just a year later, the *Nashville Tennessean* revealed that Wilkinson had been an informant for the FBI since 1974, raising the question of whether all his activities had actually been designed to bring the entire Klan movement into disrepute. (This was especially so given that Wilkinson never faced any major criminal charges, despite all the illegality he seemed to have been involved in.) In his defense, Wilkinson claimed that he had only told the FBI what they could find out from the press already, and that he had never been paid for the information he provided.

In 1980, Tom Metzger, the Grand Dragon of California, who had helped Duke organize his Klan Border Watch, split from the organization to create his own California Knights of the Ku Klux Klan. Metzger had grown frustrated both with Duke's showmanship and with his perceived lack of militancy. (The revelations about *Finders-Keepers* and *African Atto* had not helped either. "I'll never forgive him for writing those books," Metzger would say, many years later.) Metzger was a Catholic, born in Warsaw, Indiana, in 1938. After serving in the U.S. Army, he moved to Los Angeles, California, in 1961, where he eventually established a television repair business. He had been a member of the John Birch Society, as well as an ardent supporter of George Wallace, before moving more profoundly to the anti-Semitic and racist right. During the early 1970s Metzger stopped paying his taxes in protest against the Vietnam War and established a short-lived group known as the White Brotherhood. He joined the Knights of the Ku Klux Klan in 1975.

Metzger considered himself to be a "twenty-first-century Klansman." He dressed his California Knights in black uniforms instead of white robes, while his security detail was equipped with riot helmets, clubs, the chemical spray Mace, and black-lacquered plywood shields inscribed with "KKK" in white letters. Displaying his fondness for a good street brawl, in the spring of 1980, Metzger led a group of about 40 Klansmen to John Landes Park in Oceanside, California, "to rid the city of Mexicans." Wielding bats, chains, and nightsticks, the Klansmen were met by a hail of rocks thrown by anti-Klan protestors. Seven people were injured in the resulting melee. In San Diego, he also picketed the arrival of refugees from Vietnam, known as the "Vietnamese boat people." Yet like Duke, Metzger also believed in the possibility of using the electoral system to achieve political power, at least for a time.

In June 1980, Metzger ran in the Democratic Party primary for California's 43rd congressional district on a strident antiimmigration and pro-white rights platform. "Let me raise a little hell for you," declared his radio ads. Metzger won, receiving 32,344 votes—37 percent of the total—only to be soundly defeated by his Republican opponent in the general election by 254,000 votes to 35,000. Two years later—after publicly, if disingenuously, renouncing his Klan connections—Metzger launched an even more ambitious bid for the U.S. Senate. His opponents in the Democratic primary included the governor of California Jerry Brown and novelist Gore Vidal. Metzger may have only received 2.8 percent of the votes cast, but this still represented the support of over 75,000 Californians. Next, Metzger formed the White American Political Association intended to help "pro-white" political candidates get elected, but this was superseded, in 1983, by the much more militant and youth-oriented White Aryan Resistance, or "WAR." *WAR* was also the title of the group's newsletter, and as John George and Laird Wilcox have noted, "In its pages Metzger and other writers [engaged] in some of the most outspoken and vehement racist and anti-Jewish rhetoric in the neo-Nazi movement."

Another disillusioned Duke associate who struck out on his own was the Texas Grand Dragon, Louis Beam. He was born in Baytown, Texas, in 1946, and grew up in nearby Lake Jackson. He enlisted in the U.S. Army when he was 19 and spent 18 months as a helicopter gunner in the 25th Aviation Battalion during the Vietnam War, receiving the Distinguished Flying Cross for his service. The war was the defining experience of Beam's life. He returned to the United States in 1968, determined both to continue the fight against communism and also to "militarize" the Ku Klux Klan. He first joined the Texas realm of Shelton's United Klans of America, going on to become a leading member of its Bureau of Investigation. In June 1971, he and three other United Klansmen of America (UKA) were indicted for the bombings of the local headquarters of the Socialist Workers Party and a radio station in Houston, although he escaped conviction. In 1976, Beam moved to Duke's Knights of the Ku Klux Klan.

While Duke conducted his public relations efforts, Beam worked diligently behind the scenes on recruitment and the creation of a new paramilitary infrastructure for the Klan. As the historian Kathleen Belew notes in *Bring the War Home* (2018), this process began in 1977 when Beam used a Texas Veterans Land Board grant to buy 50 acres of swampland in Double Bayou, Texas, so he could establish Camp Puller, "a Vietnam War-style training facility designed to turn Klansmen into soldiers." Three additional Klan camps were created in the Lone Star State—Camp Bravo in the small city of Liberty; Camp Winnie, 60 miles west of Houston; and Camp Alpha, at a secret location—and there were others spread around the country, including Bill Wilkinson's Camp My Lai, in Alabama, named for the site of a notorious massacre of civilians by U.S. servicemen during the Vietnam War. At Camp Puller, Beam instructed his recruits on "kill zones," ambush tactics, and the effective use of explosives, as well as providing advice on the best methods of decapitation and strangulation. Active-duty servicemen were also often present.

Beam had begun trying to recruit soldiers from the Fort Hood military base in Killeen, Texas, in 1978. The following summer, both he and Duke spoke at a rally in nearby Euless. Attired in paramilitary uniforms and armed with rifles and pistols, a group of these soldiers provided the "honor guard." (Camp Pendleton, a Marine base near Oceanside, in California, was another site of Klan recruitment.) The existence of Camp Puller became public knowledge in the fall of 1980, when the parents of a group of high school Explorer Scouts who had received "training" there raised the alarm; apparently there had even been talk of the scouts accompanying the Klan on its Border Watch patrols. Faced with the negative publicity, Beam shut down the camp in November, only to quietly re-open it again five months later.

By this time, Beam and his now independent Texas Klansmen were deeply embroiled in a concerted campaign against a group of Vietnamese fishermen and their families in Galveston Bay. The fishermen were refugees who had fallen into dispute with the white fishermen of the area. The whites accused the new arrivals of overfishing and of ignoring the state's fishing regulations. Subsequent investigations proved that this was not the case and that the U.S.-born fishermen actually violated more fishing regulations than the Vietnamese did. At root, the Vietnamese fishermen just seemed to work harder and put in more hours than their white counterparts. In any event, with the encouragement of the white fishermen, the Klan eventually got involved. (The case also attracted the attention of the National States' Rights Party and its *Thunderbolt* magazine.) After weeks of tension, in early 1981, on two successive nights— January 10 and 11—two Vietnamese shrimping boats were set ablaze. A few weeks later, on February 14, Beam organized a Klan rally at nearby

Santa Fe, Texas, during the course of which he set fire to a small wooden rowboat with the name "U.S.S. Viet Cong" painted on its side. The following month, robed members of the Texas Knights of the Ku Klux Klan went out on an armed boat patrol around the Bay, an effigy of a lynched Vietnamese refugee hanging from the boat's rigging.

With the aid of the Southern Poverty Law Center (SPLC), a civil rights advocacy group, the Vietnamese Fishermen's Association filed a harassment lawsuit against the Klan in April 1981. A temporary injunction was granted the following month, and this was made permanent on June 4, 1982. The presiding judge, Gabrielle McDonald, found that the Klan's paramilitary exercises not only intimidated the Vietnamese fishermen, but also violated a state law banning the existence of private armies. She ordered both the Texas KKK and its paramilitary offshoot, the Texas Emergency Reserve, to cease all combat-related training and to stop parading in public with firearms. She also closed down all of the Klan's paramilitary training camps, including Camp Puller. Seeing the writing on the wall, Beam had resigned from the Klan the previous July. He moved to Idaho, to become an "ambassador at large" for the Aryan Nations and—as discussed in chapter 4—one of the leading white supremacist theorists of revolutionary violence in the country.

In 1985 the French director Louis Malle made a film about the Klan's "war" against the Vietnamese fishermen of Galveston Bay called *Alamo Bay*, starring Ed Harris. The Texas Klan disliked the film so much that they held rallies at local theaters to prevent people from seeing it. Ten years later, Bruce Springsteen also addressed the subject in his song "Galveston Bay" on his acclaimed album *Devils and Dust* (1995).

The emerging paramilitarism of the Klan was also evident in the activities of a former Green Beret and Vietnam veteran, Glenn Miller, who had been discharged from the Army in 1979 for distributing Nazi literature, after 20 years of service. He was briefly a member of the National Socialist Party of America, another offshoot of the National Socialist White People's Party, before establishing his own Carolina Knights of the Ku Klux Klan in 1980. The Carolina Knights became the Confederate Knights of the Ku Klux Klan, and then, in 1985, changed its name again to the White Patriot Party. Throughout, Miller stressed the importance of military-style training, as he amassed a small arsenal of weaponry, recruited active-duty soldiers, and dressed his charges in camouflage gear, all in preparation for the "race war" he believed was imminent.

The most bizarre example of this tendency occurred in April 1981 when Duke's successor, Don Black, attempted to overthrow the government of the small Caribbean island of Dominica. The plan, code-named Operation Red Dog although it was known more dismissively in law enforcement circles as the "the Bayou of Pigs"—had been hatched by Mike Perdue, a Texas mercenary, in conjunction with Dominica's deposed prime minister Patrick John. In addition to Black and Perdue, eight other men were involved, most with some kind of military training, five of them Klan members. (Two of the mercenaries were Canadian, and one, Bob "Mad Merc" Prichard, had been trained at one of Glenn Miller's paramilitary camps.) In addition to $150,000, Black had been promised some territory on the island for use both as a Klan training base and as an overseas hideout for those on the run. Unfortunately for the plotters, the coup unraveled before it had even really begun, when the merchant seamen they had paid to transport them to the island turned out to be undercover agents of the Bureau of Alcohol, Tobacco and Firearms (ATF). The ten men were charged with weapons offenses and with violating the U.S. Neutrality Act. All except Alabama Klansman Michael Norris were sentenced to at least three years in federal prison, with the jury acquitting Norris only because they believed his claim that he thought he had been working for the CIA.

The most significant and consequential act of Klan violence during this period occurred in Greensboro, North Carolina, on November 3, 1979, when a caravan of white supremacists—part of a neo-Nazi/Klan alliance called the United Racist Front (URF)—attacked a "Death to the Klan" rally that had been organized by the Communist Workers Party (CWP). Five anti-Klan protestors, four white men and one Black woman, were killed, and nine more were wounded. The assault had its origins in an earlier confrontation in July, when members of the Communist Workers Party—then named the Workers Viewpoint Organization—and other local civil rights' activists had disrupted a screening of *The Birth of Nation* (1915) by the North Carolina Knights of the Ku Klux Klan that was taking place at a community center in China Grove, a town 25 miles north of Charlotte. (*The Birth of a Nation* remained a popular film on the Klan circuit. David Duke had attended a screening in nearby Winston-Salem in February; and Tom Metzger had shown it in Oxnard, California, the previous year, also eliciting protests.)* Armed with clubs, the protestors had stormed the community center, burned the Klan's Confederate flag, and traded insults with the shotgun-wielding Klansmen, all while chanting "Kill the Klan." Police in attendance had prevented any more serious violence from taking place. In October, the Communist Workers Party issued an open letter to the North Carolina Knights, describing the Klan as "one of the most treacherous scum elements produced by the dying system of capitalism" and challenging the Klansmen to "attend our rally in Greensboro." Eager to get their revenge, the Klansmen were only too happy to oblige.

The presence of neo-Nazis at Greensboro should have come as no surprise; after all, the "Nazification of the Klan" had been under way for some time. Indeed, in September 1979, various Klans and other white supremacist groups, including the National States' Rights Party and the National Socialist Party of America, had converged on the small town of Louisburg, North Carolina, for a planning session—the creation of a unified white power movement having been a goal of racist activists in the United States for many years. Violence and paramilitary training were also very much on the agenda. During the meeting, for example, another former soldier, Harold Covington, the 26-year-old leader of the North Carolina branch of the National Socialist Party of America, had brandished an AR-15 semiautomatic rifle in the air before making the confident assertion that: "Piece by piece, bit by bit, we are going to take back this country!"

Forty Klansmen and neo-Nazis went to Greensboro on November 3. Traveling in a group of nine cars, at about 11:20 a.m. they approached 50 or so Communist Worker Party demonstrators who had gathered outside Morningside Homes, a Black housing project in the city, where a rally was taking place before the main "Death to the Klan" march that was planned for the afternoon. Insults were exchanged, and a group of demonstrators approached the leading cars, hitting them with sticks and

---

* In Spike Lee's critically acclaimed film *BlacKkKlansman* (2018), Duke played by Topher Grace, attends a screening of *The Birth of a Nation* at a meeting of the Klan in Colorado Springs, after he has unwittingly admitted a Black undercover police officer named Ron Stallworth into the Klavern. Lee's film was based on Stallworth's memoir *Black Klansmen* (2014).

their fists. The caravan halted. One of the Klansman, Rayford Caudle, got out of his vehicle and calmly walked back to his trunk to retrieve a variety of shotguns, rifles, and semiautomatic weapons, which were then distributed to six other men. (Because three television news crews were covering the rally, there is extensive footage of exactly what happened that Saturday morning.) Over the next 88 seconds, the now fully armed Klansmen proceeded to fire on the demonstrators, swiftly killing Cesar Cauce, Dr. Michael Nathan, Dr. James Waller, William Simpson, and Sandra Smith. Once the shooting had started, a number of the CWP demonstrators began shooting back, leading the Klansmen to contend that they had only been firing in self-defense. In the view of Ed Boyd, one of the cameramen on the scene, however: "It wasn't any shootout. It was a military execution." (In 1983, PBS produced a documentary on the massacre called *88 Seconds in Greensboro*, directed by William Cran.)

Of the 40 members of the United Racist Front who took part in the attack, 16 were arrested, but only 6—4 Klansmen and 2 National Socialist Party of America members—faced charges. On November 17, 1980, after six days of deliberation and despite extended viewings of the available television footage, an all-white jury found the defendants not guilty, essentially accepting their position that they had been acting in self-defense. The radical left-wing beliefs of the CWP had also clearly been a factor in the jury's verdict. One juror explained that she was "really worried about the spread of communism." Another declared: "From the beginning it was the Communists who did the attacking. It was the Communists who started beating the cars with sticks. From then on, it was a case of self-defense." What had not been revealed, however, was that two government informants, Ed Dawson and Bernard Butkovich, were not only closely involved with the United Racist Front, but had also provided advanced warning to the authorities of the group's plans.

With the backing of the FBI, Dawson had actually helped form the North Carolina Knights back in 1969, although it was now run by Virgil Griffin, a local mill worker. Dawson had subsequently become an informer for the Greensboro police. Having obtained a copy of the Communist Workers Party's parade permit, which was issued on October 19, for reasons that still remain unclear, he then embarked on a vigorous campaign to make sure that his fellow Klansmen would be out in force at the "Death to the Klan" march in November. As one Knight

later told the *Greensboro Daily News*, "We'd never have come to Greensboro if it wasn't for Ed Dawson berating us." On October 31, Dawson
informed the police that the United Racist Front would be going to the
march heavily armed, and he repeated that warning on the morning of
November 3. Butkovich, meanwhile, was an undercover ATF agent in
the Winston-Salem branch of the National Socialist Party of America.
He had personally played a key role in the formation of the United Racist Front, and, like Dawson, had attended the planning sessions for the
group's confrontation with the Communist Workers Party. More than
that, though, he had encouraged the United Racist Front to violently
attack the demonstrators and offered to provide illegal explosives, including hand grenades, to help its members do so. According to the journalist
Elizabeth Wheaton, Butkovich had also warned the ATF of the impending attack.

Needless to say, all of this conjured up the specter of the FBI's
COINTELPRO campaign of the 1960s, the murder of Viola Liuzzo
especially. With the help of the American Civil Liberties Union, in May
1982 some of the survivors of "the Greensboro massacre" issued a lawsuit against the Klansmen and neo-Nazis who had been involved, as well
as the ATF, the Justice Department, the State Bureau of Investigation,
the Greensboro police, the City of Greensboro, and Dawson and Butkovich. Before the civil suit could be heard, however, another criminal trial
took place. In April 1983, federal prosecutors had indicted nine members
of the United Racist Front, this time including Dawson and Virgil Griffin, on charges of conspiracy to violate their victims' civil rights and conspiracy to violate federal statutes—this second prosecution was prompted
in part by the national outcry that had greeted the "not guilty" verdicts of
the first trial, but the survivors' civil suit also undoubtedly played a role.
A year later, in April 1984, another all-white jury again found the defendants not guilty.

The civil trial was finally heard in 1985. The plaintiffs sought $48 mil-
lion in damages. They had to settle for $351,500. This was paid by the
City of Greensboro—the judge having dismissed all the charges against
all the federal agencies involved—which also covered the costs of the
Klansmen and neo-Nazis who had been sued. On June 17, 2009, the City
Council formally issued a "statement of regret" about the incident, and
six years later it installed a historical marker to the massacre on the cor-

ner of Willow Road and McConnell Road, near where the killings had taken place.

As Kathleen Belew notes, the Greensboro shootings "had the effect of consolidating and unifying the white power movement" in the United States. They pushed the Klan and neo-Nazi groups closer together, encouraged an even greater shift toward paramilitarism and violence—the so-called "revolutionary turn" of the movement (examined in detail in chapter 4)—and spurred a significant upsurge in recruitment activities. But they also encouraged even greater resistance to the Klan, as well as to white supremacists more broadly, much of which was extremely effective.

Both the Anti-Defamation League and the NAACP stepped up their monitoring and legal activities, for example, as did the Southern Poverty Law Center. In 1980 the SPLC had taken the leading role in the establishment of a new National Anti-Klan Network, composed of a wide range of educational, religious, and legal groups such as the National Council of Churches, the Southern Christian Leadership Conference, the United States Student Association, and the National Organization for Women. Its aim, it said, was to counter the Klan by seeking to coordinate local efforts to "force elected officials to use our tax dollars to prosecute violent racists and fight racism through education and other affirmative actions." Following the events at Greensboro and other acts of increasing Klan violence, in 1981 the SPLC also created a new "Klanwatch project," designed to collect as much data as possible on white supremacist activity in the United States and to use that data not just for educational and informational purposes, but also to help support its legislative and legal endeavors.

As previously noted, the Southern Poverty Law Center was instrumental in helping to shut down Louis Beam and the Texas KKK in Galveston. In 1984 it also brought an end to Bill Wilkinson's reign as an Imperial Wizard after it secured a number of federal indictments against his Invisible Empire Klan in the Decatur case. Wilkinson resigned from the organization shortly thereafter, although it took until 1990 for the SPLC's separate civil suit to be settled. In 1985, the SPLC obtained a court order against Glenn Miller and his Carolina Knights prohibiting them from "training and operating a paramilitary organization," or "harassing, intimidating, threatening, or harming any black person or white person who associates with black persons." (The order was the reason behind the Knights' name change to the White Patriot Party.) And in 1987 it won a historic $7 million verdict against Shelton's United Klans of America for the 1981 lynching of Michael Donald in Mobile, Alabama, putting it out of business as well. As Wyn Craig Wade writes, the SPLC's aggressive—and relentless—legal strategies had turned the civil rights group into "one of the most persistent and successful Klan fighters of the twentieth century." This was not without controversy however, as critics of the Southern Poverty Law Center raised questions about its fund-raising methods and expressed concerns about whether its activities might have a "chilling effect" on the right to freedom of speech in the United States.

Thousands of local activists, like those in the Communist Workers Party, were also involved in the campaign against the Klan and their allies. One of the most interesting of these activist groups was the John Brown Anti-Klan Committee, which was founded in 1977 and continued to operate until 1992. It had grown out of the John Brown Book Club, a study group formed by a number of Black rights and prison rights activists in the mid-1970s. Both were named for the radical nineteenth-century abolitionist John Brown, who had famously led an armed raid on the federal armory at Harpers Ferry in Virginia, in 1859, with hopes of sparking a slave rebellion. The John Brown Anti-Klan Committee had chapters across the United States, in cities including New York, Boston, Washington, Houston, Chicago, and Los Angeles. It published pamphlets like *Smash the Klan!*, a newsletter called *Death to the Klan!*—which had a circulation of about 10,000—organized protests, marches, and teach-ins, and also confronted the Klan directly, including Louis Beam in Texas and Tom Metzger in California.

According to one of the group's cofounders, Susan Rosenberg, what set the John Brown Anti-Klan Committee apart from other anti-Klan organizations was: "We believed that the KKK was not the 'lunatic fringe' of the racist movement but rather the vanguard of an enormous popular current of white racist sentiment. And we believed that without an active anti-racist movement to oppose the racists and support Black-led efforts, we could not have a radical or progressive movement in the United States." Among the "allies" the committee worked with was the Black nationalist group, the Republic of New Afrika; the pro-Chicano

Brown Berets; and radical white groups such as the Prairie Fire Organizing Committee, which had grown out of the Weather Underground, and
the May 19th Communist Organization.

Throughout this time, two men, Willis Carto and William Pierce,
each representing a different wing of the white supremacist movement,
were actively pursuing their goals. Carto took the more mainstream or
populist approach. Pierce preferred more revolutionary methods. Each
needs to be considered.

Willis Allison Carto was born in Fort Wayne, Indiana, in 1926. After
graduating from high school, he was drafted into the U.S. Army, serving
in Japan and the Philippines during World War II, and receiving the
Purple Heart. He dropped out of law school in 1949, finding work first
with the Procter & Gamble Company and later with a small loan company in San Francisco called the Household Finance Corporation. It was
in California that Carto began his almost 50-year-long career as a political organizer and publisher. In started in 1955 with the newsletter *Right:
The National Journal of Forward-Looking Americanism*, which promoted
a wide range of anti-Semitic, anti-communist, and pro-segregationist
views. Two years later came the organization Liberty Lobby.

Liberty Lobby was a vehicle for bringing the disparate elements of
the American far right together. Headquartered in Washington, D.C.,
it would be "a pressure group for patriotism," Carto explained. It would
counteract the influence of "minority pressure groups" in Congress,
undertake its own research and educational efforts, and "restore constitutional government to the people of the United States." In addition
to its lobbying activities, the organization published the monthly newsletter *Liberty Letter*—which had 200,000 subscribers by 1970—as well
as a number of other publications including *Liberty Lowdown*, *Western
Destiny*, and the *Washington Observer*. In 1966, Carto also acquired the
American Mercury, once the flagship journal of the noted satirist H. L.
Mencken, but since 1952 a largely anti-Semitic outlet for the wealthy
munitions' manufacturer Russell McGuire.

The person who had had the most important impact on Carto's politics
was an obscure philosopher named Francis Parker Yockey, the author
of a mammoth—and, to many, largely incomprehensible—626-page
book called *Imperium: The Philosophy of History and Politics* (1948) that
Carto republished in 1962. The book's supposed grand theme was the

decline of Western civilization, but its real aim was to help promote a worldwide fascist revival. As Carto's biographer, George Michael, summarizes, "Yockey saw German National Socialism as a project to renew the vitality of the West" and regarded it as his life's mission to "refashion the Nazi ideology to fit postwar conditions." Carto played down the Nazism—although he was certainly not averse to working alongside those who advocated it—but otherwise fully embraced Yockey's philosophical and racial concerns.

In 1968, to support George Wallace's bid for the presidency Carto created the Youth for Wallace organization, which became the National Youth Alliance shortly after Wallace's defeat. A few years later, in 1975, he replaced the *Liberty Letter* with a new weekly newspaper, the *National Spotlight* (later renamed *Spotlight.*) It soon established itself as the leading publication on the American far right, with 330,000 subscribers by the end of the decade. The ever-restless Carto next launched the nationally syndicated radio program *This is Liberty Lobby*, and then, in 1978, a kind of clearing house for the growing Holocaust denial movement called the Institute for Historical Review (IHR). Mimicking the trappings of legitimate academic enterprise, the institute held an annual conference and published a journal called the *Journal of Historical Review*. In 1981 it offered a $50,000 reward to anyone who could prove that Jewish people had been gassed at Auschwitz. A Holocaust survivor named Mel Memelstein sought to collect the money, but it took a four-year legal battle before the IHR agreed to pay him the $50,000, plus an additional $40,000 in damages.

Carto's mainstream political ambitions were made abundantly clear in 1984 when he established a new political party to contest that year's presidential election. The Populist Party's inaugural campaign did not go well, however. Carto had recruited Bob Richards, a former Olympic pole-vaulting champion, to top the ticket, with Maureen Salaman, an alternative medicine advocate, as his running mate. They received a mere 66,168 votes. Undeterred, Carto plowed on, and in 1988 the Populist Party's candidate for the presidency was none other than David Duke (see further below).

In contrast to Carto, William Pierce eschewed electoral politics completely. Born in Atlanta in 1933, he was raised in Texas after his mother remarried following the death of his father when he was just eight years old. A gifted student, he was awarded a doctorate in physics from the University of Colorado at Boulder and went on to become a tenured professor at Oregon State University in 1962. It was while he was at Oregon State that Pierce first began to develop his interest in racism and white nationalism. Having left academe to work as a research physicist for the Pratt & Whitney Aircraft company in Connecticut, in 1966 Pierce joined George Lincoln Rockwell's American Nazi Party, becoming the editor of its new publication *National Socialist World*. Pierce was also a key figure in the National Socialist White People's Party until he became disillusioned with Matt Koehl's leadership in the aftermath of Rockwell's assassination. As Leonard Zeskind writes, Pierce agreed completely with the party's core philosophy that "the entirety of the American political and social order needed to be destroyed in order to create a purely Aryan racial state similar to Hitler's Germany. But he wanted an organization with a distinctly American persona to start this revolution and the party of Rockwell seemed unable to escape the uniforms of its origins."

Pierce turned first to Willis Carto, becoming the chairman of his National Youth Alliance in 1969. Within a year the two men had fallen out, however, with Pierce eventually gaining control of the organization and renaming it the National Alliance in 1974. He would lead it until his death in 2002. Initially, Pierce used the National Alliance to pursue two particular areas of interest: college recruitment and revolutionary violence. The former proved difficult in the campus climate of the early 1970s, however, so Pierce turned increasingly to the latter. Unexpectedly, his greatest impact as a revolutionary theorist came in the form of two novels, both written under the pseudonym of Andrew MacDonald: *The Turner Diaries*, which was initially published in installments in the National Alliance's newspaper *Attack!*, before appearing as a paperback in 1978; and *Hunter*, published in 1989.

The Turner Diaries tells the story of Earl Turner, a 30-year-old electrical engineer turned guerrilla fighter who becomes part of a racist group known as the Organization that is trying to overthrow the federal government—referred to as "the System" throughout the book—sometime in the near future. It is presented in the form of Turner's diary entries, which have been recovered after the successful completion of this white revolution. (Turner's final diary entry takes place as he prepares to fly a small plane loaded with a nuclear warhead into the Pentagon.)

A paean to race war, terrorism, and genocidal violence, the novel has often been described as a "blueprint for revolution" and a "handbook" for the white supremacist movement, and within 20 years it had sold over 500,000 copies. (As discussed in detail in the following chapters, its impact has been profound, influencing the actions of groups such as The Order—named for an elite group of militants within the Organization—and the Aryan Republican Army, as well as the Oklahoma City bomber, Timothy McVeigh.)

Intended to be more "realistic," *Hunter* depicts the violent actions of a Vietnam veteran and Defense Department contractor named Oscar Yeager. The novel opens with Yeager on a killing spree of interracial couples in Washington, D.C., but through his involvement with a rogue FBI agent and an anti-Semitic group called the National League—a thinly disguised National Alliance—he soon comes to realize that he needs to broaden his targets to include Jews, civil rights activists, and various liberal politicians if the "system" is to be truly brought down. It many ways, *Hunter* functions as a kind of prequel to *The Turner Diaries*, but it can also be seen as making the case for "lone wolf" acts of terrorism as part of a strategy of leaderless resistance, although this is something Pierce has denied. (This will also be examined further in subsequent chapters.)

Tom Metzger's White Aryan Resistance also continued to expand its reach and influence throughout the 1980s, as it too sought a "white revolution." It did this in part through the effective use of technology: in the creation of the public access television show *Race and Reason*; and by the establishment of its WAR "telephone hotline" that offered daily "hate-o-grams" to those who called in, for example. (It was also an early adopter of the World Wide Web in the 1990s.) Having studied at the feet of David Duke, Metzger also proved extremely adept at exploiting the mainstream media, especially the afternoon talk-show circuit, with his protégés appearing regularly on shows such as *Geraldo*—hosted by Geraldo Rivera—*The Jerry Springer Show*, and *The Oprah Winfrey Show*. The most notorious of these appearances occurred in November 1988, when a mass brawl broke out on *Geraldo* after Metzger's son, John, referred to the chairman of the Congress of Racial Equality, Roy Innis, an "Uncle Tom." Rivera's nose was broken in the resulting melee.

Above all, though, Metzger tried to reach out to the young, especially young skinheads, to spearhead the revolution. He began with an organization called the White Students Union, which aimed its recruitment efforts at high schools and colleges—again Duke's influence is notable—and which from 1987 was led by John Metzger. But, overall, he was much more successful in tapping into the racist skinhead scene. Music was crucial to this, and so Metzger began promoting white power bands around the country at events such as "Aryan Fest" and "Aryan Woodstock." As Martin Durham recounts, during a "Reich 'n Roll" concert in 1989, Metzger claimed that white power music was "the most powerful message in the country today for the White race," before declaring: "If the Jews can use music against us, we will destroy them with our music." By the 1990s the predominant producer and distributor of white power music in the United States was Resistance Records, which had been founded in 1993 by George Burdi, also known as George Eric Hawthorne. The label was acquired by Carto in 1997 and then sold to Pierce in 1999, becoming a lucrative part of his National Alliance operation. (Not all skinheads are racists, it is important to point out. Indeed, a flourishing anti-racist skinhead movement exists in both the United States and the UK, which is often known by the acronym SHARP, or SkinHeads against Racial Prejudice.)

The Anti-Defamation League estimated that there were 3,500 racist skinheads in operation by the end of the 1980s, but Metzger's success in mobilizing them was not without its costs. This became very clear in November 1988, when a large group of skinheads beat a 28-year-old Ethiopian student named Mulugeta Seraw to death with a baseball bat on the streets of Portland, Oregon. Three of those involved, Kenneth Mieske, Kyle Brewster, and Steve Strasser, were tried and convicted for the killing. But the ADL and the Southern Poverty Law Center also issued a civil lawsuit on behalf of Seraw's family that utilized the contentious legal doctrine of vicarious liability to contend that both John and Tom Metzger, as well as WAR as a whole, had responsibility for the murder. The case hinged on the testimony of Dave Mazzella, who had been dispatched by the Metzgers to Portland in order to organize the city's skinheads for WAR. In October 1990, a jury found both WAR and the Metzgers liable, and awarded Seraw's family $12.5 million in damages. As the Southern Poverty Law Center's lead trial lawyer, Morris Dees, explained to the New York Times, the amount of the award had "no real relation to WAR's assets." "A judgement of several hundred thousand dollars would have done the job in terms of getting what these defendants have to give," he said. "The reason we asked for so much, and the reason the jury gave it to us, is the signal it would send to the organized hate business. We're going to clean their clock." The Metzgers were indeed bankrupt, but WAR was not put out of business completely. It would continue to operate, although in a much-diminished form, well into the 2000s.

If Metzger had long abandoned his electoral endeavors, the same could not be said for his erstwhile colleague David Duke. On the contrary, as already noted, in 1988 Duke made a bid for the presidency under the auspices of Carto's Populist Party—he had actually begun the campaign in the Democratic Party primaries, but changed horses once it became evident that he was getting nowhere. His running mate was the retired Green Beret James "Bo" Gritz, who would go on to play a prominent role in the militia and Patriot movements of the 1990s. Duke received only 48,267 votes—0.05 percent of those cast—but the publicity was immense. The following year, this time running as a Republican, he successfully, if narrowly, obtained a seat in the Louisiana state legislature—representing the 81st District in Jefferson Parish—after defeating John Treen by 224 votes. Although Duke had carefully toned down his anti-Semitic and racist rhetoric for the campaign, it was nonetheless a stunning victory. One of his most long-standing goals had been achieved.

Duke's victory obviously had a great deal to do with the local situation in Louisiana— Jefferson Parish was 96.7 percent white, for instance—as well as Duke's particular history in the state, but the broader political climate of the 1980s should not be ignored either. As many observers have pointed out, the presidency of Ronald Reagan was one that seemed especially encouraging to the forces of the far right. In August 1980, for example, Reagan had officially launched his national campaign at the Neshoba County Fair in Philadelphia, Mississippi, not far from the scene of the murders of James Chaney, Andrew Goodman, and Michael Schwerner in 1964. Rather than using the occasion to deplore the violence of the Klan, or express his support for the civil rights movement, he had chosen to declare his enthusiasm for states' rights instead. Well-versed in the art of the dog whistle, Reagan also firmly opposed affirmative action and sought to gain backing for his "reform" of the welfare system through stereotypical invocations of freeloading, Cadillac-driving "wel-

fare queens." Not surprisingly, then, the Klan and other white suprema-
cist organizations keenly endorsed Reagan's candidacy, with Imperial
Wizard Bill Wilkinson even going so far as to suggest that the 1980
Republican platform "reads as if it were written by a Klansmen." (As
Hilary Moore and James Tracy note, much like Donald Trump in 2016,
Reagan eventually rejected the Klan's support, but he "took his sweet
time" in doing so, "using silence to send a message.")

Nor did things improve during Reagan's time in office. The National
Anti-Klan Network was repeatedly critical of the administration's seeming indifference to Klan violence, for example, while Leonard Zeskind
argues that as far as the president, his attorney general, Ed Meese, and
the head of the Justice Department's Civil Rights Division, William
Bradford Reynolds, were concerned, "the principal civil rights battle was
not against racist violence but against affirmative action for black people
and women in hiring and education." The African-American scholar
Manning Marable went even further with his criticism, writing in 2000,
that Reagan's election had been one of three "green lights" that had
been "largely responsible for unleashing racial terror" on Black Americans during the 1980s. The other two, Marable said, were the Supreme
Court's decision in the affirmative action case of *Bakke* in 1978 and the
"Greensboro massacre."

As for Duke, he continued on with his pursuit of high political office
into the 1990s, running for the U.S. Senate in 1990—and again in 1996—
the governorship of Louisiana in 1991, the presidency (again) in 1992,
and the House of Representatives in a special election in 1999. During the
2000s, he would also become an enthusiastic supporter of both the Tea
Party movement and Donald Trump.

The Ku Klux Klan underwent a significant revival during the 1970s
and early 1980s. Duke, of course, was at the heart of this, although his rise
to prominence was accompanied by no small degree of controversy and
contention. One of Duke's key aims was the "mainstreaming" of white
supremacy within the American body politic, an aim he shared with Willis Carto among others, and which he sought to accomplish through a
careful public relations strategy centered on the skillful exploitation of
a widespread sense of white grievance. Duke may not have achieved
his goal of restoring the Klan to the "golden age" it had enjoyed in the
1920s, but his impact was nonetheless considerable, not least through the

so-called "Nazification of the Klan," a process he helped to initiate. This, in turn, contributed to a notable uptick in Klan violence, culminating in the horrific events at Greensboro in 1979, although other prominent Klan leaders such as Bill Wilkinson certainly needed no encouragement from neo-Nazism to embrace the bullet and the gun.

Duke's Klan Border Watch initiative also provided an early indicator of the shift toward paramilitarism that would become such a prominent feature of the extreme right in the 1980s, although Louis Beam was the real pioneer in this respect, alongside the even more influential William Pierce. Indeed, there were a whole range of other white supremacist groups in operation during the 1980s, including the Covenant, the Sword, and the Arm of the Lord; the Christian-Patriots Defense League; and The Order—also known as The Silent Brotherhood, or Brüder Schweigen—that had turned not just to paramilitarism, but also to armed revolution to achieve their goals. It is these groups, as well as the impact of racist theologies such as Christian Identity, that we consider next.

4

Religion and Revolution

The Posse, Identity Christianity, and The Order

ON FEBRUARY 13, 1983, GORDON KAHL, a farmer, tax resister, and member of a radical right-wing group called the Posse Comitatus, shot and killed two federal marshals who were trying to arrest him. Four months later Kahl himself was killed in a raid on the remote Arkansas property where he was hiding out. On October 28, 1983, four members of a white supremacist group called The Order—or the Silent Brotherhood—robbed a pornographic bookstore in Spokane, Washington, the beginning of a revolutionary-inspired crime spree that went on to include the murder of Alan Berg, a Jewish talk show radio host, in Denver, and the $3.6 million robbery of a Brinks armored car in California. On June 30, 1984, Richard Wayne Snell murdered Louis Bryant, a Black Arkansas state trooper. The previous year Snell and two colleagues had also killed a Texarkana pawnshop owner, whom they mistakenly thought was Jewish. Snell was a member of the Covenant, the Sword, and the Arm of the Lord, whose survivalist compound and illegal weapons business was presided over by charismatic racist Christian Identity minister James Ellison. Over 300 federal agents would stage a four-day siege of the property in April 1985 in an attempt to shut it down. Two years later, 14 white supremacist leaders and activists, including 4 members of The Order, would be indicted for seditious conspiracy against the U.S. government.

These figures and these groups—together with the various issues their activities raise—are the subject of this chapter, alongside other related figures and organizations such as Henry Lamont Beach, Jim Wickstrom, Wesley Swift, the Christian-Patriots Defense League, and the Aryan

Nations. The chapter addresses the so-called "revolutionary turn" of the white supremacist movement in the United States that occurred around 1983 and was precipitated, in the main, by the thinking of William Pierce, Louis Beam, and a former Klansman called Robert Miles. Miles's idea of a "Fifth Era Klan" is also examined, as is the critical role played by religious beliefs during this period, Identity Christianity most prominently, but others as well. Significantly, these beliefs offered not just an underlying theological rationale for racism, but also a moralistic justification for violence. Finally, issues of apocalyptic thinking, nuclear anxiety, and the "farm crisis" of the 1980s are considered, as is the role that women played within these groups.

We begin with the Posse Comitatus, formed by William Potter Gale in 1971. Posse Comitatus is a medieval term, Latin for the "power of the county." In the American context, at least in terms of how Gale promoted the idea, this meant that the local sheriff was the highest legal power in the land; that the federal income tax was illegal; and that the nation should be governed by what was called the "organic" Constitution, which is to say, the original Constitution, plus the Bill of Rights, but not any of the subsequent amendments, such as the Fourteenth Amendment, which granted citizenship to former slaves and guaranteed every citizen "the equal protection of the laws." In fact, as far as Posse adherents were concerned, there was a clear distinction to be made between (white) "sovereign citizens" and so-called "Fourteenth Amendment citizens." Gale was also a believer in Identity Christianity, which held, in sum, that whites were descended from the "lost tribes" of Israel, that Jews were the spawn of Satan, and that African Americans and other racial minorities were "pre-Adamic," or "mud people." (The origins of this theology are discussed in detail below.)

Gale was born in St. Paul, Minnesota, on November 20, 1916, to Charles and Mary Agnes Gale. Ironically, given the deeply anti-Semitic politics he would pursue for most of his adult life—and although he would try to keep it a secret—as Daniel Levitas revealed in *The Terrorist Next Door* (2002), his father was Jewish. Charles Gale had abandoned his faith before Bill was born, but as Levitas points out, because of the convoluted theology of Identity Christianity, this meant that "Bill Gale was a Jewish anti-Semite who spent a lifetime trying to convince other anti-Semites that they, too, were Jewish." In 1922, the Gale family moved to California, and after graduating from high school, Bill enlisted in the U.S. Army. In 1937 he was married to Josephine Catherine Dvornich—with whom he would have three children—and honorably discharged from the Army.

Following a spell running a restaurant in Los Angeles called Bill's Cafe and Cocktail Lounge, Gale reenlisted in the Army during the Second World War. He served first in Australia, as director of supply for the Army's Pacific Section Headquarters, and then in Japan, as part of General Douglas MacArthur's occupation staff. In 1950 Gale retired from the Army, having been declared medically unfit for service due to hepatitis. Despite his own repeated claims to the contrary, he had not reached the rank of full colonel upon his retirement, but only that of lieutenant colonel. Nor had he been responsible for the training and leading of bands of guerrilla fighters in the Philippines, another of his much-repeated claims. Nonetheless, his wartime experiences still provided him with a great deal of credibility once he entered the world of far-right politics. First, though, Gale underwent a conversion to Christian Identity. He was introduced to the religion in 1953 by former Texas Klansman San Jacinto Capt, but it was the former Methodist clergyman Wesley Swift who became Gale's real mentor and who formally "ordained" Gale as an Identity minister in 1956. (Swift's critical role in Identity's spread in the United States is addressed later in the chapter.)

The following year, as chairman of the small right-wing Constitution Party, Gale decided to make a run for the governorship of California. Deeply disturbed by the recent events at Little Rock, Arkansas, and in order to generate some publicity for his campaign, in December 1957 Gale invited the Mississippi judge and leading Citizens' Council advocate Tom Brady to address a meeting of the party in Sacramento. Despite this support, Gale was unable to generate the 50,000 names that were necessary to have him placed on the ballot. As Levitas notes, the campaign was nonetheless notable in at least two respects. One, it began the process of moving Gale away from mainstream politics—although he would make another, equally ineffective bid for the governorship in 1962; and, two, it saw his first publicly recorded use of the term "Posse Comitatus," a full 14 years before he set out to create a whole new organization centered around the concept.

In sending troops to Little Rock, President Eisenhower was in clear violation of the 1878 Posse Comitatus Act, Gale asserted. The president had illegally "invaded" the "sovereign state of Arkansas," was obviously guilty of "high crimes and misdemeanors," and should be immediately arrested and tried for his crimes. It was true that the 1878 Act was intended to prevent the federal government from using the U.S. Army to enforce the nation's domestic laws, but the prohibition was not absolute. Troops could be so dispatched if they were "expressly authorized by the Constitution or by act of Congress," and controversial as it may have been, there was nothing illegal or unconstitutional about what Eisenhower had done.* In addition, while inventive legal reasoning would become one of the hallmarks of the Posse movement in the years to come, it is also worth noting that the Posse Comitatus Act was a product of the racist milieu from which it had sprung. Signed into law by Rutherford B. Hayes, the act was really the work of Southern Democrats in Congress who wanted to prevent the Army from being used to protect the rights of Black Americans during Reconstruction. As such, it was firmly rooted in the doctrines of white supremacy and states' rights, something that doubtless made it even more appealing to Gale.

In 1958, Gale and Capt created a short-lived group called the Christian Defense League, which was intended, they explained, to speak for "white Christians" in the same way that the National Association for the Advancement of Colored People spoke for Blacks and the Anti-Defamation League spoke for Jewish people. Two years later, Gale formed the explicitly paramilitary California Rangers. Like its counterpart in Missouri, Robert DePugh's Minutemen, the Rangers were ostensibly a "volunteer civil defense organization" designed to protect the nation from communist invasion. In practice, however, each group attracted a large number of racists and anti-Semites and seemed just as hostile to the federal government as they were to any foreign enemy. Indeed, in a report published in 1965, California's Attorney General Thomas Lynch described the Rangers as a "secret underground guerilla force" that constituted a "threat to the peace and security of the state." Yet as Jeffrey Kaplan has written, regardless of how it was judged, because of its "localist orien-

---

* The Posse Comitatus Act was amended in 1956 to cover the Air Force as well. In 2011 President Obama signed the National Defense Authorization Act, which controversially allowed detained American citizens to be taken into military custody within the United States if they were determined to be a terrorist or a terrorist supporter. And in 2020 the law became news again, when President Trump threatened to invoke the Insurrection Act of 1807—another exception to the Posse Comitatus Act—in the wake of widespread protests following the death of George Floyd in Minneapolis on May 25 that year.

tation" and also because of Gale's subsequent "status" in the American racialist movement, the California Rangers was important in providing an organizational model not just for Gale's own Posse Comitatus idea, but also the broader tax protest movements of the 1980s and the militia movement of the 1990s.

In 1963 Gale moved to Lancaster, the same small town in the Mojave Desert where Wesley Swift lived. There he established his own Ministry of Christ Church. In 1965 he remarried, to Roxanne Lutrell—he had divorced Josephine three years earlier—and that November began publishing a new monthly newsletter, *IDENTITY*, which he used to promote a range of pro-segregationist, pro-Constitution, anti-communist, and anti-tax articles, alongside his various theological explications and justifications. He also taped his weekly sermons, distributing them around the country in a further attempt to expand the reach of his ministry. It wasn't until 1971 that Gale returned to his ideas about "volunteer Christian Posses."

In a series of articles in *IDENTITY* beginning that summer, which were often written under the pseudonym "Colonel Ben Cameron"—the name a reference to one of the central characters in *The Birth of a Nation* (1915)—Gale carefully set out his case for the Posse Comitatus. "In the formation of this constitutional republic," he explained, "the county has always been and remains to this day, the TRUE seat of the government for the citizens who are the inhabitants thereof. The County Sheriff is the only legal law enforcement officer in these United States." It was therefore incumbent upon every sheriff to mobilize all the men aged between 18 and 45 in their area to enforce the laws of the land—although others could volunteer should they wish—and if the sheriff refused to do so, then the local citizenry should take it upon themselves to establish their own Posse and remove the sheriff from office. In addition, Gale went on, if any government official violated the Constitution—or even "Natural Law"—they should be arrested and put on trial by a citizen jury. And if then found guilty they should "be removed by the Posse to a populated intersection of streets in the township and at high noon be hung there by the neck, the body remaining until sundown, as an example to those who would subvert the law."

In 1972 Gale offered further guidance on how to establish these groups when he announced the formation of the United States Christian Posse

Association (USCPA). A minimum of "seven Christian citizens," all living in the county in which the Posse was to be organized, was required
for a "charter" from the USCPA to be granted, he said, although in
practice—as he would soon discover—his new association had very little
control over how the movement he had started would actually develop.
(Not surprisingly given the beliefs underpinning it, a deeply felt sense of
autonomy was very much the order of the day for most Posse members.)
Indeed, it was not Gale but another anti-Semite, Henry Lamont "Mike"
Beach, who more effectively expanded the reach of the Posse Comitatus
movement during the 1970s.

Beach had been a state liaison officer in William Dudley Pelley's Silver
Shirts in the 1940s. He was retired from his dry-cleaning repair business
and living in obscurity in Portland, Oregon, when he came across Gale's
ideas and decided to steal them. In 1973 he established the Citizens Law
Enforcement and Research Committee (CLERC) and began publishing
what he called the Posse *Blue Book*—the title seemingly a reference to
the foundational text of Robert Welch's John Birch Society. As Daniel
Levitas has shown, the contents of Beach's *Blue Book* were lifted wholesale—and completely uncredited—from the articles Gale had already
published in *IDENTITY*. Unlike Gale, however, Beach was as much
interested in making money from the concept of the Posse Comitatus
as he was in spreading the word. Copies of the *Blue Book* cost 25 cents
apiece, for example, and each new Posse recruit was expected to pay a
$3 membership fee. Beach also sold signed Posse "charter certificates,"
badges, car-door decals, and taped speeches, among other merchan-
dise. He was so shameless that he even claimed to have formed the first
Posse group back in 1969, a fiction that would find its way into countless
accounts of the founding of the movement.

Yet while Gale was understandably upset with Beach's blatant "rip-off,"
the fact remains, as Levitas writes, that "Gale could not have popularized
the Posse as successfully as did Beach." By 1976, the former Silver Shirt
claimed there were 100,000 members of the Posse movement spread across
the country. The FBI put the figure at anywhere between 12,000 to 50,000,
with perhaps an additional 120,000 to 500,000 sympathizers, but the figures were still impressive. (Despite Beach's promotional skills and desire
for recognition, secrecy remained a prominent feature of the movement as
a whole, so exact figures are difficult to come by.) The group attracted a

range of constitutional fundamentalists, racists, Christian Identity adherents, gun rights advocates, and tax protestors, as well as disaffected members of the Birch Society, former Minutemen, and other conservative populists. It was especially strong in states such as Colorado, Idaho, Oregon, Washington, Nebraska, North Dakota, Montana, California, and Texas, but beginning in the late 1970s and early 1980s it spread with particular rapidity in the rural Midwest, spurred in part by the actions of another important popularizer, James Wickstrom, and, more substantively, by the widespread "farm crisis" that was gripping the region.

Wickstrom had been introduced to the movement by Thomas Stockheimer, another Posse leader, in 1975. He was an Identity believer, a tax resister, and a former traveling salesman who had served briefly in the Army during the Vietnam War, although not in combat. In 1978 he set up a religious compound in Tigerton Dells in Wisconsin as the base both for his Mission of Jesus the Christ Church and his Christian Liberty Academy school; he had previously taught history and geography at Dan Gayman's paramilitary-style Church of Israel, in Schell City, Missouri. Despite the fact that there was no single national organization to belong to, in 1979 Wickstrom declared himself to be the Posse's "National Director of Counterinsurgency" and set about traversing the Midwest in search of new recruits. As a result, as James Coates notes, by the early 1980s he had become "the most visible Posse leader in America."

Wickstrom had a forceful personality and was undoubtedly a talented salesman, but he was also fortunate in that many of the farmers and other rural residents he encountered on his travels were already ripe for recruitment. The farm crisis that began in the late 1970s and lasted until the end of the 1980s was the product of a number of interrelated factors, including high inflation, rising interest rates, overproduction, soaring costs, declining export markets, and government policies that favored corporate farming over that of family-run businesses. Saddled with expensive loans they were now unable to repay, many farmers were forced to sell off parts of their land, but this only led to a further drop in farm values, as well as a corresponding rise in the number of bank foreclosures, since it was the value of their land that been used as collateral for the loans they had taken out in the first place. Around 625,000 family farms went out of business between 1981 and 1988. The results were devastating, not just for farmers, but for the whole rural economy. By

1987 the Center on Budget and Policy Priorities reported that nearly 17 percent of rural Americans were living below the poverty line. Not surprisingly, the rates of depression, suicide, alcoholism, and domestic violence in the region all increased dramatically.

This was the environment that Wickstrom—and others—sought to exploit. He placed advertisements for the Posse in various farm newspapers and magazines, went on extensive speaking tours, did local press and television interviews, and sold his own newsletter, *The Posse Noose*. Both his and Bill Gale's taped sermons were also broadcast regularly on the powerful 100,000-watt KTTL radio station in Dodge City, Kansas, which could reach as far as Colorado and Oklahoma. In one 1982 broadcast, Gale declared:

> You're damn right I'm teaching violence! You better start making dossiers, names, addresses, phone numbers, car licence numbers on every damn Jew rabbi in this land, and every Anti-Defamation League leader, or [Jewish Defense League] leader in this land . . . and you better start doing it now. . . . You get these roadblock locations, where you can set up ambushes, and get it all working now. If you have to be told any more than that, you're too damn dumb to bother with!

Wickstrom's broadcasts were equally graphic and equally offensive. "The Jews are like a pen full of pigs," he proclaimed in November 1982:

> You bring them into a country, it's just a matter of time, they eat everything up. . . . Who caused and planned the wars? Who passed all these abortion laws to kill our children? . . . These Jews don't think they are going to drink of the cup of wrath. They're going to take a big swig, believe me. . . . [The Bible] didn't say you're gonna vote them out. It said, "Thus with violence shall that great city Babylon"—that international communist system—"shall be thrown down and shall be found no more." . . . And all the disco-bongo-congo from the Congo is gonna be gone. All the nigger jive and the tootsie-wootsie is going to go!

Nor were Gale and Wickstrom content just to incite violence. They also actively sought to teach people how to carry it out. As Leonard Zeskind recounts, beginning in 1982, the two men started a paramilitary training camp on a farm near Weskan, Kansas, which they euphemistically advertised as an "Ecological Seminar." Over the course of three days, Gale instructed the 55 fee-paying participants, which included members

of both the American Agricultural Movement and the Farmers Liberation Army, on matters such as "killer teams, knife fighting, usable poi-
sons, and explosives." According to Zeskind, both Wickstrom and Gale
later ran separate bomb-making seminars as well.

The American Agricultural Movement had been formed in 1977 in
response to the emerging farm crisis. In 1979 it drew tens of thousands of
farmers to Washington, D.C., for a massive "tractorcade" protest, but by
1983 the involvement of Posse members and other right-wing extremists
caused a major split in the group. The Farmers Liberation Army was
a smaller group of militant farm activists formed by a Kansas farmer,
Keith Shive, in 1981, and it was much more closely aligned with the
Posse movement. Willis Carto also tried to exploit the farm crisis. In
the August 1984 issue of *The Spotlight*—which was widely read on the
farm circuit during this time—he suggested that the Populist Party was
the only viable way "to revitalize the family farm." Yet he was also an
enthusiastic advocate of the Posse Comitatus movement. For example,
the inaugural issue of what was still the *National Spotlight*, in September
1975, had described the emergence of the Posse as "a heartening sign of
public determination to see [that] law enforcement is restored." David
Duke was a supporter too. He told *Newsweek* the same year that the Klan
worked "with Posses wherever we can," explaining how "we get their
material and funnel it to our groups."

The activities and ideology of the Posse Comitatus did not go unnoticed by government authorities, of course. In the mid-1970s, the Internal Revenue Service (IRS) established a special Illegal Tax Protestor
Program to try to deal with the group. In 1980 it identified 17,222 illegal
tax protestors, based on a count of the number of people who had either
stated their political views directly on their tax forms, or had failed to file
their tax returns as a deliberate expression of political protest. By 1983
that number was 57,754. The agency added hundreds of "tax-protest
coordinators" and auditors to deal specifically with Posse cases and prosecuted offenders vigorously, while Congress also increased the penalties
for politically motivated tax avoidance. Yet by 1986 the number of cases
had only declined to 52,000. (To be sure, the "tax protest movement" was
wider than the Posse, as evidenced by the national "tax revolt" launched in
California in 1978 by Howard Jarvis and Paul Gann, as well as the best-
selling success of books such as Frederick "Tupper" Saussy III's *The*

Miracle on Main Street [1980] and Irwin Schiff's *How Anyone Can Stop Paying Income Taxes* [1982], but the group was very much at the heart of it.)

The FBI first become aware of the organization in 1972 when its Portland, Oregon, office reported on what it called an "association of long-time Right-Wing extremists" who were "preaching hate against the Negroes and the Jews, and calling for the repudiation and overthrow of the existing law enforcement and judicial systems of this nation." By the mid-1970s, the bureau had expanded its investigations into the group across 14 states, as it became increasingly concerned about the Posse's potential for vigilante violence. However, in the wake of the Church committee's revelations about COINTELPRO in 1975, as well as the uneven response of some of its local field offices, by the late 1970s the FBI had largely backed away from its surveillance of the movement, its own warnings going largely unheeded. It took the 1983 case of Gordon Kahl to change this.

Kahl was born on January 20, 1920, and grew up with his four siblings on the family's 240-acre farm in North Dakota. An aircraft gunner during the Second World War, his service was recognized with a Bronze Star, a Silver Star, and two Purple Hearts. According to James Corcoron, in his book *Bitter Harvest: The Birth of Paramilitary Terrorism in the Heartland* (1995), it was during the war that Kahl also became an anti-Semite, following his reading of Henry Ford's *The International Jew: The World's Foremost Problem* (1920). By the 1950s Kahl had also become a Christian Identity believer. He joined the Posse in 1973 and was promoted to the position of state coordinator for Texas in 1974. (He and his family would escape North Dakota's brutal winters for the Lone Star State as often as they could.)

To further their recruitment efforts, in 1976 Kahl and five other Posse members appeared on local television in Midland, Texas, to encourage citizens to stop paying their income taxes. As a result—although this was something he largely seemed to welcome—Kahl was indicted for his own failure to pay taxes for the years 1973 and 1974. He was convicted in June 1977 and sentenced to a year in jail, with five years' probation, the terms of which included that he both *start* paying his taxes and *stop* associating with the Posse. Upon his release from Leavenworth prison in August 1979, Kahl ignored both injunctions. Nor did he deliver any of the monthly probation reports he was supposed to.

In November 1980 the IRS filed a lien against Kahl's farm for the now $35,000 he owed in back taxes, penalties, and interest charges—the original bill had been $7,074—and a warrant was issued for his arrest because of his probation violations. In early 1981 the government seized part of Kahl's land in order to prepare it for sale by auction. Undeterred, Kahl continued to recruit for the Posse, meeting regularly with farmers across the Midwest—including members of the Farmers Liberation Army—where he was often accompanied by his eldest son Yorie and another North Dakota farmer, Scott Faul. On February 13, 1983, the three men were at a meeting in the small town of Medina, North Dakota, to discuss the creation of a Posse "township" in the area. That evening, driving away from the meeting, they ran into a roadblock that had been set up by federal marshals. A vicious gunfight ensued, in which two of the marshals, Kenneth Muir and Robert Cheshire, were killed. Three other officers were wounded, as was Kahl's son. Faul and Kahl escaped.

Faul turned himself in the following day, but despite a massive manhunt, Kahl managed to elude capture for four months. He was sheltered first by Arthur Russell, who owned a farm near Mountain Home, Arkansas; and then by Leonard and Norma Ginter, in their bunker-like residence in Smithville, in the foothills of the Ozark Mountains. While he was in hiding, Kahl wrote a detailed letter to explain his actions, which he dispatched to an Aryan Nations compound in Idaho (the group is discussed in detail below). Describing himself as a "Christian patriot," Kahl claimed that he had only acted in self-defense and that the shootout had been part of a "struggle to the death between the people of the Kingdom of God and the Kingdom of Satan." "We are a conquered and occupied nation," he went on, "conquered and occupied by the Jews, and their hundreds or maybe thousands of front organizations doing their un-godly work."

Thanks to information provided by Arthur Russell's daughter, Karen, who was keen to obtain the $25,000 reward on offer for his arrest, the FBI eventually tracked Kahl down to the Ginters' property. On June 3, 1983, a heavily armed law enforcement team made up of 6 FBI agents, 15 federal marshals, 3 state police officers, and 4 county lawmen, surrounded the house. Another shootout occurred that resulted in the death of the local sheriff Gene Matthews. Unsure whether Kahl had been killed in the initial gunfight, the federal agents unleashed a further barrage of gunfire and also dispatched tear gas, smoke grenades, and even diesel fuel into the house in the hope of "smoking" out the fugitive. A devastating inferno ensued, with Kahl's body burned beyond all recognition.

Gordon Kahl's death turned him into both a hero and a martyr; not just for the Posse movement, but for the whole anti-government and white supremacist right. He was joined in this status by Arthur Kirk, another Posse adherent, who died on October 23, 1984, in a gunfight with a Nebraska state SWAT team, after he had refused to repay the $100,000 he owed on an overdue farm loan and then chased three deputies from his property with an M-16 rifle. As for Yorie Kahl and Scott Faul, they were both convicted of second-degree murder for the killings of Marshals Muir and Cheshire and sentenced to life in prison.

Identity Christianity was central to the belief system of the Posse Comitatus, but it was a significant feature of many other racist groups as well. Indeed, to a considerable extent, the theology provided a unifying element to much of the white supremacist movement in the United States. It had its origins in the nineteenth-century doctrine of British Israelism which held that the British—although perhaps other Anglo-Saxon and Nordic peoples as well—were the lineal descendants of the "ten lost tribes" of Israel, which were said to have been removed from the Holy Land by the Assyrians around 722 BCE. (This view was expressed in the Scotsman John Wilson's 1840 book *Lectures on Our Israelitish Origin*, for example.) The idea first spread to the United States in the 1870s and the 1880s, but its impact became more pronounced during the 1920s and 1930s thanks to the efforts of Howard B. Rand, the head of the Anglo-Saxon Federation of America; William J. Cameron, a writer and editor for Henry Ford's *Dearborn Independent* newspaper, as well as his personal publicist; and the Oregon Ku Klux Klan leader Reuben H. Sawyer. It was during this time that Identity also first began its shift toward outright racism and anti-Semitism, a process that was completed in the 1940s and 1950s through the ministries of Gerald L. K. Smith and Wesley Swift.

Smith had begun his political career as the trusted lieutenant of Louisiana Governor Huey Long, but following Long's assassination in 1935, he moved increasingly to the far right. A spellbinding public speaker and committed organizer, he ran for the presidency as the leader of the America First Party in 1944 but replaced that organization with a new one called the Christian National Crusade in 1947, while both his political and his religious views were vehemently expressed in his long-running magazine *The Cross and the Flag*. Based in Los Angeles, Smith became the center of the Christian Identity community on the West Coast. Among those he attracted was Wesley Swift, who had founded his Anglo-Saxon Christian Congregation Church in Lancaster, California, sometime in 1948, later changing its name to the Church of Jesus Christ Christian in order to emphasize his view that Jesus had not actually been Jewish. And it was Swift, Michael Barkun writes, who became "the single most significant figure in the early history of Identity," responsible more "than anyone else . . . for popularizing [the religion] in right-wing circles by combining British-Israelism, a demonic anti-Semitism, and political extremism." It was Swift, as we have already seen, who mentored William Potter Gale, for example, and he did the same for other figures such as Richard Girnt Butler, Kenneth Goff, and Richard Warner. And they in turn would act as "teachers" for the next generation of Identity leaders such as Dan Gayman, Thom Robb, and David Lane.

At the heart of Identity's racist theology was the "two-seeds doctrine." This is the belief that Eve was impregnated both by Adam and by the Devil—or by one of his evil underlings—in the Garden of Eden: the first union producing the true Israelites, the sons of Abel, who are really the white race; and the second, the sons of Cain, who became known—erroneously—as the "Jews." Identity believers further suggest that before God created Adam and Eve, He also created a group of subhuman, "pre-Adamic" peoples—essentially all non-whites; the "mud people"—who lived outside of the Garden of Eden prior to the Fall. It was the descendants of Cain who killed Jesus, the theology maintains, and they remained intent on the destruction of all white Christians.

Other religions were also popular on the racist right, including the pre-Christian belief system of Odinism, with its veneration of the Viking-era Norse gods; Wotanism, a religion of nature; Occultism; and even Satanism. In the late 1970s, William Pierce created a new doctrine of Cosmotheism, a pantheistic religion premised, in the words of George Michael, "on the notion that the white race should wilfully seek an evolutionary path that will enable it to reach divinity." Another new religion, Creativity, was established by former John Bircher and longtime neo-Nazi Ben Klassen. Although originating in the 1970s, it wasn't until 1982 that Klassen was able to establish the physical head-quarters of his Church of the Creator, in Otto, a small town in the Appalachian Mountains in North Carolina. He also began publishing a new monthly magazine called *Racial Loyalty*, which had a circula-tion of 15,000, or so he claimed. Not content with issuing "the Sixteen Commandments" of Creativity, he also propounded "five fundamental beliefs," which he recommended that his followers memorize and repeat as a sacred ritual five times a day. They were:

1. WE BELIEVE that our Race is our Religion.
2. WE BELIEVE that the White Race is Nature's Finest.
3. WE BELIEVE that Racial Loyalty is the greatest of all honors, and racial treason is the worst of all crimes.
4. WE BELIEVE that what is good for the White Race is the highest virtue, and what is bad for the White Race is the ultimate sin.
5. WE BELIEVE that the one and only, true and revolutionary White Racial Religion—Creativity—is the only salvation for the White Race.

Klassen was also an advocate of "RAHOWA"—or Racial Holy War—which he once characterized as "total war against the Jews and the rest of the goddamned mud races of the world" (the phrasing an indication that Identity had had an influence on him too). George Burdi, the founder of Resistance Records, discussed in chapter 3, took the acronym RAHOWA for the name of the white power band he formed in 1989. Klassen com-mitted suicide in 1993, and his church was eventually taken over by Matt Hale and renamed the World Church of the Creator in 1996.

Mainline Protestant and Christian fundamentalist beliefs were also frequently expressed by American white supremacist groups, not sur-prisingly, perhaps, given that "Christian teachings" and "the Bible" had provided plenty of justifications for slavery and segregation in the past. But whatever form these theological expressions took, the effect was usu-ally the same: the sanctification of racism and—more often than not—racial violence.

Religious beliefs, Christianity Identity beliefs most prominently, were also an important feature of a number of white supremacist survivalist groups that emerged during this time. The most notable of these was the Covenant, the Sword, and the Arm of the Lord (CSA). Its remote compound, accessible by a single road, was located on 244-acres of land on the shores of Bull Shoals Lake in the Ozark Mountains on the Arkansas-Missouri border. It had begun life as the Zarephath-Horeb Community Church, established by the charismatic Identity minister James Ellison in 1976. (Zarephath was the name of the ancient city where the prophet Elijah was said to have resurrected a widow's son from the dead and was also seen as a place of refuge for weary soldiers; and Horeb was the biblical name for Mount Sinai, the place where Moses received the Ten Commandments.) By 1978, however, following Ellison's deep immersion in Identity end-times prophecies concerning Armageddon, the once quiet and peaceful community had transformed itself into the heavily armed and increasingly confrontational CSA.

Initially, the commune's members, who never numbered more than 100—although Ellison claimed the compound could house up to 5,000 in an emergency—had supported themselves through logging, but once it became the CSA, other enterprises came to the fore, most of them involving arms and weaponry. Covenant members began attending the nation's gun shows, for example, selling survivalist material, including gun accessories, and hate literature such as the *Protocols of the Elders of Zion*, *Who's Who in the Zionist Conspiracy*, and *A Straight Look at the Third Reich*. They also promoted the CSA's "Endtime Overcomer Survival Training School," where, for a fee of $500, attendees could learn all about urban warfare and "Christian martial arts," as well as wilderness survival, weapons selection, first aid skills, and even natural childbirth techniques. The course culminated with a run through "Silhouette City," modeled on the FBI's training facility at Quantico, where the camouflaged students got to rappel down buildings and sprint through fake streets littered with burning tires and wrecked cars, all while shooting at pop-up, cutout targets of gun-toting villains, including prominent Jewish leaders such as Golda Meir and Menachem Begin.

The Covenant, the Sword, and the Arm of the Lord's machine shop was used to build silencers, homemade hand grenades, land mines, and transform semiautomatic rifles into fully automatic machine guns, with the CSA quickly becoming well known in "far-right circles as one of the best sources" for such illegal weaponry, Levitas notes. By 1982, Ellison

had proclaimed himself "King James of the Ozarks," embraced polyg-
amy, and begun issuing "divinely inspired prophecies." He also committed the group to theft and armed robbery as a way to help support the
organization; practices he justified biblically as "Plundering the Philis-
tines," based on his reading of the First Book of Samuel. Other acts of
Covenant violence included the 1983 fire bombings of Jewish-owned
businesses and the Beth Shalom synagogue in Bloomington, Indiana, and
a gay community church in Springfield, Missouri, the same year.

By this time the organization had also become deeply embedded in
the wider white supremacist movement, with strong ties to the Klan,
the Posse, Aryan Nations, and—discussed below—The Order. Gordon
Kahl was a visitor to the CSA compound, for example, and it is widely
suspected that one of the group's members, Richard Wayne Snell, had
acted as Kahl's courier while he was on the run. Snell was a particularly violent member of the CSA, although he lived with his wife on an
80-acre farm in Muse, Oklahoma, where he earned his living as an army
surplus dealer, rather than at Zarephath-Horeb. In revenge for Kahl's
"murder" in late 1983, he and two other Covenant members attempted
to blow up a natural gas pipeline in Fulton, Arkansas, with hopes of
fomenting widespread civil unrest. When this failed, on November 3 the
three men robbed and murdered a Texarkana pawnshop owner, William Stumpp, whom they mistakenly believed to be Jewish. The following year, on June 30, Snell shot and murdered a Black Arkansas state
trooper, Louis P. Bryant, who had pulled him over in a routine traffic
stop. Snell was sentenced to life imprisonment for Bryant's murder but
received the death penalty for Stumpp's killing. He was executed on
April 19, 1995, the same day as the Oklahoma City bombing. James Ellison was also outraged by Kahl's death. "I'm sorry I wasn't with Gordon
Kahl when they found him. I just wish I'd been there," he informed the
attendees at the 1983 Aryan World Congress in Idaho. "I'm here to tell
you that the sword is out of the sheath, and it's ready to strike. For every
one of our people they killed, we ought to kill a hundred of theirs."

The CSA was also deeply involved, at least for a while, with another
prominent Christian Identity survivalist group called the Christian-
Patriots Defense League (CPDL). The group had been formed in 1977
by an apocalyptic-minded multimillionaire named John R. Harrell who
had made his fortune in the 1950s and 1960s selling mausoleums and

agricultural real estate. Harrell promoted the idea of a "Mid-America Survival Zone," a 20-state expanse of land in the middle of the country bordered by the Appalachian Mountains on one side and the Colorado Rockies on the other, where he believed those who followed him would have the best chance of riding out the End Times, nuclear war, a communist invasion, or some other catastrophic event. To help prepare for such eventualities, the CPDL held twice yearly, three-day, private, all-white "Freedom Festivals" at Harrell's 55-acre farm near Louisville, in southern Illinois. The festivals attracted a range of white supremacists for training in activities such as "street action," "knife fighting," and the "concealment of valuables and weaponry" and were keenly promoted by William Pierce and Willis Carto, among others.

In addition to the Christian-Patriots Defense League, Harrell also established a Citizens Emergency Defense System, a kind of private militia headed by Lieutenant Colonel Gordon "Jack" Mohr, a distinguished veteran of both the Korean War and the Second World War, which operated from two compounds: one in Missouri and the other in West Virginia. Another organization, the Paul Revere Club, handled fund-raising activities, while the Christian Conservative Church of America took care of spiritual matters—its aim, Harrell explained, was "to blend Christianity and Patriotism together to effectively oppose Zionism and Communism." CSA members provided the security for the Christian-Patriots Defense League's Freedom Festivals until 1982, when Harrell soured on the increasingly cultlike turn of the group. Indeed, Harrell's letter explaining the split between the two organizations made explicit reference to the 1978 "Jonestown massacre," when 909 members of Jim Jones's Peoples Temple committed murder-suicide in Guyana. "In the beginning Mr. Ellison's intentions were proper," he wrote,

> but as time progressed they altered and changed to the point where he may well be engaged in practices and actions that could endanger his entire unit, plus set the stage to bring public reproach and damage to the overall patriotic effort nationwide. . . . Some who have lived there honestly state and believe it could eventually evolve into a Jim Jones type of tragedy unless numerous changes are made.

This did not come to pass, although the CSA compound was the subject of a four-day government siege in 1985, which finally brought about its dissolution (see below).

Together with the Covenant, the Sword, and the Arm of the Lord, and the Christian-Patriots Defense League, other survivalist groups active on the extreme right during the 1970s and 1980s included Robert Millar's Elohim City in Oklahoma, as well as Dan Gayman's and Jim Wickstrom's previously mentioned compounds in Schell City, Missouri, and Tigerton Dells, Wisconsin. What they all shared in common—in addition to the racism, anti-Semitism, and paramilitarism—was a profound sense of the need to prepare for the dark times to come. Part of this was religiously motivated, of course, and it is important to note that in contrast to those premillennial evangelical and fundamentalist Christians who believed in the "rapture"—the moment during the apocalypse when the faithful would be lifted into the air to meet with Jesus preceding the "battle of Armageddon" predicted in the Book of Revelation—Identity Christians generally took the view that they would have to remain on earth and fight it out with Christ's enemies during a period of "tribulation" before being saved (a theological position known as postmillennialism). But they were also responding to the broader economic, social, and political conditions of the period that were affecting all Americans, not the least of which was the widespread fear of nuclear war brought on by the heightened tensions of the Cold War.

"We may be the generation that sees Armageddon," Ronald Reagan told the televangelist Jim Bakker during the 1980 presidential election campaign; while in a speech to the National Association of Evangelicals in March 1983, he referred to the Soviet Union as "the focus of evil in the modern world"—an "evil empire." Eight months later, in November 1983, the United States and NATO undertook a large-scale military training exercise called "Able Archer 83." Fearing the exercise might actually be a ruse to provide cover for a sneak nuclear attack, the Soviets responded by placing their own nuclear fleet on alert. "The international situation at present is white hot, thoroughly white hot," a Politburo member informed the Soviet Congress, according to the historian Jules Tygiel. Nuclear anxiety was also evident in the culture at large, in films such as *The Day After*, about the devastating effects of a nuclear attack on the heartland town of Lawrence, Kansas, which aired on network television across the United States on November 20, 1983; and in the publication of books such as *The Fate of the Earth* by Jonathan Schell in 1982, for example.

Nor were white supremacists and Christian Identity believers the only ones to embrace survivalism and paramilitarism during the early 1980s, as James William Gibson makes clear in his study *Warrior Dreams: Violence and Manhood in Post-Vietnam America* (1994). On the contrary, such attitudes are evident in everything from the success of movies such as *First Blood* (1982), *Red Dawn* (1984), and *Rambo: First Blood Part II* (1985); the popularity of magazines such as *Soldier of Fortune*, which began in 1975 and had a readership of almost 200,000 by the mid-1980s; the novels of Tom Clancy; and the appearance of paintballing and combat pistol shooting as mainstream leisure activities. All of which is to say that these "extremists" were as much a part of the culture as they were separate from it.

It is also important to point out that as these white supremacists ensconced themselves in their isolated and heavily armed compounds to prepare for what was to come—whether nuclear war, race war, a communist invasion, or the biblical apocalypse—at root their withdrawal represented an acknowledgment of defeat: a turning away from the world as it *was* and a recognition—implicit at least—that they did not have the power or the numbers to turn it into the place they wanted it *to be*; that neither hard-core racism, anti-Semitism, or Identity Christianity was likely to represent the future of the United States or its governmental structures. A similar (implicit) recognition was at work in the larger-scale proposals of other white supremacist groups to create a "separate homeland" for white Americans in some distinct part of the country, proposals that went under various names, including the "White Aryan Republic," the "White Aryan Bastion," the "10% Solution," and the "Northwest Territorial Imperative."

One of the primary advocates of this idea throughout the 1970s and 1980s was Richard Girnt Butler and his group Aryan Nations, based in Hayden Lake, near Coeur d'Alene, in northern Idaho. Butler was born in Bennett, Colorado, on February 23, 1918, but his family moved to Los Angeles when he was 13. He served in the Army Air Corps during World War II and became a staunch anticommunist and supporter of Senator Joseph McCarthy during the 1950s. He was introduced to the doctrine of Identity Christianity by William Potter Gale in the 1960s, by which time Butler was working as an aeronautical engineer for the Lockheed Corporation. Gale in turn introduced Butler to Wesley Swift.

Having become an ordained Christian Identity minister—and the head of the Christian Defense League—in 1970 Butler took over Swift's ministry in Lancaster following Swift's death in a Mexican clinic, where he had gone to seek treatment for diabetes. (This was much to Gale's chagrin, who had been eyeing the position for himself.) The dynamic Swift was a hard act to follow, however, and Butler, in truth, was not much of an orator. With his congregation dwindling, in 1974 Butler and his wife Betty relocated to Idaho, where Butler first established his own Church of Jesus Christ Christian, and then, in 1977, its political arm, the Aryan Nations. A number of factors account for Butler's decision to move to Hayden Lake, including the fact that as well as being beautiful, land there was cheap, and that he and his family had been regular vacation visitors to the Coeur d'Alene area for a number of years. Perhaps more importantly, it was also both remote and overwhelmingly white.

In many respects the Aryan Nations "headquarters" Butler created at Hayden Lake served as a forerunner for the survivalist compounds that would be established later by the likes of Ellison, Harrell, and others. As well as Butler's home, there was a bunkhouse, a chapel—decorated with Aryan flags and a large stained-glass window—a meeting hall, a steepled bell tower, several cabins, a trailer that served as a schoolhouse, and office space, which housed the group's printing press and other equipment. Following an unsolved bomb attack on the property in June 1981—relations between local citizens, anti-racist activists in the area, and Aryan Nations members were far from cordial, it should be noted—a 29-foot watchtower was erected, a sentry station added, and armed guards began more conspicuously to patrol the entrance to the compound, with its welcome sign reading "Whites Only." (The 20-acre site was not big enough to accommodate paramilitary training exercises itself, so shooting practice and other related activities had to take place on other land nearby.)

The Aryan Nations was never large, but it was influential. Butler claimed a membership of 6,000 in the early 1980s, although the real figure was probably closer to 1,000, and less than 100 people could live comfortably at Hayden Lake itself at any one time. Making good use of its printing press, the organization produced a steady stream of pamphlets, leaflets, and newsletters with titles such as *Calling Our Nation* and *Aryan Nations Newsletter*. It also sold a wide range of Christian Identity tracts and other hate literature while plying a lucrative trade in Butler's recorded sermons—the Aryan Cassette Service—which cost subscribers $2.50 a tape. A prisoner outreach program was overseen by Butler's secretary, Janet Hounsell, thus helping the group to forge a close relationship with the notoriously violent white supremacist prison gang, the Aryan Brotherhood. And Butler also did much to popularize the term "ZOG," or "Zionist Occupied Government," as a white supremacist descriptor for federal authorities and its agencies.

In addition, as already noted, Butler keenly promoted the idea of a "territorial homeland" for "white Americans." Initial plans had been for a huge swath of the United States to be given over to "Christian-Patriots," but by 1980 Butler and his followers had settled on what became known as the "10% Solution," which is to say, the control of Idaho, Montana, Wyoming, Washington State, and Oregon. Yet perhaps Butler's most important contribution to the white supremacist movement of this period was his annual Aryan World Congress, held at Hayden Lake from 1975 onward. (Butler organized the Aryan World Congress until his death in 2004. The only exception was 1985, when several members of The Order were put on trial, an event addressed later in the chapter.)

The Congress was Butler's attempt to bring unity to the fractured elements of the American racist right while simultaneously elevating his own status within the movement. Part social gathering, part political rally, part survivalist training camp, and part religious revival, the three-day summer event regularly attracted anywhere between 300 and 500 participants at its peak. They included Klansmen, Posse Comitatus members, tax resisters, neo-Nazis, Identity adherents, CSA and CPDL members, and—to quote the journalist and author James Coates—"a godly number of lone wolves, right-wingers too cranky to join any group but fully in accord with the Aryan Nations' theology of hate." (Because the Congress was a social event, wives and children attended too, and one of the highlights of the "festivities," alongside the volleyball and spaghetti dinners, was a gigantic evening cross burning.) At the 1982 Congress, 59 participants, including Butler, the Klan leader Thom Robb, and the revolutionary theorist and pastor Robert Miles, signed a charter for what they called "Nehemiah Township," a self-governing community of "Aryan Freemen." It rejected all existing local, state, and federal laws should they run counter to the law of God—which the members of the township would determine for themselves, as and when the need arose, of course—and which would be protected by its own armed forces, a Posse Comitatus and a militia. The following year, white power leaders were alleged to have issued a formal declaration of war against the U.S. federal government.

This startling claim was made by FBI informants and government witnesses during the Fort Smith sedition trial in 1988 (see below), although no documentary evidence to support the contention was ever produced. Even without such evidence, however, as Kathleen Belew has argued, it is clear that "something happened in July 1983," because after this point the white power movement became "decidedly revolutionary." Following the 1983 Aryan Nations World Congress, she writes, "the movement shifted nationwide to call for revolution against the Zionist Occupational Government . . . bombing of public infrastructure, undermining of national currency, assassination of federal agents and judges, and attempts to break away into a white separatist nation." The group that came to epitomize the "revolutionary turn" of the American white supremacist movement was The Order, but the shift was precipitated by the thinking of three key figures: William Pierce, Louis Beam, and the aforementioned Robert Miles.

As noted in chapter 3, Pierce had helped to push the white supremacist movement in a more violent direction through both his leadership of the National Alliance and, more particularly, through his authorship of *The Turner Diaries* (1978). As also previously noted, after leaving David Duke's Knights of the Ku Klux Klan in 1980, Louis Beam had moved to Hayden Lake to become an "ambassador at large" for the Aryan Nations. There he began reassessing the history of the Klan and setting forth his ideas on how the white power movement as a whole should develop in the future. These ideas were presented in two publications, both of which were published by Aryan Nations. The first, written in conjunction with Robert Miles, was called the *Inter-Klan Newsletter & Survival Alert*; and the second, authored by Beam alone, was called *Essays of a Klansman*. Each first appeared in 1983, and each made the case for a shift to clandestine, revolutionary activity and violence. (Richard Wayne Snell had a copy of *Essays of a Klansmen* in his car when he was arrested for the murder of Louis Bryant in 1984, and it would also have a significant impact on the Patriot movement that developed in the 1990s.)

One of Beam's ideas was for a "point scoring system," whereby militant racists could ascend to the status of an "Aryan Warrior" when they carried out particular acts of violence. The killing of an ordinary Black person would garner them one thousandth of a point. A Jewish demonstrator was worth two thousandths of a point, but the director of the FBI, a federal judge, or some other senior government official would gain the assassin one sixth of a point. This reflected Beam's belief that it was largely a waste of time to focus on "the enemy's pawns," and that only by directly challenging the "system's" leadership and infrastructure would the revolution come to pass. Acknowledging the recent problems the Klan and other groups had encountered from their infiltration by federal agents, the use of government informers, the passage of anti-paramilitary training legislation, and the opposition of watchdog groups such as the Anti-Defamation League and the Southern Poverty Law Center (see chapter 3), Beam also suggested a new organizational model for the movement, which he termed "leaderless resistance."

Beam traced the idea to a 1962 essay by one Colonel Ulius Louis Amoss, who had proposed both it and guerrilla warfare as a way of counteracting a communist invasion of the United States. Rather than a traditional, top-down, pyramid-like organizational structure, in which leaders issued orders that were then carried out by those below them, what was needed, Beam argued, was a "phantom cell" model of organization, in which every member already knew what they were supposed to do without any central direction being required. "Since the entire purpose of Leaderless Resistance is to defeat state tyranny," he wrote,

> all members of phantom cells or individuals will tend to react to objective events in the same way through usual tactics of resistance. Organs of information distribution such as newspapers, leaflets, computers, etc., which are widely available to all, keep each person informed of events, allowing for a planned response that will take many variations. No one need issue an order to anyone. Those idealists truly committed to the cause of freedom will act when they feel the time is ripe, or will take their cue from others who precede them.

In other words, those operating above ground—producing newsletters, engaging in speeches, publishing books, making sermons, or posting on computer bulletin boards—would provide the general ideological and political direction, but it would be for those in the underground, dispersed and untraceable, to carry out the necessary "actions." Not coincidently, Beam and Butler, both engineers, were hard at work creating a computer network called Aryan Liberty Net at precisely this time.

Robert Miles also believed in the concept of leaderless resistance, although he often used the metaphor of a "web" to describe it. "In any web, each intersecting point is tied to many other points," he explained. "In a chain type organization, one link is suspended by only the one above it. Let one link fail, and the function of the entire chain fails. Let one strand, on the contrary with a web break, and the function of the web is unimpaired." Miles also rejected the idea of public paramilitary training camps, arguing that if racist activists needed such training they should join the military, or a gun club, rather than making themselves both visible and vulnerable in this way.

Born in 1925 in Bridgeport, Connecticut, Miles was another of the patriarchs of the movement. He had served with the U.S. Navy during the Second World War, became a member of Robert Shelton's United Klans of America in the 1960s, and spent six years in the federal prison, in Marion, Illinois, for the 1971 fire-bombing of ten empty school buses in Lansing, Michigan, in protest against school integration. Upon his release in 1979, he became another "ambassador at large" for the Aryan Nations. He also ran his own "Dualist" Mountain Church, based on his farm in Cohoctah, Michigan, where he published a monthly newsletter, *From the Mountain*, and oversaw a prison outreach program, which had its own newsletter called *Beyond the Bars . . . The Stars!* As Martin Durham notes, although superficially similar to Identity Christianity, Miles's Dualism was actually somewhat different. As Miles saw it, for example, the ongoing battle between God and the Devil predated Christianity altogether. He also believed that God had dispatched whites to earth in order to conquer it for Him in the face of evil angels composed of "dirt, dust, and mud."

Miles's twice-yearly gatherings at Cohoctah, one in the spring and one in the fall, although smaller in scope than Butler's Aryan World Congress or Harrell's Freedom Festivals, were also important. Among those in attendance in April 1986, for example, were William Pierce, Thom Robb, the Alabama Klan leader Don Black, and the head of the White Patriot Party, Glenn Miller.

In addition to his support for leaderless resistance—and the Northwest Territorial Imperative—another of Miles's contributions as a white supremacist theorist was his concept of the "Fifth Era Klan." The First Era Klan was the Reconstruction Klan, he explained, the Second Era encompassed the 1920s, and the Third Era in the 1960s. David Duke's "Television Era" represented the Fourth Era, and it was this period that Miles really took to task. "The Fourth Era was an excellent supersalesman," he wrote, but it had not been "able to deliver the product which it had so competently sold." What was needed in the Fifth Era, he argued, was a truly revolutionary organization. (Despite all of its problems and all the new organizations that had appeared in its wake, it is still striking how attached racists like Miles and Beam remained to the concept and symbolism of the Klan.) Miles even made his own esoteric contribution to Klan Kulture when he decided that the Fifth Era needed its own numerological designation: "33/5," with the 33 representing the letter K, the eleventh letter of the alphabet, multiplied by three for KKK; and the 5 denoting the new, underground era into which the organization was hopefully heading.

As Leonard Zeskind notes, both Beam and Miles routinely used the word "Order" as a substitute for "Klan," and, of course, "the Order" was the name of the white supremacist group at the center of Pierce's novel, *The Turner Diaries*. Led by Robert Jay Mathews, in September 1983, just two months after the most recent Aryan World Congress, a real-life revolutionary organization called The Order burst onto the scene.

Mathews was born in Marfa, Texas, in 1953, but grew up mostly in Arizona. He became a member of the John Birch Society when he was still in his early teens and formed his own anticommunist and survivalist organization, the Sons of Liberty, in 1972, aged 19. Two years later he was sentenced to six months of probation for tax resistance activities after he had provocatively listed ten (nonexistent) dependents on a W-4 form. In 1974, Mathews left Arizona for the tiny town of Metaline Falls in Washington State, not far from the Canadian border, where he found work for a mining company. In 1975 he met his wife Debbie through a personal ad he had placed in *Mother Earth News*. They were married the following year.

By 1980 Mathews had joined William Pierce's National Alliance and began attending Aryan Nations events at Hayden Lake, which was about a three-hour drive from Metaline Falls. With Debbie unable to have children, in 1981 the couple adopted a son, Clint, who was baptized by Richard Butler at his Church of Jesus Christ Christian shortly thereafter. In 1982 Mathews began promoting the idea of a "White American Bastion" in the Pacific Northwest, but despite placing ads in *The Spotlight*, he was only able to persuade one couple to actually move to the area. At the September 1983 National Alliance Convention in Arlington, Virginia, Mathews received a standing ovation after he delivered a rousing speech about the "vanguard of an Aryan resurgence," and later that month he put his words into action when he formed The Order, also known as Brüder Schweigen, or the Silent Brotherhood.

As Kevin Flynn and Gary Gerhardt report in their book on the organization, in forming The Order, Mathews was influenced not just by Pierce, Miles, Beam, and Butler, but also by the "murder" of Gordon Kahl, which had taken place that June. The initial group consisted of Mathews and eight others. Four of the men, Daniel Bauer, Denver Parmenter III, Randolph Duey, and Bruce Pierce, were members of Aryan Nations; Richard Kemp and William Soderquist were recruited from the National Alliance; David Lane was a former Klansman; and Kenneth Loft was Mathews's close friend and neighbor. The Order quickly grew to about 50 members, organized in Beam-like cells, and drawn from all corners of the white supremacist world, including the Covenant, the Sword, the Arm of the Lord, the Posse Comitatus, and the Knights of the Ku Klux Klan. Among the most notable of these later recruits were Randall Radar, who had overseen the paramilitary training of the CSA and did the same for The Order; Gary Yarbrough, who had come to Aryan Nations through Butler's prison program; and Tom Martinez, another National Alliance member, whose mistakes handling counterfeit currency would ultimately have dire consequences for the group.

Mathews had a six-step strategy that drew on the key ideas of his various mentors. Step one was paramilitary training. Step two was fundraising, which was to be achieved through robberies and a counterfeiting operation. Step three was the purchasing of supplies and weapons. Step four was the distribution of money and arms to other white supremacist groups. Step five was called "security" but really amounted to the assassination of key figures on a "hit list." And step six was the expansion of the group into separate cells to avoid detection and prosecution. The Order's overall goal was the creation of a white separatist "homeland" in the Pacific Northwest, but Mathews was under no illusion that his small band of "Aryan warriors" would achieve this goal by itself. His aim was not to "win" the revolution, it was clear, but merely to start it; to disrupt the operations of ZOG and to rouse other "patriots" from their ignorant slumbers.

The Order's "operations" began with the robbery of a pornographic bookstore in Spokane, Washington, on October 28, 1983. The raid may have only netted the group $369, but it was fully in keeping with the practices of the fictional Order in *The Turner Diaries*, which had also specifically targeted "immoral" places to attack. Next, on December 18, Mathews—acting alone—robbed $25,952 from a Seattle bank, although an exploding dye pack ruined much of the take, forcing the group to deploy liberal amounts of turpentine and paint thinner in an attempt to wash it clean. In January 1984 Bruce Pierce and Gary Yarbrough stole $3,600 from another bank in Spokane, and then, on March 16, The Order robbed its first armored car, coming away with $43,345 in six large money bags. The group robbed the same armored car company again on April 23, this time clearing $230,379.

As part of a diversion plan—as well as another act of morally justifiable violence—two days earlier, on April 21, Yarbrough had bombed The Embassy Theater, an XXX-rated movie house in downtown Seattle, causing a small amount of damage. On the afternoon of the 23rd, the group then called in another bomb threat to the theater to draw police to the area. On the way to the robbery, they also tossed several boxes of nails onto the highway with the intention of causing a massive traffic jam to further aid their chances of escape. On April 29, the group next bombed a synagogue in Boise, Idaho.

On June 1, 1984, The Order carried out its first murder. The victim was one of their own, an Aryan Nations member named Walter West, who they were afraid talked too much. He was hit in the head with a sledgehammer, shot, and then buried in the woods in Kaniksu National Forest. Shortly thereafter, on June 18, at 9:15 in the evening, Alan Berg, a controversial Jewish talk radio show host, was murdered in the driveway of his home in Denver, Colorado. Berg had a reputation for baiting racists and anti-Semites live on air, and he had been pushed to the top of The Order's "hit list" by David Lane in particular, who had once appeared on his show. (Other prominent figures targeted for assassination by the group included civil rights lawyer Morris Dees, the television producer Norman Lear, the oil magnate Armand Hammer, former U.S. Secretary of State Henry Kissinger, and banker David Rockefeller.) The murder was carried out by Bruce Pierce using a converted MAC-10 submachine gun that had been obtained from the CSA's gun shop. Mathews and another Order member Richard Scutari acted as lookouts, while Lane was the getaway driver.*

On July 19, 1984, Mathews and six other members of The Order carried out their most audacious heist yet, the robbery of a Brinks armored truck on Highway 101, just outside of Ukiah, California. They drove away with over $3.6 million. The group paid itself salaries and "bonuses" from the proceeds of its operations (and its members also gave themselves code names and established false identities). In addition, they bought arms, electronic equipment, and other matériel, as well as two plots of land where they could conduct further paramilitary training: 300 acres in Missouri and 110 acres in Idaho. But true to their credo, a significant amount of money was also distributed to other members of the white power movement, including, or so federal prosecutors believed, William Pierce, Louis Beam, Robert Miles, Richard Butler, Glenn Miller, Dan Gayman, and Tom Metzger. (The exact amounts are unknown and were understandably disputed by those alleged to have received them. Indeed, in the end the FBI was able to account for only $600,000 of the Ukiah take.)

At the same time as the robberies and murders were taking place, The Order was also involved in an extensive counterfeiting operation. As Kathleen Belew notes, as with its namesake in *The Turner Diaries*, the group saw counterfeiting "not only as a source of income but also as a way to wage war on the Federal Reserve by flooding the market with fake money," thus eventually undermining "public confidence in paper currency [and] fomenting revolution." Yet it would also lead to the group's undoing. On June 28, 1984, Tom Martinez was arrested by the U.S. Secret Service for distributing counterfeit currency; almost unbelievably he had returned to the same Philadelphia liquor store, in his own neighborhood, where he bought a lottery ticket with a fake $10 bill the previous day. (Mathews had given him $30,000 in counterfeit bills earlier in the month with clear instructions that the money should be passed far

---

* Berg's killing provided the basis for Eric Bogosian's Pulitzer Prize-nominated 1987 play *Talk Radio*, which was turned into a film by Oliver Stone in 1988.

from his home.) Rather than go to jail, Martinez decided to become an informer for the FBI. Another mistake, which also aided the FBI, had occurred during the Ukiah robbery, when in his haste Mathews had dropped a 9-mm semiautomatic pistol that had been bought by Andrew Barnhill using his real name from a gun shop in Missoula.

With Martinez's help, in November 1984 the FBI tracked down Mathews and Yarbrough to the Capri Motel in Portland, Oregon. Yarbrough was captured, but Mathews shot his way out and went on the run, fleeing to a safe house in Whidbey Island, in Puget Sound, a short ferry ride from Seattle, where he holed up with other Order members and their families. As he recuperated from a gunshot wound to his right hand, Mathews drafted a formal "Declaration of War" against the "Zionist Occupation Government of North America." It referenced the killings of both Gordon Kahl and Arthur Kirk and promised to "avenge" their deaths and to "drive the enemy into the sea." "Through our blood and God's will, the land promised to our fathers of old will become the land of our children to be," he went on, claiming "a territorial imperative which will consist of the entire North America continent north of Mexico." "This is war!" he declared, and "for Blood, Soil, and Honor, and for the future of our children, we commit ourselves to Battle."

Having received an anonymous phone call advising them of Mathews's location, on December 7, the FBI dispatched 150 of its agents to Whidbey Island. The other Order members all surrendered, but Mathews refused to turn himself in. A 36-hour standoff ensued. It was brought to an end when an FBI helicopter dropped three M-79 illumination flares into the safe house igniting Mathew's store of ammunition and explosives. In an outcome eerily similar to the death of Gordon Kahl, Mathews was incinerated; and like Kahl, Mathews quickly became a "martyr" to other white supremacists.

Over the next few months an enormous law enforcement task force composed of the FBI, the Secret Service, the U.S. Marshals Service, the Bureau of Alcohol, Tobacco and Firearms, and the IRS rounded up most of the rest of The Order. Ironically, given the group's preferred name of the Silent Brotherhood, many of those arrested followed Martinez's example and informed against their colleagues, including founding members Dan Bauer and Bill Soderquist. On April 15, 1985, a federal grand jury issued a 21-count racketeering and conspiracy indictment against 23 members of the group, under the 1970 Racketeer Influenced and Corrupt Organizations Act, more commonly known as the RICO Act, which had been designed originally to combat organized crime in the United States. Eleven of those indicted pleaded guilty. The remaining ten defendants went on trial that September—two others, David Tate and Richard Scutari, had been more difficult to capture and would be tried separately, later in 1985 and 1986. On December 17, an all-white jury found all the defendants guilty, and they were sentenced to between 40 and 100 years in federal prison.

The successful pursuit of The Order precipitated a much wider crackdown on the white supremacist movement in the United States. On April 19, 1985, just four days after indictments against The Order had been laid, more than 300 federal offices raided the Covenant, the Sword, and the Arm of the Lord's compound in Arkansas, uncovering an enormous stash of illegal weaponry and ammunition, including stockpiles of cyanide gas. Ellison and seven other men were convicted that September of a range of offenses, including conspiracy to commit arson, with Ellison being sentenced to 20 years in prison. On October 9, 1986, William Potter Gale and eight of his associates were charged with conspiracy, interference with federal tax laws, and the mailing of death threats to the IRS, arising from their involvement in a new group called the Committee of the States that Gale had launched in 1982. (The Committee was pretty much the Posse Comitatus, just in another form.) Gale and four codefendants—two others had already pleaded guilty and two more had agreed to appear as witnesses for the prosecution—were found guilty on all counts in October 1987. Gale was sentenced to three concurrent one-year terms in prison and five years' probation but died from emphysema on April 28, 1988, aged 71, before his sentence was completed.

The biggest trial—indeed, arguably the most significant political trial in the United States since the Great Sedition Trial of 1944 (*United States v. McWilliams*), which had involved the unsuccessful prosecution of 30 far-right agitators, including Gerald Winrod, William Pelley, Elizabeth Dilling, and four former leaders of the German-American Bund, for being involved in a supposed conspiracy to overthrow the U.S. government and establish a fascist one in its stead—took place in Fort Smith, Arkansas, in 1988. Fourteen white supremacist leaders and activists, including Louis Beam, Robert Miles, and Richard Butler, CSA member

Richard Snell, and five members of The Order—Bruce Pierce, David Lane, Richard Scutari, Andrew Barnhill, and Ardie McBrearty—were charged with various offenses such as conspiracy to murder federal officials, conspiracy to manufacture illegal weapons, and, most seriously of all, seditious conspiracy, which is to say, conspiracy to "overthrow, put down and to destroy by force the government of the United States and form a new Aryan nation." Notable by their absence in the charges were William Pierce and Tom Metzger, while James Ellison and Glenn Miller appeared as witnesses for the government.

Evidence to support the seditious conspiracy charge included the attempted Klan invasion of Dominica in 1981 (see chapter 3), the Covenant, the Sword, and the Arm of the Lord's botched natural gas pipe bombing of 1983, the various criminal activities of The Order, and Beam's establishment of the Liberty Net computer bulletin board. However, in reality, the government's case was weak—it needed to demonstrate the existence of a single, clearly directed and highly coordinated conspiracy, rather than just a similarly inclined series of otherwise independent criminal acts—was poorly prosecuted, ran constantly into serious constitutional issues of "freedom of speech," and was hardly helped by the shambolic and utterly unconvincing performances of its two "star witnesses," Ellison and Miller. After seven weeks of trial, on April 8, 1988, following three days of deliberations, the jury found the defendants not guilty on all counts. The white power movement was jubilant. Far from being defeated, it had emerged from the proceedings victorious and ready to push forward into a new decade.

The white supremacist movement in the United States during this time remained both overwhelmingly male in terms of its composition and also hypermasculine with respect to its codes, orientation, and practices. Yet as scholars such as Kathleen Blee, Abby Ferber, and Kathleen Belew have emphasised, women nonetheless still played an important role in it—albeit usually in their "traditionally assigned" positions as wives, daughters, and mothers. The wives of William Potter Gale, Richard Butler, Louis Beam, and Robert Miles—Roxanne Gale, Betty Butler, Sheila Beam, and Dorothy Miles—all played crucial roles in the racist careers of their husbands, for example, as did Tom Metzger's wife Kathleen. Women were also important to The Order, although again largely in supportive or background ways, rather than as leaders in their own right. "They disguised male activists and drove getaway cars, trafficked weapons and matériel, created false identity documents, destroyed records when pursued by federal agents, and helped to produce the symbols and rhetoric that defined the group," Belew notes.

Jean Craig, the mother of Bob Mathews's second, polygamous wife, Zillah, went further, however. She tracked the movements of Alan Berg in Denver for months in order to lay the groundwork for his murder and was sentenced to 45 years in prison alongside other members of the group. (Despite bearing Mathews's child—a girl called Emerant—Zillah, in contrast, testified against both her mother and her "husband" during the 1985 trial, leading many in the movement to regard her as a "traitor" to her race.) The widows of "martyrs" were also celebrated. As Blee writes of the "racist icon" Mary Snell, the wife of Richard Wayne Snell: "She [became] esteemed for her 'lady-like-toughness' in lobbying for Richard's release, for maintaining his racist newsletter in his absence, and for preserving the memory of Richard's racist cause after his death."

More broadly, because "racial purity" and a fear of miscegenation and immigration were part of its driving concerns, women also played an important symbolic and practical role in the movement as the "propagators" of the white race. Indeed, in this respect it was widely agreed that (white) women were to be both venerated and protected, although again only in a very traditional way. As one Aryan Nations pamphlet from 1979, titled "The Aryan Warriors Stand," expressed it, for example, "Every child that an Aryan mother brings into the world is a battle waged for the existence of her people." "The thoughts of Aryan woman are dominated by the desire to enter family life," it went on,

> Aryan woman brings true love and affection, and a happy, well-run home to refresh and inspire her man. Aryan woman is treated with chivalry and respect by Aryan man. . . . It is the duty of the Aryan state to safeguard the mother and the child. . . . Aryan woman guards the purity of her blood in which reposes her racial instinct and strength, the guarantor of Aryan culture.

Similarly, Robert Mathews, who had required the original members of The Order to swear their oaths of allegiance while gathered in a candlelit circle around a six-week-old baby girl, complained in his "Declaration of War" about the "mongrel hordes" who were intent on conquering the nation either through "the force of arms, or the force of the groin." And David Lane, who underwent a conversion to Odinism while in prison for his part in The Order's crimes, issued a 14-word slogan with the same theme that would have widespread resonance for the racist right, not just in the United States but around the world. His wife Katja, whom he married in prison in 1994, would help popularize both it and Lane's other writings through their 14 Word Press. It was: "We must secure the existence of our people and a future for White children."

The impact of the activities of The Order on the white supremacist movement in the United States was considerable. As Leonard Zeskind succinctly puts it, "The Order changed everything." Mathews and his cohorts had *acted*. They had taken on the might of ZOG, and Mathews had been willing to lay down his life for the cause. The date of his death, December 8, became celebrated as the "Day of the Martyrs." White power activists made pilgrimages to Whidbey Island, songs and poems were written about him, and "We Love The Order" banners became a common sight at subsequent marches and rallies. William Pierce began circulating tapes of the speech Mathews had delivered to the National Alliance meeting in 1983, stressing the "symbolic importance of what Mathews had done"—his "courage, his strength, and [his] willingness to sacrifice it all for the white race." A short-lived group called The Order II— or Brüder Schweigen Strike Force II—was even established, setting off a number of bombs in the Coeur d'Alene area.

More fundamentally, The Order's commitment to violent revolution— as well as the consequences of the government's crackdown on it— forced a reckoning within the movement between those who wanted to continue the fight (although not necessarily in the same way, or with the same results), those who wanted to withdraw further into their protected enclaves, and those who wanted to shift to more politically oriented activities. Pierce, for example, while full of admiration for Mathews's "heroism," nonetheless thought that the country wasn't yet ready for revolution and that The Order's actions had come too soon. Dan Gayman returned the money he had received from the group and retreated back to his Church of Israel in Schell City. And David Duke, not surprisingly, led the charge for "nonviolent political action." ("Is this the way American civilization will topple," he lamented in the *NAAWP News*, following Mathews's death, "as more and more whites flip off their TV sets, quit their jobs, trash their word processors and desert the suburbs in favor of weapons and revolution?") The rise and fall of The Order also pushed the idea of a territorial "homeland" to the top of the racist political agenda, spurring a move toward a more explicit embrace of "white nationalism" to be examined in chapter 5.

The activities of the Posse Comitatus were also significant. As James . Ridgeway has written, the group managed to attain "mythic stature, and become a political metaphor to such an extent that Posse symbolism pervaded mainstream politics across the Midwest" in the late 1970s and 1980s. It became both a "symbol of resistance to the spreading 'tyranny' of the state" and a "symbol of the patriot, of the sovereign who, in order to maintain his freedom, has become an outlaw in his own country." As such it profoundly influenced the development of the Patriot movement during the decade that followed, as we shall shortly see. It also did an enormous amount to spread the ideas of Identity Christianity throughout the nation, complete with its theological and moralistic justifications for racism and violence.

The final issue of Louis Beam's and Robert Miles's *Inter-Klan Newsletter & Survival Alert*, published in April 1985, contained a stark message. "The Second American Revolution will be a revolution of individuals," it declared,

> a revolution without exact precedent in recorded history. Because individuals can accomplish complex acts of resistance without peril of betrayal or even detection by the most advanced snooping devices, missions FORMERLY ASSIGNED TO GROUPS MAY BE UNDERTAKEN BY INDIVIDUALS EQUIPPED TO FIGHT ALONE.

It was a clear call for "lone wolves" to act, and many would, including the Oklahoma City bomber Timothy McVeigh.

5

Terror in the Heartland

Ruby Ridge, Militias, and Oklahoma City

ON THE MORNING OF APRIL 19, 1995, a massive truck bomb exploded outside the Alfred P. Murrah Federal Building in downtown Oklahoma City. One hundred and sixty-eight people were killed, the worst domestic terrorist attack in American history. The bombing was carried out by a Gulf War veteran named Timothy McVeigh, with the assistance of two former Army friends, Terry Nichols and Michael Fortier. McVeigh in particular was closely connected with, and profoundly influenced by, the white supremacist underground in the United States, and the suspicion has long remained that there may have been a much wider conspiracy at work behind the bombing. This chapter examines McVeigh, the bombing, and the conspiracy theories associated with it in detail, but it also explores the roots of the bombing, beginning with the government raid on a white supremacist and Christian Identity adherent Randy Weaver at Ruby Ridge in Idaho in 1992.

Following this raid, about 160 far-right and racist activists, including Louis Beam and Richard Butler, gathered at Estes Park in Colorado to decide how they would respond. A number of ideas emerged, most notably the creation of armed citizen militias and the revival of Beam's strategy of leaderless resistance. Shortly thereafter another significant government raid took place, this time in Waco, Texas, home to the Branch Davidian religious sect. Gun control legislation was also enacted. All these events spurred the development of a new militia movement that began to emerge in earnest in early 1994, some of which was clearly racist, but much of which was not. All these developments need to be considered. Let us begin, though, with Randy Weaver.

Randall Claude "Randy" Weaver was born in January 1948 and grew up in Jefferson, Iowa. After graduating from high school and following a short stint as a school bus driver, he enlisted in the U.S. Army in 1968. He was trained as a combat engineer and as a member of the Special Forces—better known as the "Green Berets"—although much to his frustration he never went to Vietnam. In 1971 Weaver married Vicki Jordison and the couple moved to Cedar Falls, Iowa, to raise a family. His initial hopes of joining the FBI or the Secret Service having failed to come to fruition, Randy found work at the John Deere tractor factory in nearby Waterloo. Over the next few years, driven to a considerable extent by Vicki's interests and research, the Weavers became increasingly concerned with the Biblically prophesied End Times, survivalism, and right-wing conspiracy theories. In September 1983 the family—Randy, Vicki, their two daughters, Sara and Rachel, and son, Samuel, or Sammy—left Iowa for Idaho, where they built a remote cabin on Ruby Ridge in the Selkirk Mountains, 40 miles south of the Canadian border, so that Vicki could homeschool their children without interference from the government and they could all prepare for the Great Tribulation to come.

Richard Butler's Aryan Nations compound at Hayden Lake was only an hour's drive from Ruby Ridge, and Randy began to make regular visits to its annual World Congress. He and Vicki also became fully versed in the religion of Christian Identity. In 1988 Weaver ran for sheriff of Boundary County on a Posse Comitatus-like platform of enforcing only those laws the local citizens approved of. Yet despite distributing promotional business cards reading "Vote Weaver for Sheriff" on one side and "Get out of jail free" on the other, he lost in the Republican primary by 383 votes to 102. The following year Weaver was ensnared in a Bureau of Alcohol, Tobacco and Firearms (ATF) "sting operation," when he sold two illegally sawed-off shotguns to an undercover informant Kenneth Fadley, whom Weaver had met at Hayden Lake under the name Gus Magisono. (Unaware of Fadley's real identity, Butler had assigned "Magisono" to provide security for Gordon Kahl's widow at the 1989 Aryan Nations World Congress.) The Bureau offered to drop the weapons charges if Weaver would also become an informant for the ATF, which was investigating both the Aryan Nations and a suspected illegal white supremacist gun-running operation.

Weaver refused, and in December 1990 he was indicted on the gun charge. Released on an unsecured bond of $10,000 following his arrest in January, Weaver retreated to Ruby Ridge with his family and a friend, Kevin Harris, aged 24, whom the family had unofficially "adopted" nine years earlier. On February 3, 1991, with her husband's trial imminent, Vicki sent an alarming letter to the U.S. Attorney for Idaho, Maurice Ellsworth, whom Weaver referred to as the "Servant of the Queen of Babylon." "Whether we live or whether we die," Vicki wrote, "we will not bow to your evil commandments." She also quoted Bob Mathews, the "martyred" leader of The Order, by adding: "A long forgotten wind is starting to blow. Do you hear the approaching thunder? It is that of the awakened Saxon. War is upon the land. The tyrant's blood will flow." Predictably, perhaps, Weaver failed to appear for his trial on February 20. As a result, a warrant was issued for his arrest, and the case was turned over to the U.S. Marshals Service.

Although there had been some confusion over the dates—Weaver had originally been told his trial would take place in March, later received notification that it would be on February 19, only for it to be shifted to the 20th—the Weavers interpreted the apparent confusion not as an indicator of bureaucratic incompetence, but as simply further evidence of the evil machinations of the Zionist Occupational Government, and there is little to suggest that Randy was ever really intending to appear at court. Indeed, in another letter from June 1990—this one sent to the Aryan Nations and addressed to "all our brethren of the Anglo-Saxon race"— Vicki had made it abundantly clear that her family would "not make deals with the enemy." "This is war against the white sons of Issac," she wrote. "We have decided to stay on this mountain. You cannot drag our children away from us with chains."

Keen to avoid another Bob Mathews or Gordon Kahl showdown, for over a year the U.S. Marshals Service surveilled the Weavers' property, establishing listening posts in the woods, and conducting high-altitude flyovers, as friends and neighbors kept the Weavers stocked with food and other supplies. In October 1991 Vicki gave birth to the couple's fourth child, a girl Elisheba, in the "birthing shed" on the property. On August 21, 1992, six members of the Marshals' Special Operations Group was conducting another surveillance operation when they disturbed Striker, the family's Labrador retriever. The dog's barking attracted the attention of Randy, his son; Sammy, now aged 14; and Harris, all of whom were armed. The marshals shot the dog and Sammy fired at the marshals. The marshals returned fire and Sammy was killed. So too was U.S. Marshal William F. Degan, shot in the chest by Harris, while another marshal, Arthur Roderick, was slightly injured. After the shoot-out, the federal agents retreated down the mountain. Weaver and Harris then recovered Sammy's body, taking it back to the "birthing shed," and an 11-day siege began.

The FBI's elite counterterrorism Hostage Rescue Team was brought in to take control of events. Based on a preexisting "threat assessment" that had been carried out by the Marshals Service, which emphasized that "the entire Weaver family, including the 12- and 14-year-old children, were armed at all times," and that Randy and Vicki Weaver might use their children as a "first line of defense" in any assault by law enforcement agencies—an assessment based, in part, on Vicki's "Queen of Babylon" letter—FBI officials decided to alter the "rules of engagement" for dealing with the family. All agents were authorized to use deadly force against any adult seen with a weapon in the vicinity of the Weaver's cabin. This new, military-style, "shoot-on-sight" policy would have immediate and deadly consequences. On Saturday, August 22, the day after the shootings of Sammy Weaver and Marshal Degan, Randy, his daughter Sara, and Harris went to check on Sammy's body in the shed outside the cabin. FBI snipers were already hidden in various places around the property. As Randy Weaver reached to open the shed, he was shot in the arm. Randy and Harris turned to run back into the cabin as Vicki Weaver held the door open for them. Another sniper, Lon Horiuchi, fired at Harris. The bullet went through Harris's arm and struck Vicki Weaver in the face, killing her instantly. She had been holding ten-month-old Elisheba in her arms.

It would take another six days for the outside world to learn that Vicki had been killed. In the meantime, the FBI set up a roadblock down the hill from the Weaver cabin as it brought in hundreds of other law enforcement personnel and heavy equipment, including armored personnel carriers, bulldozers, and helicopters. The roadblock soon became the site of extended and vehement protest as scores of people gathered to offer their support for the Weavers. Local friends and neighbors took part regularly in these gatherings, but they were outnumbered by a wide range of white supremacists and Identity believers, including members of the Aryan Nations, skinheads, and future militia leaders. Bob Mathew's widow, Debbie, attended, along with her ten-year-old son, Clint, who held up a sign reading "Baby Killers!" Other signs read: "Death to ZOG," "Government Lies/Patriot Dies," "Christians Against Tyranny," "FBI Burn in Hell," and "The Weavers Today! Our Families Tomorrow." Away from Idaho, other white supremacists, including Tom Metzger and Willis Carto, also got involved. Carto's *Spotlight* published a series of articles on the siege, with headlines such as "Confrontation in Idaho Harbinger for America," for example.

The FBI attempted to open negotiations with Randy, sending an armed robot up to the cabin with a phone attached to its arm, along with tape-recorded messages from friends and other family members urging him to surrender. To put added pressure on the survivors, at night the agency aimed high-intensity lights on the cabin in an attempt to induce sleep deprivation, while the surrounding area was cleared of brush and trees, as tanks circled. The Weavers and Harris—who was badly injured—refused to engage. On August 25, five skinheads were arrested as they tried to smuggle rifles and semiautomatic weapons up to the cabin on a back road. The following day, retired Lieutenant Colonel James "Bo" Gritz and his sidekick, Jack McLamb, a former Phoenix police officer, appeared on the scene to offer their services.

Gritz was an almost mythical figure. The most decorated Green Beret in the Vietnam War, who General William Westmoreland referred to as "The American Soldier" in his autobiography, Gritz claimed to have personally killed 400 communists. During the early 1980s he spent three years searching for missing American POWs in the jungles of Southeast Asia, the project largely funded by billionaire Texas businessman H. Ross Perot. Although he failed to find any remaining Vietnamese prison camps, Gritz's exploits had apparently made him the model not only for Sylvester Stallone's Rambo character, but also that of John "Hannibal" Smith, the fictitious leader of television's *The A-Team* (played by George Peppard). By the late 1980s, Gritz had also become a staple figure on the American far right. He received extensive laudatory coverage in *The Spotlight*, was a popular speaker on the Christian Patriot circuit, and became good friends with Identity pastor Pete Peters, who helped to finance Gritz's 1991 autobiography, *Called to Serve*. In 1988 Gritz had been the Populist Party's vice presidential candidate under David Duke. In 1992, when he arrived at Ruby Ridge, he was running as the Party's presidential candidate under the slogan "God, Guns, and Gritz."

The events at Ruby Ridge had coincided with Pete Peters's annual Family Bible Camp Conference in Cedaredge, Colorado. When Peters learned that Gritz was en route to Idaho, he asked Gritz to deliver a letter to Randy Weaver. "Please know that the murder of your son has not gone unnoticed," it began (Vicki's death was yet to be disclosed). "Five hundred Christian Israelites from 40 states gathered at my 1992 camp in Colorado are right now praying for you and the Gideon situation you face," Peters went on, referring to the Israelite leader who, according to the biblical Book of Judges, had defeated a much larger army of Midianites. Gritz claimed to have been Weaver's commander in the Special Forces—although it was not clear whether the two men had actually ever met—and offered to help talk Randy and his family out. The FBI was initially reluctant, but with little progress being made, they finally agreed, largely because Weaver had stated his willingness to meet with Gritz. On August 30, Gritz and McLamb persuaded Weaver to allow Harris to leave the cabin so that he could get medical treatment, and the following day the two men walked Randy and his three surviving children out. After Weaver had been taken into custody, Gritz went down to visit the still-assembled protestors. Addressing a group of skinheads, he informed them that "Randy told me to give you guys a salute." He then raised his right arm in a typical, straight-arm, Sieg Heil gesture, adding, "He said you'd know what that meant." Gritz would first explain that he had given his Nazi salute only because Weaver had asked him to. He later denied that he had given any salute at all and said that he had just been waving at the crowd. The television coverage, which captured one of the skinheads returning Gritz's stiff-arm gesture with one of his own, suggested otherwise.

Weaver and Harris went on trial in 1993. Both were charged with the murder of William Degan, as well as conspiracy to murder. Weaver was also charged with illegally selling sawed-off shotguns and with failing to appear for his original trial. Weaver's lawyer was Garry Spence, who had made his name acting for the family of activist Karen Silkwood, who had exposed dangerous practices in the American nuclear industry before dying in mysterious circumstances in 1974 (her story was made into a widely acclaimed film *Silkwood* by Mike Nichols in 1983, with Meryl Streep in the title role). Spence turned the trial on its head. Weaver was not a dangerous "white supremacist," the attorney contended; he was just a harmless "white *separatist*." All he and his family had wanted was to be "left alone," but instead they had been pursued relentlessly by the federal government and then subjected to totally unnecessary and overwhelming government force. Spence was also able to dispute the FBI agents' claims as to what exactly had happened in the woods, including who had fired first, and he was helped considerably in his defense by the government's admission that the FBI had falsified evidence, by re-staging photos of the crime scene and fabricating a photo of a bullet.

Harris was acquitted on all of the charges against him. Weaver was convicted only for his failure to appear in court on the original shotgun charge, the jury accepting his defense that he had been entrapped by the ATF into selling the illegal weapons. On October 19, 1993, he was sentenced to 18 months in prison. In August 1995, Weaver's family received $3.1 million in settlement of a civil damages claim against the federal government. Harris received $380,000 in a separate settlement.

Criticism of the government's handling of the events at Ruby Ridge was widespread. During the trial, the judge had accused the FBI of showing "callous disregard for the rights of the defendants and the interests of justice." A subsequent investigation by the Justice Department's Ruby Ridge Task Force reproached the bureau for failing to gather sufficient evidence and for not ordering the Weavers and Harris to surrender before engaging them in a firefight. It also concluded that the shot that had killed Vicki Weaver had been unwarranted because both Harris and Weaver were running for cover at the time and so had posed no "imminent threat" to any of the agents present. Similar criticisms were voiced during the 14 days of hearings into the siege that were held by the Senate Subcommittee on Terrorism, Technology, and Government Information in October 1995. The final reports of both the Senate subcommittee and the Ruby Ridge Task Force also condemned the FBI's decision to alter its rules of engagement during the siege.

Media coverage of the affair was extensive, and a great deal of sympathy for what had happened to Randy Weaver and his family was expressed. A July 1993 editorial in the *New York Times*, although not going as far as to endorse Spence's description of the Weavers as "white separatists," nonetheless seemed to accept much of the lawyer's other arguments, along with the general sentiment of bemused outrage at what had transpired. It read, in part:

> Randy Weaver was a white supremacist. He lived as a heavily armed recluse in a cabin on a ridge in rural Idaho. Neither of these things is against the law in the United States. . . . And serious questions [remain] about how Federal agencies deal with religious and political eccentrics who may hold distasteful views but aren't necessarily a threat to society. . . . There are a lot of lunatics out there in the woods. But it is not the job of Federal law enforcement agencies to behave in a way that seems designed to confirm their paranoia—especially when there is no proof they have violated any laws.

Daniel Levitas is among those who have objected most strongly to use of "separatist" to describe the Weavers. "The separatist label is an utter falsehood," he writes in *The Terrorist Next Door* (2002). "Weaver and his wife fervently believed in the superiority of white, Anglo-Saxon Christians—the true people of Israel—over Satanic Jews and subhuman blacks." Other writers, including Kathleen Belew and Leonard Zeskind, have criticized the *New York Times* and other similar coverage of Weaver as essentially "harmless," arguing that it seriously underestimates the danger that Weaver—and others like him—actually pose to the United States.

Nowhere was the impact of Ruby Ridge felt more keenly than in the world of the racist and white supremacist right, however. On September 22, 1992, Louis Beam launched United Citizens for Justice, a support group for Weaver and his family, in Naples, Idaho, a hamlet not far from Ruby Ridge. Its immediate aim was to press for murder charges to be brought against the federal agents involved in the siege. Beam played down his racist associations as he attempted to recruit local residents to the organization, telling a crowd of 200 in nearby Sandpoint on October 6 that he had been minding his own business "in a small East Texas community raising black-eyed peas and blond-haired children until I heard about the events in North Idaho," rather than the fact that he was a former Klan leader and "ambassador at large" for the Aryan Nations, for example. Beam was joined in this endeavor by Chris Temple, a long-standing Identity believer, writer for the monthly Identity newspaper

Jubilee, and one of the Montana coordinators for Bo Gritz's presidential campaign. A friend of Weaver's, John Trochmann, a retired snowmobile salesman and future founder of the Militia of Montana, was also brought in as one of the co-chairs of the organization.

Following up on the letter he had sent to Weaver during the siege, on October 23 Pastor Pete Peters convened an emergency, three-day summit meeting of the American far right in Estes Park, Colorado, to discuss how it should respond to the events at Ruby Ridge. Among the 160 participants at this self-described "Gathering of Christian Men" were Louis Beam, Chris Temple, John Trochmann, Richard Butler, Jack McLamb, tax protestor Red Beckman, attorney Kirk Lyons—who had represented Louis Beam during the Fort Smith trial and gone on to establish a legal advocacy group called the Patriots Defense Foundation, later to be called CAUSE—Larry Pratt, head of the group Gun Owners of America, and numerous Christian Identity ministers. Others who were invited, but declined to attend, included David Duke, Willis Carto, and William Pierce, along with the attorney general of the United States, William Barr, whom Peters had asked to come so he could explain the government's actions against the Weavers in person. (Bo Gritz didn't receive an invitation because he and Peters had fallen out over Gritz's refusal to endorse Peters's position that homosexuals deserved the death penalty.)

The Estes Park meeting was an attempt, once again, to bring unity to the white power movement in the United States while also enhancing Peters' own status within it. Born in Nebraska, in 1947, Peters was the pastor of the LaPorte Church of Christ, Colorado, near the city of Fort Collins. A dedicated white supremacist, he had built up his Identity ministry in the usual way through monthly newsletters, cassette-distributed sermons, radio broadcasts, and speaking tours. His annual Bible camp conference attracted prominent figures including Beam, Carto, and Lyons, and he had served as a religious mentor to various members of The Order. In addition, Peters was the author of such paramilitarist- and gun-promoting tracts as *The Bible: Handbook for Survivalists, Racists, Tax Protestors, Militants and Right-Wing Extremists* and *Everything You Always Wanted to Know (and Preachers Were Afraid to Tell You) About Gun Control*, in which his fondness for drawn-out titles was matched only by his insistence—as expressed in *The Bible*—that he was not "writing to promote or advocate violence, but rather to stir a Christian people to such a stance that none would dare provoke violence."

Yet the strategies that ultimately emerged from Estes Park arguably owed more to other attendees than they did to Peters. The first was a renewed enthusiasm for Louis Beam's model of leaderless resistance, which he had initially advocated back in 1983. (Beam had written a revised version of his original essay on the effectiveness of "phantom cell" organizing for his new newsletter *The Seditionist* early in 1992, and this was republished in the "official" account of the proceedings at Estes Park.) The second was the embrace of armed citizen militias. The idea had been around in the wider Patriot movement since at least the late 1960s. William Potter Gale had endorsed citizen militias as a vital aspect of the Posse Comitatus movement, for example, and Bo Gritz was busily promoting their formation as part of his ongoing presidential campaign. But it was Larry Pratt, more than anybody else, who made the case for them at Estes Park.

Born in Camden, New Jersey, in 1942, Pratt had served two years in the Virginia legislature in the early 1980s, and as executive director of Gun Owners of America he headed a militant gun rights organization with over 100,000 members. In 1990 he wrote a book called *Armed People Victorious* extolling the virtues of armed citizen militias in Guatemala and the Philippines—countries he had visited regularly—because of their effectiveness, he said, in helping to crush emergent left-wing insurgencies. Critics of such groups understood them more as vigilante "death squads"—and he wanted to revive their use in the United States, believing they could be particularly useful in the fight against crime and the "War on Drugs." At Estes Park, Pratt extended his argument in the light of both Sammy and Vicki Weavers's deaths and the recent Los Angeles riots.* Armed militias were needed not just to deal with lawlessness or to provide "personal security," he maintained they were also vital to ensure

---

* The Los Angeles riots, or the Los Angeles uprising, as it has also been called, occurred between April 29 and May 4, 1992. The immediate cause was the acquittal of four Los Angeles police officers, three of whom were white, who had been charged in the vicious beating of an African-American motorist Rodney King (which was captured on videotape and broadcast extensively). But the underlying causes included years of ethnic and racial tension in the city, massive structural inequalities, and longstanding concerns about the "racist" and "militaristic" policies of L.A. police chief Daryl Gates. Sixty-three people were killed, 2,383 people were injured, and an estimated $1 billion worth of property was destroyed before the National Guard and federal troops were called in to restore order after President Bush invoked the Insurrection Act of 1807 at the request of California Governor Pete Wilson.

that the government "feared the people" and respected their rights, as well as to prevent any other "Ruby Ridges" from happening in the future.

Pratt's identification of the federal government itself as an "enemy" had been a trend within the far right for some time—as noted in previous chapters—but it became an even more potent idea with the ending of the Cold War, following the dissolution of the Soviet Union in 1991, and the accompanying elimination of communism as an all-encompassing and unifying menace. As Louis Beam put it in his updated essay on "Leaderless Resistance": "Communism now represents a threat to no one in the United States, while federal tyranny represents a threat to *every-one*." In the new, post-Cold War environment, the supposedly malign forces of "globalism" and the "New World Order" also became targets of renewed hostility, both for the racist right and for many others. Somewhat ironically, President George H. W. Bush had launched much of this concern in 1990, in the aftermath of the first Gulf War, when he expressed his hope that a "new world order" would emerge out of "these troubled times" to produce a "new era" of peace, prosperity, and justice.

Nor were leaderless resistance and citizen militias the only strategies considered at Estes Park. A third idea articulated by Chris Temple and Kirk Lyons, among others, was to use Ruby Ridge, together with the wider issues it represented—gun rights, "religious freedom," and government "tyranny" in particular—as a means of expanding the reach of the movement by building bridges with others who were not necessarily white supremacists themselves but who might share similar concerns about such matters. Temple and Lyons were thinking especially of the New Christian Right that had emerged during the 1980s, and that was led by such figures as Pat Robertson, Jerry Falwell, Jimmy Swaggart, and Jim Bakker. (One of these new evangelical leaders, James Dobson, the head of the influential pressure group Focus on the Family, had actually been invited by Peters to attend the gathering, but he had not replied to the invitation.) "We need to remember the Muslim's saying that my enemy's enemy is my friend," Temple suggested, reminding the participants of their "common goal . . . to restore Christian government in this land."

Such apparent ecumenicalism was Peters' own takeaway from the meeting too. "Men came together who in the past would not normally be caught together under the same roof, who greatly disagree with each other on many theological and philosophical points, whose teachings contradict each other in many ways," he explained after the event. "Yet, not only did they come together, they worked together for they all agreed what was done to the Weaver family was wrong, and could not, and should not, be ignored by Christian men." Louis Beam made a similar point more forcefully—and in his own inimitable style—during the summit itself. "The federals have by the murder of Samuel and Vicki Weaver brought us all together under the same roof for the same reason," he said:

> The two murders of the Weaver family have shown all of us that our religious, our political, our ideological differences mean nothing to those who wish to make us all slaves. We are all viewed by the government as the same, the enemies of the state. When they come for you, the federals will not ask if you are a Constitutionalist, a Baptist, Church of Christ, Identity Covenant believer, Klansman, Nazi, home schooler, Freeman, New Testament believer, [or] fundamentalist.

"If you think that this generation of men will maintain its present freedoms without also having to fertilize the tree of liberty with the blood of both patriot and tyrant, then you are mistaken," Beam added, to a standing ovation.

None of the principal strategies outlined at Estes Park were mutually exclusive, of course—and each could also be pursued independently of the others, as indeed they subsequently were. It is also true to say that the shooting of a white woman in the doorway of her own home while holding her infant child in her arms during a government "assault" was a boon to white supremacists in the United States in and of its own right. Yet, perhaps the most interesting development at the Estes Park meeting was the indication it provided that at least some of the movement's leaders were willing to modify their practices and their rhetoric in order to push themselves more firmly into the mainstream of American life, downplaying their racism, anti-Semitism, and even Identity beliefs, and instead emphasizing broader issues such as gun control, government "abuse," and the right to religious worship. As Morris Dees and James Corcoran have noted, in effect, even though he had not been in attendance, those who gathered at Estes Park had "borrowed a page out of David Duke's book."

Before any of the ideas developed at Estes Park could be effectively implemented, however, a deadlier and even more violent confrontation involving both the ATF and the FBI took place in Waco, Texas. This too would have a significant impact on the development of the militia movement that would shortly emerge.

The Branch Davidians, an obscure offshoot of the Seventh-Day Adventist Church, had moved to Waco in 1935, where they took up residence in a compound called Mount Carmel to prepare for the coming apocalypse. By 1990 they were led by the charismatic preacher David Koresh, who had been a member of the sect since 1981 (when he was still known as Vernon Howell). In June 1992 the ATF began an investigation of the Davidians for the manufacture and sale of illegal weapons and explosives after a postal worker had discovered some empty grenade shells in a box he was delivering. There were also concerns that some of the children in the compound were being abused, as well as rumors of a drug-making laboratory on-site. On February 28, 1993, 80 heavily armed federal agents attempted a "dynamic entry" on the compound in order to serve a search warrant for illegal weapons and an arrest warrant for Koresh. The secrecy of the operation had been compromised, however, and a fierce firefight erupted in which four ATF agents and five Davidians were killed. Twenty ATF agents and five Davidians, including Koresh, were also injured. As the ATF withdrew and attempted to regroup, the FBI was called in to take control of events, under the direction—as at Ruby Ridge—of its Hostage Rescue Team. Indeed, many of the same FBI agents who had been involved at Ruby Ridge were also present at Waco.

A standoff lasting 51 days soon developed, as over 800 officers from various law enforcement agencies descended on the Davidians' property. The electricity was cut off, high-intensity lights were erected, and speakers were set up to blast the compound with loud music, Tibetan chants, and even the sound of rabbits being slaughtered in the hope of driving the Davidians out. But neither the psychological warfare tactics nor the ongoing negotiations with Koresh were effective; although 21 children and a handful of other residents were allowed to leave in early March, approximately 90 others, including over 20 children, remained holed up in Mount Carmel as the "siege" continued on into April.

As well as engaging the considerable interest of the media, the confrontation quickly attracted the attention of various right-wing and racist groups in the United States. Louis Beam and Kirk Lyons both made visits to the site during the standoff, Beam as a credentialed journalist for *Jubilee*; during one FBI press briefing, he asked if a police state was on the way. Other attendees included the future Oklahoma City bomber Timothy McVeigh and Linda Thompson, an Indianapolis lawyer and founder of the Unorganized Militia of the United States of America, who went on to produce two influential and conspiratorial videos about the events, *Waco: The Big Lie* and *Waco II: The Big Lie Continues*. The stand-off was finally brought to an end on April 19, 1993, when armored tanks modified for demolition duty began punching holes into the Mount Car-mel complex to insert canisters of CS gas in the hope of "flushing out" the Davidians. Over 300 cannisters of gas were pumped into the compound for over six hours before a massive fire broke out. Seventy-six Davidians, including 24 children, died in the resulting inferno, which was broadcast live on American television. (McVeigh watched the coverage on a farm on Michigan and took the view that the government had "declared war" on the American people.)

It is important to acknowledge that neither Koresh nor his follow-ers were white supremacists or Identity believers—in fact, the David-ians were a multiracial and multiethnic community, with many believ-ers coming from outside the United States, from countries such as Great Britain, Australia, New Zealand, and the Philippines. For the American far right, however, the government's actions at Waco raised precisely the same issues that had been raised at Ruby Ridge: gun ownership, state "tyranny," and religious "persecution" chief among them. That the two events had occurred within just a few months of each other only fur-ther emphasized their "special symbiotic relationship," as the sociologist Stuart Wright puts it. (The trial of Randy Weaver and Kevin Harris opened just five days before the FBI's final "assault" on the Davidian's compound, and the presiding judge was so concerned about the appar-ent similarities between the two incidents that he instructed the jury not to watch any coverage of what was going on at Waco.) In addition, both Waco and Ruby Ridge fit comfortably into what members of the racist right regarded as a much wider pattern of government oppression that had started with the "murder" of Gordon Kahl in 1983 and continued on with the killing of Robert Mathews in 1984, the raid on the Covenant, the Sword, and the Arm of the Lord's compound in Arkansas in 1985, and the Fort Smith sedition trial in 1988. For the conspiratorially minded, the signs were especially ominous, it seemed.

Underpinning much of the concern about what had happened at Ruby Ridge and Waco—concerns that went beyond the world of the racist right, it is important to note—was the apparent "militarization" of American law enforcement that seemed to be increasingly taking place. In both cases the operations had been huge—the ATF's initial raid on the Davidian complex was the largest it had ever undertaken—and involved a wide array of military-style tactics and equipment, including snipers, camouflage uniforms, Bradley fighting vehicles, Abrams tanks, National Guard helicopters, and F-4 Air Force jets. At Waco, military advisers from both the U.S. Special Forces and Britain's Special Air Service, or SAS, had been on site, and at the conclusion of the "siege," the ATF had raised its own flag on the Davidian's flagpole, underneath the state flag of Texas and the flag of the United States, to signify its "victory" over the sect.

The militarization of the police and other government agencies had been going on for some time, driven largely by the "wars" against crime and drugs, but the process received a significant boost with the ending of the Cold War. In 1989, for example, just before the fall of the Berlin Wall, the National Defense Authorization Act was amended. As Stuart Wright points out, the new law "substantially enhanced the role and scope of military support for domestic law enforcement." State and local police were now able to borrow equipment from the military when dealing with drug trafficking and illegal immigration; military personnel were authorized to conduct aerial reconnaissance missions and to provide training in intelligence analysis and survival skills; and they could also deploy and monitor electronic ground sensors for civilian agencies, for example. In 1989 the government also established the 1033 Program to facilitate the transfer of surplus military weaponry and other equipment to domestic law enforcement. By 1995 an estimated $350 million worth of equipment, including armored personnel carriers, Blackhawk helicopters, sniper rifles, and gas masks, had been given to the police and various federal law enforcement agencies.

The presence of the California National Guard and federal troops on the streets of Los Angeles during the 1992 riots was another indication of the trend, and although the "problem" of police militarization was of concern to civil libertarians and various left-wing groups—and would become so again in the wake of the Black Lives Matter protests that erupted across the United States following the killing of George Floyd in

2020—it became a particular rallying cry for the militia and Patriot movements. Waco especially "galvanized the militia movement," as Kenneth Stern has written. Yet, as another keen observer of the American far right, Leonard Zeskind, has noted, the events at Waco also "became a test of the ideas enunciated at Estes Park," and by throwing their support behind Koresh and the Branch Davidians—and calling attention to the government "abuses" supposedly committed at Mount Carmel—Louis Beam and other white supremacists were consciously attempting to enlarge "the political space" they had opened up at Ruby Ridge.

As was the case after Ruby Ridge, there were numerous enquiries and investigations into what exactly had happened at Waco. In August 1999 Attorney General Janet Reno appointed former Senator John C. Danforth as special counsel to investigate. Published in November 2000, his report concluded that contrary to widespread allegations, government agents had not caused the fire that had engulfed the compound; the fire, he said, had been started deliberately by the Davidians themselves. He also concluded that the FBI had not improperly used the armed forces of the United States, nor engaged in a massive cover-up or conspiracy. (In 2018 the Paramount Network created a six-part miniseries about the events called *Waco*.)

In addition to Ruby Ridge and Waco, there was one other event crucial to the rise of the militia movement, and that was the passage of the Brady Handgun Violence Prevention Act in 1993. Named for Ronald Reagan's press secretary, James Brady, who had been shot during an attempted assassination of the president in 1981 by James Hinckley, the act was the first major piece of federal gun control legislation since the 1960s. Signed into law by President Clinton in November 1993, it imposed a five-day waiting period in the sale of all handguns and required criminal background checks on potential gun buyers. Although relatively modest in scope, for gun advocates in the United States, including the powerful National Rifle Association (NRA), the law was seen as a fundamental attack on the right of Americans "to keep and bear arms" as set out in the Second Amendment. For those on the far right, it was also taken as an additional indication of impending government "tyranny." After all, not only had guns been central to what had transpired at Ruby Ridge and Waco, but the future "disarming of the American people" had long been a major theme in movement literature, including William Pierce's

The Turner Diaries, in which the fictional Cohen Act outlaws the private ownership of all firearms in the United States as the novel begins. Such concerns were magnified even further in 1994, when the Violent Crime Control Act banned the sale of 19 different semiautomatic weapons—the "paramilitary right's weapon of choice," as Dees and Corcoran note—and placed a ten-bullet limit on gun clips.

It is not entirely clear when exactly the first militia group was formed. Sam Sherwood, a devout Mormon and occasional computer consultant, claimed to have helped organize a Constitutional Militia Association in Madison County, Idaho, in 1992, before establishing his own U.S. Militia Association in Blackfoot, Idaho, in 1993, for example. (Sherwood was the author of a 1992 book *The Little Republics* about how a post-Armageddon society should be run. Although he achieved a great deal of notoriety for a provocative statement he made at a meeting in Boise, Idaho, in March 1995, urging audience members to "Go up and look your legislators in the face, because some day you may have to blow it off," as David Neiwert and Kenneth Stern have both noted, in actuality Sherwood's main aim was to attract mainstream politicians to his anti-government and pro-states' rights cause.) At Waco, Linda Thompson, the self-proclaimed acting adjunct general of the Unorganized Militia of the United States, encouraged other "patriots" to join her in defense of the Davidians through a fax sent on the nascent American Patriot Fax Network, but it is not evident that her group actually had any other members in it at the time. (In 1994 Thompson issued an "official ultimatum" calling on all militias to travel to Washington, D.C., on September 19 to "arrest Congress" for treason, with the suspected congressmen to face trial by citizens' courts. Few other militia leaders thought this was a good idea, however, and Willis Carto's *Spotlight* also condemned it, with the result that Thompson was reluctantly forced to back down.) But there is little disputing that the most significant and most influential of all the early militias was the Militia of Montana. It was also the group with the most direct connection to Ruby Ridge and the plans that were laid at Estes Park.

The Militia of Montana was created in February 1994 by John Trochmann, his brother David, and David's son Randy. The Trochmanns originally hailed from Minnesota, where they ran a successful snowmobile business. David moved to the small town of Noxon, Montana, in

1984, and John followed him four years later. John Trochmann in particular was closely involved with the events at Ruby Ridge. His family and the Weavers were friends; John's wife Carolyn had helped Vicki Weaver to deliver her daughter Elisheba; the Trochmanns' son Caleb was Sara Weaver's boyfriend; and John and Carolyn had helped to supply food to the Weavers during the siege. In addition, David Trochmann was one of the suspected gunrunners the ATF was pursuing when it tried to entrap Randy Weaver into becoming an informer for the agency—the other was the former Klansman Chuck Howarth. And it was from the mailing list of the Weaver support group, United Citizens for Justice, of which John Trochmann was co-chairman, along with Chris Temple, that the Militia of Montana was established.

The Trochmanns also had strong ties to Identity Christianity, the Posse Comitatus movement, and the Aryan Nations. In January 1992 John Trochmann had filed an affidavit at the Sanders County Courthouse declaring his "sovereignty" as a "free white Christian man" who believed in the "organic Constitution of the United States." "I am not now, nor have I ever been, a citizen of the United States or a resident of its subordinate territories, or a property appertaining thereto, in either a legal or factual sense," he stated. He was also a regular visitor to Hayden Lake—it was during an Aryan Nations "family day" in 1990 that the Weavers and the Trochmanns apparently first met—where he helped to draw up the group's "code of conduct." But in keeping with the approach discussed at Estes Park, Trochmann downplayed all these associations and beliefs once the Militia of Montana was launched, denying he was a racist and insisting that the group was concerned only with government corruption, the "destruction" of the Constitution, and the impending imposition of "the single world government." The aging Richard Butler, who had been present at Estes Park alongside Trochmann, did not seem to have fully come to terms with the new strategy. Affronted by Trochmann's attempt to dissociate himself from the Aryan Nations, Butler issued a public statement explaining that Trochmanm had made "six or seven trips" to the compound for "Bible study" and asking: "Why lie about the number of times here?" For his part, Trochmann claimed to have visited the compound only twice, including for a bagpipe festival. "I love bagpipes," he informed a reporter for the *Jewish Week* in May 1995.

John Trochmann traveled extensively around the Pacific Northwest, making speeches, attending gun shows, visiting Preparedness Expos, and granting interviews during 1994 and early 1995; and with his full white beard, occasional cowboy hat, and rugged eloquence, he was a compelling figure. But the Militia of Montana's real contribution to the burgeoning militia movement was as an information center and propaganda outlet. It produced a newsletter, *Taking Aim*, an *Information and Networking Manual*, as well as its own version of the *Blue Book*, previous iterations of which had been produced by both the John Birch Society and the Posse Comitatus movement. It also sold a vast array of books, pamphlets, videos, and audiotapes that drew from all corners of the radical and racist right, including numerous survivalist and guerrilla warfare tracts on subjects such as "Booby Traps," "Sniper Training & Employment," "Hand to Hand Fighting," and "How to Bury Your Goods." William Potter Gale's *The Road Back* (n.d.) was on offer, as was Robert Bradley's *The Citizen Soldier: A Manual of Community Based Defense* (1994), Duncan Long's *To Break A Tyrant's Chains: Neo-Guerilla Techniques for Combat* (1991), and Tony Lesce's *Escape from Controlled Custody* (1990). Among the videos for sale were *The Countdown Has Begun (Biochip)*, *The Pestilence (AIDS)*, *Equipping for the New World Order*, and Linda Thompson's two films about Waco. One could even buy Patriot-themed songs about Waco and Ruby Ridge, or the coming of martial law.

By early 1995 the Militia of Montana claimed to be sending out 200 of its "militia formation" packets every week, and although it operated aboveground—how could it not given its role as an informational, mail-order clearinghouse—it recommended that other militias organize themselves according to the "phantom cell" structure outlined in Beam's "Leaderless Resistance" essay. Many subsequent militias did, from Washington State to Kansas, Florida to Texas, and Colorado to Utah. But others rejected such an approach, preferring to remain both publicly visible and readily identifiable. The most prominent advocate of this alternative model of organizing—indeed, at one point the largest militia group in the country with as many as 10,000 members—was the Michigan Militia.

The group, which, like many other militias, was separated into different units at the county level, was formed in April 1994 by Ray Southwell, a real estate agent, and Norman Olson, a gun store owner and Baptist minister. Both claimed that Waco had provided them with their "wake-up calls," but a dispute between Southwell and his local school board over what Southwell called its "socialistic values" had also played a part. The officially stated goal of the Michigan Militia was to confront "tyranny, globalism, moral relativism, humanism and the New World Order threatening to undermine these United States of America." To prepare for this likelihood, its members donned military-style fatigues and trained at least twice a month with loaded weapons. This embrace of paramilitarism was characteristic of the militia movement as a whole, and it greatly alarmed monitoring agencies such as the Southern Poverty Law Center (SPLC) and the Anti-Defamation League. Yet no militias would ever face prosecution under the anti-paramilitary training statues that had been passed in various states during the mid-1980s in response to the rise of groups like Beam's Texas Klan (see chapter 3).

The growth of the militia movement was spectacular. By 1996, according to the SPLC, there were 441 armed militias across all 50 states. Gauging the exact size of the movement was not easy, however. Estimates ranged in size from 20,000 to 300,000, but when militia "supporters" and the wider Patriot movement were factored in, the figure rose as high as five million.* The movement was also both highly decentralized and determinedly local. There was no single leader directing affairs, for example, nor any national organization to which all militia members could belong. As a result, while gun rights, a profound distrust of the federal government, and conspiratorial fears about the "New World Order" provided a certain degree of ideological coherence for the movement, many militia groups were animated by other concerns: abortion rights, environmental issues, educational standards, the use of public land, immigration policy, border security, gay rights, taxation, affirmative action, public morals, or the negative impact of international trade agreements like the North American Free Trade Agreement on the American economy. Because of this—and because those assembled at Estes Park had decided to intentionally conceal or downplay their support for the

---

* The Patriot movement is an umbrella term that encompasses a wide range of groups including militias, sovereign citizens, tax protestors, survivalists, Christian Identity believers, Posse Comitatus members, constitutionalists, common law advocates, radical anti-abortion activists, Klansmen, and neo-Nazis. They do not all believe the same things or act in the same way, however. As Kathleen Belew has noted, if the figure of five million was correct, it would make the Patriot movement "an even larger movement than the second-era Ku Klux Klan in the 1920s." While this is true, it is important to recognize that the Klan was considerably more visible and considerably more "accepted" and "legitimate" than were the Patriots of the 1990s.

creation of militias—gauging the extent to which the movement as a whole can be said to be racist or white supremacist is not straightforward.

As Chip Berlet and Matthew Lyons note in their book *Right-Wing Populism in America* (2000), some militias were clearly racist and anti-Semitic. Others were not and actively excluded racists from their ranks; indeed, a few militias, including the Ohio Unorganized Militia and the Missouri 51st Militia had Black, Jewish, and Latina/o members. Some of the racism and anti-Semitism expressed by militias was "unconscious and unintentional," Berlet and Lyons write; while in other cases "far-right activists hid their overt racist and antisemitic views to recruit from, or take over, Patriot and militia groups." Kenneth Stern suggests racism and anti-Semitism were "essential" to the militia movement in four ways: first, because of the involvement of key figures such as Pete Peters, Bo Gritz, and John Trochmann; second, because racist and anti-Semitic material was readily available at militia events; third, because ideas such as "states' rights" and "county supremacy" that provided much of the "fuel" of the movement were really "covers for bigotry"; and fourth, because many of the conspiracy theories that underlay the movement were "rooted" in the *Protocols of the Elders of Zion*. But he acknowledges that the movement as a whole could not be said to be "driven" by white supremacy.

Yet it was also true that the idea of armed citizen militias was promoted keenly by the likes of Tom Metzger's *WAR*, Carto's *Spotlight*, and the Identity newspaper *Jubilee*. For Leonard Zeskind, not only were the origins of the movement to be found in white supremacy, but in his view, militias "marched to the same drumbeat that other bands of white paramilitaries had heard before them." This too is the view of Kathleen Belew, who describes the militia movement as "the outward growth of the paramilitary white power movement" rather than something "new" or "distinct" in her book *Bring the War Home* (2018). Tensions between the differing elements of the militia movement—as well as the differing interpretations of it—can be traced back to Estes Park, of course. Clearly white supremacist leaders encouraged the creation and development of militias, and they also would have liked to control and direct the resulting movement. But they could not do so precisely because of the strategy they had adopted in Colorado, and they had taken this approach presumably because they understood, on some level at least, that any militia movement that emerged from Estes Park would be much smaller—both in terms of its size and in terms of its impact—were it to be an openly white supremacist one. Which is not to say that those same white supremacist leaders did not try to exploit the militias and their concerns as much as possible—they clearly did; and not surprisingly, since from the outset, Beam, Peters, and the others had "embedded themselves into the militia movement" like "a tick buried in the thick hair on a dog's neck," to quote Dees and Corcoran.

The appearance and rapid growth of armed citizen militias were not just products of America's paramilitary and white supremacist cultures, however. They were also responding to—and were supported by—broader developments in the political and cultural mainstream, both at home and abroad. The liberal internationalism pursued by the Bush and Clinton administrations was anathema to many conservatives, as well as to members of the radical right, for example. And while it may have been Bush who inadvertently initiated much of the contemporary discussion of the "New World Order" with his 1990 speech on the subject in the aftermath of the first Gulf War, it was a prominent member of the Christian Right, Pat Robertson, who really pushed the conspiracy theory into widespread circulation. Robertson was the head of the influential Christian Broadcasting Network, and his 1991 book *The New World Order* predicted the creation not just of a "one-world government," but also a "one-world army" and a "one-world economy," all presided over by a "world dictator": the Antichrist. It sold more than half a million copies.

The 1992 presidential election also illustrated that a rising tide of right-wing, populist sentiment was increasingly at work in American society. Bush, for example, had faced a surprisingly strong challenge in the Republican primaries from Patrick "Pat" Buchanan, a former special assistant and speechwriter to Richard Nixon, as well as director of communications for Ronald Reagan. A self-described "pit bull of the right," Buchanan aimed to end affirmative action policies, freeze all government spending, outlaw abortion, and build a two-hundred-mile-long "Buchanan fence" across the Mexican border. (Buchanan would run for the presidency again in 1996, with Larry Pratt of Gun Owners of America as one of the co-chairs of his campaign, but Pratt was forced to resign the position when his involvement at Estes Park was exposed.) Bo Gritz's former benefactor, H. Ross Perot, running largely on an anti-NAFTA and an anti-government "inefficiency" campaign, then faced off against

Bush and Clinton during the general election, securing 19.7 million votes, or 19 percent of the total. Clinton won 44.9 million votes and Bush 39.1 million, while in the Electoral College, the vote was 370 to 168 in Clinton's favor.

Clinton's victory was not well received either by the Republican right or the radical right. Congressional Republicans refused to cast even a single vote in favor of the new president's budget, and they mobilized both vociferously and extremely effectively to prevent the implementation of the administration's signature first-term policy goal, health care reform, which was being spearheaded by Clinton's wife, Hillary Rodham Clinton. The vicious personal hostility directed toward Hillary Clinton was especially notable, and it would continue all the way through her presidential campaign against Donald Trump in 2016. On the far right, this hostility was epitomized by the Christian fundamentalist minister Texe Marr's 1993 book *Big Sister is Watching You: Hillary Clinton and the White House Feminists Who Now Control America and Tell the President What to Do*—it was another of the books sold by the Militia of Montana. (White supremacists had a particular animus toward Bill Clinton, it should be noted, because he had been the governor of Arkansas at the time of the killing of Gordon Kahl in 1983, and had approved the federal government's raid on the Covenant, the Sword, and the Arm of the Lord's compound in 1985.)

In the November 1994 midterms the GOP won control of the House of Representatives for the first time in 40 years and the Senate for only the fourth time since the end of World War II. They had been led in the election by the Georgia congressman—and new House Speaker—Newt Gingrich, who, in conjunction with the chair of the House Republican Conference, Dick Armey (TX), had created an intensely conservative campaign manifesto called the "Contract with America." The 367 congressmen who signed up to the Contract promised to "restore the bonds of trust between the people and their elected representatives" and to bring an end to government that was "too big, too intrusive, and too easy with the public's money." In the view of Senator Phil Gramm of Texas, because of the Contract, the Republican's resultant victory needed to be understood not just an "anti-Clinton vote," but as a broader "anti-government vote."

Significant anti-government sentiment was also reflected in the opinion polls of the period. According to the research of Daniel Yankleovich,

76 percent of Americans trusted the government to do what was right "always" or "most of the time" in 1964. By 1984 that figure was down to 44 percent, and in early 1994—just as the militias were beginning to form—the number was 19 percent, a "new all-time low." Participation in the electoral process marked a similar downward trajectory: Of the 196 million Americans eligible to vote in the 1996 elections, less than 50 percent—or just over 96 million—chose to do so. The figure in 1964 had been 61 percent.

Extreme anti-government and anti-Clinton rhetoric was also a marked feature of the "mainstream" gun lobby and talk radio circuit of the mid-1990s. On April 13, 1995, Wayne LaPierre, executive vice president of the NRA, wrote a highly charged fund-raising letter to the group's 3.5 million members specifically referencing the events at Ruby Ridge and Waco, as well as the 1994 Violent Crime Control Act. "Not too long ago, it was unthinkable for Federal agents wearing Nazi bucket helmets and black storm trooper uniforms to attack law-abiding citizens," he wrote. "Not today, not with Clinton." Rush Limbaugh, whose daily broadcasts reached an estimated 20 million Americans, speculated about the need for a "second American revolution" because of the malicious actions of "bureaucrats in Washington." And G. Gordon Liddy, the disgraced former Watergate burglar and talk radio's "host of the year" for 1995—who gleefully used cardboard cutouts of Bill and Hillary Clinton for shooting practice—informed his listeners that should the "brutal thugs" of the ATF come "smashing" into their homes, the answer was simple: "Head shots! Head shots!" "Kill the sons of bitches!" he declared.

From the local to the national level, civil rights groups and watchdog agencies were intensely concerned about the rise of the militia movement, its paramilitarism, its conspiracism, its confrontational rhetoric, and its apparent racism and anti-Semitism. The Anti-Defamation League, the American Jewish Committee, and the Southern Poverty Law Center all issued reports on the militias. The SPLC also established a new Militia Task Force—an addition to its existing Klanwatch program—to monitor the movement. In October 1994, Morris Dees, the group's chief trial counsel, wrote a letter to Attorney General Janet Reno urging her to "alert all federal law enforcement authorities to the growing danger" posed by the militias, warning of the existing "substantial evidence" that white supremacists were "infiltrating the leadership of these organizations." In the Pacific Northwest, one of the hotbeds of early militia activity, groups such as the Coalition for Human Dignity, based in Portland, Oregon, and the Montana Human Rights Network also tried to raise the alarm. The latter also prepared a practical guide for activists and local community members called "What to Do When the Militia Comes to Town." Calling citizen militias a "chilling echo" of the Silver Shirts and the Klan, the guide argued that the "lesson that emerges from history is that these groups are hindered more by the attitudes of the community than they are by laws," and that it was "fear and silence" that allowed "hate groups to flourish."

Yet despite such warnings, it would take the Oklahoma City bombing for most Americans to become aware of both the militia movement and of the dangers posed by the anti-government extremists in their midst. As noted earlier, the bombing was carried out by Timothy McVeigh, with the assistance of two former army buddies, Terry Nichols and Michael Fortier, although the suspicion that there was a much wider conspiracy at work, one involving members of a white supremacist gang called the Aryan Republican Army and residents of Robert Millar's Identity compound at Elohim City, has remained strong.

McVeigh was born in Lockport, New York, on April 28, 1968. His parents, Bill and Mildred, had a troubled marriage. They first separated in 1979, when Tim was 11, and finally divorced in 1986, when he was 18, his mother moving to Florida with his sisters Patty and Jennifer. Shortly thereafter McVeigh graduated from high school, and after brief periods attending a nearby business college and working as a security guard, McVeigh joined the U.S. Army in May 1988. He met Nichols and Fortier during basic training at Fort Benning, Georgia, before moving on to Fort Riley, Kansas. McVeigh had been obsessed with guns from a young age, but it was while he was at Fort Riley that he first exhibited his burgeoning interest in white supremacy: reading and promoting *The Turner Diaries*, and joining the North Carolina Ku Klux Klan (for which he received a complimentary "White Power" T-shirt). In 1991 McVeigh was shipped out to the Gulf War as part of the 1st Infantry Division— the legendary Big Red One—where he fought as a gunner on a Bradley fighting vehicle. An exemplary soldier and outstanding gunner, he received numerous decorations, including the Bronze Star and the Army Achievement Medal, for his service during operation Desert Storm.

In the spring of 1991 McVeigh tried to enlist in the Special Forces, but he failed the 21-day assessment and selection course on day two because of blistered feet. He was invited to try again but—disillusioned and disgruntled—instead decided to leave the Army altogether. Discharged at the end of 1991, McVeigh returned to his father's home in Pendleton, New York, where he joined the New York National Guard and found low-paid work once again as a security guard and at a gun store. He also continued his extensive reading of radical right-wing literature.

In February 1992 McVeigh hinted at his newfound political direction in a letter to his local *Union-Sun and Journal* newspaper. "What is it going to take to open the eyes of our elected officials?" he asked. "America is in serious decline. We have no proverbial tea to dump. Should we instead sink a ship full of Japanese imports? Is civil war imminent? Do we have to shed blood to reform the current system? I hope it doesn't come to that, but it might." The following year McVeigh left New York and began an itinerant, two-year odyssey across the United States, often as part of the gun show circuit, as he bought and sold weapons, books, pamphlets, bumper stickers, and even, at one point, his own military uniform, while immersing himself deeper and deeper into the paramilitary and white supremacist underground—the gun show circuit, in the view of William Pierce being a "natural recruiting environment" for the racist right. Indeed, according to Stuart Wright's count, in the two-year period between the events at Waco and the bombing at Oklahoma City, McVeigh attended more than 80 gun shows in 40 states.

In June 1993 McVeigh moved to a trailer park in Kingman, Arizona, where Michael Fortier lived with his wife Lori. He also spent time in Decker, Michigan, with Terry Nichols on a farm owned by Terry's brother James. Both Terry and James Nichols held far-right, anti-government views, close to those of the Posse Comitatus movement. During a dispute with Chase Manhattan Bank over his credit card debt, Terry had referred to himself as "a common law individual," and James had surrendered both his driver's license and his Social Security card, for example. (Later, McVeigh and the Nichols brothers attended at least one meeting of the Michigan Militia, while Fortier claimed that McVeigh had tried to establish his own militia in Arizona. For its part, the Michigan Militia said that it had rejected McVeigh and the Nichols because their views were too "radical.") In April 1994 McVeigh traveled to Waco during the siege of the Branch Davidians, where he sold bumper stickers reading "Fear the Government That Fears Your Gun," "A Man with a Gun Is a Citizen. A Man without a Gun Is a Subject," and "When Guns are Outlawed, I Will Become an Outlaw." He was there at the same time as Louis Beam.

McVeigh, like many others in the Patriot movement, was outraged by Ruby Ridge, so much so that he would pass out cards at the gun shows he attended with the name and home address of Lon Horiuchi, the FBI sniper who had killed Vicki Weaver. But it was Waco that truly radicalized him, and this, together with the passage of the Brady Bill and the subsequent assault weapons ban, that moved him out of what he called the "propaganda stage" and into the "action stage." Spurred on by his reading of both Beam's "leaderless resistance" essay and Pierce's *The Turner Diaries*, McVeigh sought to "retaliate" for Waco with the bombing of the Murrah building, which housed offices of the ATF and several other federal agencies.

In September 1994, McVeigh and Terry Nichols stole 229 sticks of Tovex—a water-gel explosive composed of ammonium nitrate and methylammonium nitrate—544 blasting caps, and 93 lengths of fuse cords from a quarry in Marion, Kansas, close to Nichols's home. A month later, at McVeigh's direction, Nichols robbed the Arkansas home of a gun dealer that McVeigh had worked with named Roger Moore, coming away with $60,000 worth of goods, including $8,700 in cash. They purchased the 50-pound bags of ammonium nitrate fertilizer and other materials needed to make the bomb from various stores in the Midwest and assembled it in the back of a rented Ryder truck in Geary Lake State Park, near Junction City, Kansas, on April 18, 1995. Fortier was aware of the plans and helped to store some of the bomb materials but did not take part in the bombing itself. Nichols too apparently had cold feet but was coerced into continuing to take part in the bomb's assembly by McVeigh, who threatened to kill his wife and child if he backed out.

Both the fertilizer bomb and the targeting of a federal building were modeled on *The Turner Diaries*. So too was the timing of the attack. In Pierce's novel, the Organization's bomb explodes at 9:15 a.m., specifically designed to kill and injure as many people as possible at the start of a workday. McVeigh's bomb exploded at 9:02 a.m. on April 19, 1995—the second anniversary of the ending of the government's "siege" at Waco—with the same intent. One hundred and sixty-eight people died in the attack, including 19 children in the building's day care center. McVeigh drove away from the scene in a 1977 yellow Mercury Marquis. He was pulled over by an Oklahoma state trooper just over an hour later because he didn't have a license plate on the car, and he was arrested after the officer discovered he was also carrying a loaded gun. McVeigh was wearing a white T-shirt with a picture of Abraham Lincoln and the words "Sic Semper Tyrannis"—Latin for "Thus ever to tyrants"—on the front, the phrase John Wilkes Booth had shouted out after he had assassinated the president. On the back was a picture of a tree dripping with blood and a quote from Thomas Jefferson: "The Tree of Liberty must be refreshed from time to time with the blood of patriots and tyrants." It was the same quote Louis Beam had invoked at the Estes Park gathering in 1992. On the passenger seat was an envelope stuffed with anti-government literature, including excerpts from *The Turner Diaries*, although this would not be discovered until two days later, after the FBI became involved.

The Oklahoma police did not initially suspect McVeigh in the bombing. This changed once the FBI located the rear axle of the Ryder truck in the wreckage of the Murrah building and used its vehicle identification number to track it back to a body shop in Junction City, where McVeigh had rented it. After questioning the body shop's personnel, two composite sketches were drawn up: a thin-faced and crewcut "John Doe One," which seemed to match McVeigh; and a heavier-set and more olive-skinned "John Doe Two." A sweep of local businesses revealed that McVeigh had checked into the nearby Dreamland Motel under his own name, and that he also had given James Nichols's Michigan farmhouse as his address. FBI agents quickly flew down to Oklahoma to take McVeigh into custody. Learning of the news, Terry Nichols turned himself in to police in Kansas shortly thereafter. Neither of the Nichols's brothers nor Michael Fortier matched the description of John Doe Two.

McVeigh was indicted on 11 counts: one count of conspiring to use a weapon of mass destruction, one count of using a weapon of mass destruction, one count of destruction by explosives, and eight counts of first-degree murder for the deaths of eight federal officers. In June 1997, he was found guilty on all of them, and three months later he was sentenced to die by lethal injection. The execution was carried out at the maximum-security federal prison at Terre Haute, Indiana, on June 11, 2001. In a separate trial, Terry Nichols was found guilty of conspiring with McVeigh to plan the bombing and of the involuntary manslaughter of the eight federal agents who had been killed, but he was acquitted of actually carrying out the attack. He was sentenced to life in prison, with no chance of parole. (Both McVeigh and Nichols's trials were presided over by Richard Matsch, the same judge who had been in charge of the proceedings against The Order in 1985.) In 2004 Nichols was tried at the state level on 160 counts of first-degree murder for the non-federal officers who had died, and although he was found guilty, he was again spared the death penalty because the jury was unable to reach a unanimous verdict on his sentence. Michael and Lori Fortier agreed to cooperate with the government, and both testified against McVeigh and Nichols at their trials. In May 1998 Michael Fortier pleaded guilty of failing to warn the authorities of the bomb plot, of transporting stolen firearms, and of lying to federal officials. He was sentenced to 12 years in prison but was released in 2006—a year and a half early—and went into the federal Witness Protection Program, along with his wife and two children.

McVeigh's lawyer, Stephen Jones, had intended to defend his client on the basis that there had been a much wider conspiracy behind the bombing. But McVeigh—either because he wanted to take full credit for the attack, because there was no wider conspiracy beyond himself, Nichols, and Fortier or because he wanted to protect the others who had been involved—refused to go along with it. McVeigh's preference was for a "necessity defense," whereby he would admit his guilt but contend that the bombing had been fully justified because of the impending federal "tyranny" the country was facing—the abuses at Waco and Ruby Ridge, gun control, the general militarization of American law enforcement, and so on. Jones eventually decided against this, however, reasoning—undoubtedly correctly—that such a defense was unlikely to be persuasive for the jury. (Jones, it should be noted, was not McVeigh's first choice for his attorney; he had really wanted Randy Weaver's lawyer, Garry Spence, to defend him, but Spence had refused.) However, the idea that there were others involved in the Oklahoma City bombing would not go away.

Both at the time, and ever since—in books such as Mark Hamm's *In Bad Company: America's Terrorist Underground* (2002); Stuart Wright's *Patriots, Politics, and the Oklahoma City Bombing* (2007); Andrew Gumble and Roger Charles's *Oklahoma City: What the Investigation Missed—and Why It Still Matters* (2012); and Stephen Jones's own *Others Unknown:*

The Oklahoma City Bombing Case and Conspiracy (1998); as well as in the report of an independent commission established by Republican Oklahoma state congressman Charles Key in 2001; and material gathered for the defence of Terry Nichols in his 2004 state trial—considerable doubt has been cast on the official position that McVeigh acted largely alone in carrying out the bombing, with assistance coming only from Nichols and Fortier.

It has been argued that McVeigh and Nichols lacked the necessary technical expertise to make the bomb. There were witnesses who stated that rather than driving to Oklahoma City in the Ryder track alone, as McVeigh claimed, he had been traveling in a convoy of vehicles. There were additional witnesses who said they saw McVeigh in the company of other men, and possibly a woman, outside the Murrah building just before the explosion took place. The owner of the Dreamland Motel said that not only had she heard male voices coming from McVeigh's room at a time when he and Nichols were still in Oklahoma City, stashing the Mercury getaway car, but that McVeigh had also had a second Ryder truck on the premises. (A Chinese restaurant delivery driver also claimed to have delivered food to someone other than McVeigh at McVeigh's room in the motel.) The prosecution could not even prove that McVeigh had actually rented the Ryder truck in person, or that he had done so alone—McVeigh's fingerprints were not found on the body shop's counter, nor on the rental agreement, which had been signed in the name of "Robert Kling." Then there was the matter of John Doe Two. The FBI argued that there was no John Doe Two, that his identification—and all the other sightings of additional people who might have been involved— was explicable as simple witness misidentification and the notorious fallibility of human memory. But this did not really put the matter to rest, and the existence of a mysterious lower left leg that had been discovered in the Murrah building's rubble, clad in a military-style boot, and remained unaccounted for, only fueled the speculation further. Had this been John Doe Two? Or was John Doe Two someone else entirely?

The suspicion that others had been involved in the bombing centered on Robert Millar's Christian Identity compound at Elohim City and the members of a white supremacist gang called the Aryan Republican Army (ARA). Elohim City—Hebrew for "City of God"—had been established by Millar in 1973 on a 400-acre site near Sallisaw, Oklahoma. About 75 men, women, and children lived on the compound, often in polygamous and even incestuous relationships, and the community supported itself through a trucking company and a small sawmill. While Millar insisted that he and his followers were peaceful and just wanted to be left alone, the compound also served as a safe haven and gathering place for movement activists. Members of The Order had hidden out there in the 1980s, for example, and Millar had hosted Tom Metzger and Kirk Lyons, among other white power leaders, on the site. Millar and the CSA leader James Ellison were especially close. Indeed, it had been Millar who had anointed Ellison "King James of the Ozarks" back in 1982, and Ellison went to live at Elohim City on his release from prison in 1995, marrying one of Millar's many granddaughters. Other former Covenant members moved to the compound as well, and Millar also served as the personal minister for convicted murderer Richard Wayne Snell during his time in prison and then took his body back to Elohim City to be buried following his execution.

Several members of the Aryan Republican Army also either lived at—or were regular visitors to—Elohim City, including Mark Thomas, Kevin McCarthy, Scott Stedeford, and Michael Brescia. Modeled on The Order, the ARA was led by the cross-dressing Pete Langan and his violent associate, Richard Guthrie, and they hoped to use the proceeds of their bank robberies—22 of them between October 1994 and January 1996—to help finance a white supremacist revolution in the United States. (Imitating the bank-robbing surfergang in the 1991 movie *Point Break*, members of the group wore masks of presidents Nixon and Carter, Santa Claus outfits, and even FBI caps and badges during their raids. The press dubbed them the "Midwest Bank Bandits.") In January 1995 Langan and Guthrie produced a bizarre recruitment video called *The Aryan Republican Army Presents: The Armed Struggle Underground*, with Langan dressed as the gun-waving figure "Commander Pedro." He stressed the importance of phantom cell organizing and declared war on the Zionist Occupied Government in Washington, while also doing his best, as Mark Hamm notes, to make "revolutionary action" seem like "fun." Guthrie was arrested in Cincinnati in January 1996 and quickly gave up his associates. He committed suicide in jail before he could testify against them, but the rest of the gang were all given lengthy prison sentences. Langan was sentenced to life and while in prison transitioned to become a woman and activist, renouncing his former racist and political views. (In 2017, Donna Lagan joined with hundreds of other activists to challenge the Trump administration's policies on transgender prisoners.)

McVeigh's connections to Elohim City were not insignificant. A couple of weeks before the bombing, on April 5, 1995, he had called the compound asking to speak to Andreas Strassmeir, Millar's head of security, a former German army officer better known as "Andi the German." The two had first met at a gun show in Tulsa in April 1993. Strassmeir had bought McVeigh's Desert Storm uniform for $2 and given McVeigh his business card, telling him to drop by Elohim City any time. McVeigh still had the card in his wallet when he was arrested two years later, and he seems to have visited the compound at least twice: once in October 1993 and then again on September 13, 1994, the day the Clinton administration's assault weapons ban went into effect. Strassmeir was also a close match for the John Doe Two sketch, but he was spirited out of the country by Dave Hollaway, the deputy director of Kirk Lyons's CAUSE Foundation—the acronym stood for Canada, Australia, the United States, South Africa, and Europe, the places Lyons believed the rights of the white majority were under attack—in January 1996, before the FBI could interview him. McVeigh claimed that he only called Strassmeir on April 5 because he was looking for a safe place to hide after the bombing. (The two men never actually spoke, but McVeigh left a message, saying, "Tell Andi I'll be coming through.")

Andreas Strassmeir is an elusive figure. The son of a prominent German politician and grandson of a leading member of the Nazi Party, in addition to being a former German army officer, Gumbel and Charles suggest that he may have also worked for German or even Israeli intelligence—he had spent three summers on a kibbutz in Israel during his youth—before going rogue and becoming a "true believer" in the American white supremacist cause. He had ended up in Elohim City at the behest of Kirk Lyons, who had grown weary with his freeloading and asked Millar to take him in.

The ATF had a paid informant inside Elohim City named Carol Howe. She issued numerous warnings to her supervisors that a plot was being hatched within the compound to bomb a federal building, either in Tulsa or Oklahoma City, on April 19, 1995. She identified Strassmeir, as well as her former boyfriend, Dennis Mahon, the local head of

White Aryan Resistance, together with someone she knew only as "Tim Tuttle"—a known alias of McVeigh's—as being involved in the plot. She also issued warnings about the activities of the Aryan Republican Army, which she believed Stressmeir was connected with. Howe was not allowed to testify during McVeigh's trial, but she did appear as a witness during Nichol's—the ATF maintained that Howe was unreliable, and that her warnings had not been as specific as she claimed; it is also the case, however, that following the debacles at Ruby Ridge and Waco, there was considerable reluctance within the bureau to launch any kind of raid on Elohim City.

In a letter in October 1993 McVeigh told his sister Jennifer, who shared many of his political beliefs, that he had established a new "network of friends" that he could count on if he ever got into any trouble, and in November 1994 he told her that he had helped to plan a bank robbery and asked her to launder some of the money from it. For those who believe in the existence of a wider conspiracy, this is taken as further evidence of McVeigh's involvement with the Aryan Republican Army. Hamm, for example, argues that McVeigh, Fortier, and the Aryan Republican Army all belonged to the same paramilitary cell, and that it was the ARA that helped McVeigh to carry out the bombing. Stuart Wright contends that there were at least two cells at work: One composed of McVeigh, Nichols, and Fortier and the second comprising members of the ARA, and that this second cell helped to carry out the attack and finance it. Nichols seemed to add weight to this theory in 2005, when he claimed that the gun dealer Roger Moore had supplied both the Aryan Republican Army and McVeigh with explosives. In an interview in 2004 Pete Langan also claimed that it was Richard Guthrie, not Nichols, who had robbed Moore, while others have suggested that the entire episode may have been staged. Because none of these possible links were ever pursued officially, Gumble and Charles regard Moore as "perhaps the luckiest man in the entire [Oklahoma] investigation."

According to Wright, the bombing was planned at a meeting organized by Strassmeir at Elohim City on September 13, 1994, which was attended by "approximately seventy Patriot activists," including McVeigh. Wright argues that the meeting "resurrected" an earlier plan to bomb the Murrah building that had been drawn up by James Ellison and Richard Wayne Snell in 1983, and was designed not just to commemorate the two-year anniversary of the events at Waco, but also to "honor" the execution date of Snell that was coincidentally scheduled for April 19, 1995. Snell watched coverage of the bombing just before his execution, and his last words were addressed to the governor of Arkansas Jim Tucker. "Governor Tucker, look over your shoulder," he said. "Justice is on the way. I wouldn't trade places with you or any of your political cronies. Hell has victory. I am at peace."

When Ellison first proposed bombing the Murrah building, he had explained to his followers: "We need something with a large body count to make the government sit up and take notice. I want the government to know that the right wing has spoken, that the Second American Revolution has begun." McVeigh had the same motivation, and when asked directly by Wright—who was working with the defense team because of his scholarly expertise on Waco—why he had bombed the building during the daytime, rather than at night when it would have been largely empty, his reply directly echoed Ellison. "Because in order to really get the attention of the government, there has to be a body count," he said.

McVeigh took the secrets he had about the Oklahoma City bombing— if any—to the grave. Yet, as Kathleen Belew has argued, whether or not any wider conspiracy took place—or whether or not it could be proved legally—the official explanation that McVeigh acted largely alone still had significant consequences, because it turned the bombing into a "singular event" carried out by a "lone madman, acting in concert with only a few co-conspirators," rather than what it really was: "the culmination of decades of white power organizing" and an apparent vindication of Beam's strategy of leaderless resistance. McVeigh's whole life history, his associations, and all the "ideas that shaped his life and actions, points to his long participation in the white power movement and as a soldier of its cell-style underground," she says. As Andrew Gumbel and Roger Charles make clear, the official explanation also suited the FBI and the other federal agencies involved, because it served to downplay all the failures, missed leads, institutional missteps, and bureaucratic infighting that had taken place during the investigation. The overall effect of all this—especially given McVeigh's own desire to take responsibility for the bombing—was to largely obscure the underlying and supportive role played by the white supremacist right in bringing about the attack.

The impact of the Oklahoma City bombing was considerable. Not surprisingly, a swift and extensive crackdown on anti-government extremism took place almost immediately. In April 1996, for example, the Anti-Terrorism and Effective Death Penalty Act was passed. Among its provisions, the new law significantly increased the penalties for those involved in terrorist acts and placed major—and controversial—restrictions on the habeas corpus rights of prisoners. Congress also authorized a $1 billion increase in the amount of money allocated to the fight against domestic terrorism, with the FBI receiving an additional $468 million. A number of terrorist plots were also thwarted in 1996: Twelve members of the Arizona Viper Militia were arrested for planning to blow up government buildings in Phoenix; seven members of the West Virginia Mountaineer Militia were indicted for planning an attack on an FBI facility in Clarksburg, West Virginia; and three members of a Georgia militia were charged with conspiring to carry out attacks on the Summer Olympics in Atlanta. The FBI also successfully—and peacefully—brought an end to an 81-day siege in Jordan, Montana, involving 11 members of a Posse Comitatus-like group called the Free-men, who had barricaded themselves inside a 960-acre ranch called "Justus Township." (Bo Gritz, Jack McLamb, and Randy Weaver had all shown up to offer their services to the FBI during the standoff.) A similar standoff in Fort Davis, Texas, in the spring of 1997, involving members of an armed separatist group called the Republic of Texas—which believed that Texas had been illegally annexed by the United States in 1845 and that the state was therefore an independent "sovereign nation"—also ended without bloodshed.

As for the broader impact of the bombing on the Patriot movement, at first there was a notable uptick in Patriot group membership, driven it seems by the large amounts of publicity it was receiving. But once the McVeigh and Nichols trials got underway—and as the movement became more closely identified with murder and terrorism—any such positive impact disappeared. According to the Southern Poverty Law Center, there were only 194 Patriot groups in operation in the United States by 2000, down from 858 in 1996 (and 224 in 1995). Militias were hit particularly hard by the bombing, even though neither McVeigh nor Nichols had actually ever belonged to one. Just two months after the attack, in June 1995, the Senate Judiciary Subcommittee on Terrorism, Technology, and Government Information held a day of hearings on the militia movement. All the militia leaders called to testify, including John Trochmann of the Militia of Montana and Norman Olson of the Michigan Militia, denounced the bombing and did their best to dissociate themselves from it, but the effort was not really successful. As Steven Chermak has demonstrated in his book *Searching for a Demon* (2002), the movement was simply never able to recover from all the negative coverage it received as a result of the bombing, both in the press and in the culture at large.

On the other hand, there was also a notable increase in racist "lone wolf" terrorist attacks in the wake of the Oklahoma City bombing. For example, Larry Wayne Shoemake, a National Alliance supporter, shot eight Black Mississippians at a restaurant in Jackson in April 1996, killing one and seriously wounding the others, before killing himself. Three years later, Benjamin Smith, a member of the neo-Nazi World Church of the Creator, went on a three-day, drive-by shooting spree in Illinois and Indiana. He attacked six Orthodox Jews in Chicago on July 2, killed an African-American man Ricky Brydsong in Skokie the same evening, wounded a Black minister in Decatur the following day, and then murdered a 26-year-old Korean student Won-Joon Yoon on July 4. As the police closed in, Smith, too, committed suicide. The following month, Buford Furrow, a member of the Aryan Nations, fired 70 shots into a Jewish Community Center in Los Angeles, wounding five people, including three children. After leaving the Center, he then shot and killed Joseph Santos Ileto, a postal worker, because Ileto was employed by the U.S. government and looked "non-white." Furrow was the ex-boyfriend of Debbie Mathews, the widow of The Order leader Rob Mathews. The two had apparently lived together for two years, having met at Butler's compound in the mid-1990s. In 2001 Furrow was convicted of all the charges against him and sentenced to life in prison.

Yet perhaps the greatest impact of the Oklahoma bombing on the American white supremacist movement—because of both the widespread crackdown and the enormous revulsion it generated—was that it pushed the "mainstreaming" strategy outlined at Estes Park even further to the fore. Building on the use of euphemistic phrases such as "racialist" and "white separatist," white supremacists in the twenty-first century would increasingly deploy terms like "white nationalist" and the "alt-right" to describe themselves as they attempted both to advance their racist agenda and to capitalize on broader developments on the American political scene. It is this that we turn to examine next.

6

Facing the Present

White Nationalism, Obama, Trump, and the Alt-Right

IN THE AFTERMATH OF THE OKLAHOMA CITY bombing and the government crackdown that followed, there was a marked decline in the violent and revolutionary wing of the white supremacist movement, as racist groups sought to insinuate themselves more fully into the political mainstream. As part of this development, many of these groups began describing themselves as "white nationalists" rather than white supremacists. They claimed that they were seeking only to protect and promote their own threatened "white identity" rather than to dominate and subjugate other races. They spoke of "white rights" and "racial pride" and "racial self-determination" and argued that their own "identity politics" were just as legitimate as those of other racial and ethnic groups such as Blacks and Latina/os. Generally speaking, they decried violence, avoided crude racial slurs, and sought to adopt a more intellectual and "reasonable" approach to the nation's racial issues. Among the most prominent of these new groups were Reno Wolfe's National Association for the Advancement of White People (NAAWP), David Duke's National Organization for European American Rights (NOFEAR), Jared Taylor's New Century Foundation—and its *American Renaissance* magazine— and Don Black's *Stormfront* website. They were aided and abetted in their activities by the work of so-called "academic racists," including Kevin McDonald, Michael Hart, Michael Levin, and Peter Brimelow, as well as by neo-Confederate groups such as the Council of Conservative Citizens and the League of the South.

The shift to a discourse of white nationalism was in part a consequence of the ending of the Cold War, which had helped unleash a wave of ethnic nationalism around the globe, but it was also a matter of simple rebranding: an opportunistic and cynical attempt to make the ideas of the white supremacist right more palatable to a larger group of American citizens at the dawn of a new century. Yet in the immediate years of the twenty-first century—and especially in the wake of the "war on terror" unleashed in the aftermath of the terrorist attacks of September 11, 2001—white nationalism made little real headway. The election of the nation's first Black president, Barack Obama, in 2008 changed the situation considerably. The membership of racist groups increased dramatically during Obama's presidency, and the rise of the Tea Party movement during this period both reflected the racist hostility to the new president and facilitated it. Patriot and militia groups also staged a resurgence.

At the same time, 2008 witnessed the first stirrings of the "alt-right," a new and somewhat amorphous collection of initially largely online racists, that would come to greater prominence during Donald Trump's 2016 election campaign, as well as his subsequent presidency. Leading members of the alt-right such as Richard Spencer—who coined the term—also wanted to normalize racism in the United States, hoping that it would eventually lead to the creation of a white ethnostate. As the movement grew, it began to draw not just white nationalists such as Jared Taylor and David Duke into its orbit, but also explicitly neo-Nazi groups such as Matthew Heimbach's Traditional Workers Party and Andrew Anglin's *Daily Stormer* website, as well as Klan groups, militias, and anti-feminist organizations such as the Proud Boys. Indeed, the range of groups operating under the alt-right umbrella is huge. Others include Identity Evropa (which became the American Identity Movement in 2019), the anti-immigrant VDare, the publishing house Counter Currents, and various websites, blogs and podcasts with names such as *The Right Stuff*, *Occidental Dissent*, and *The Political Cesspool*. Then there is the so-called "alt-lite": which is to say, various individuals or groups who claim to reject the explicitly racist and white nationalist politics of the alt-right but who share similar concerns on issues such as immigration, multiculturalism, or political correctness. Included among this grouping are the right-wing news outlet *Breitbart News*, led by former Trump adviser Steve Bannon; the conspiracy theorist Alex Jones; the conservative author and media pundit Ann Coulter; and the now disgraced British-born provocateur Milo Yiannopoulos.

All these developments are the subject of this chapter, as is the presidency of Donald Trump. Remarkably, Trump has been accused not just of giving support and encouragement to the American white supremacist movement, but of being a white supremacist himself. As such, it is important to consider why this is the case and whether or not such criticisms are justified.

Let us begin, though, with Reno Wolfe, David Duke, Jared Taylor, Don Black, and the emergence of the white nationalist movement in the United States.

As noted in earlier chapters, the idea of imitating the language and activities of civil rights' activists in the service of racism and white supremacy was nothing new. An organization called the National Association for the Advancement of White People had been established by Byrant Bowles as early as 1953, was re-established by William Miller in 1964, and then again by David Duke in 1980. Duke's version of the NAAWP had largely petered out by the early 1990s, but it was revived for a fourth time in January 1998 by Reno Wolfe. "We are a civil rights organization specifically founded for white people to counter reverse discrimination," Wolfe declared. Rejecting the label of white supremacy, Wolfe argued that he and his followers were simply people who were proud of their white culture and their white heritage and wanted it to be protected. "Our adversaries have tried to make the word white a dirty word," he explained to one interviewer. "But there's nothing dirty about it. There's nothing bad about being white. . . . My grandparents were white . . . [my] whole family has been white, so I have a white heritage, a white past. Why should I be ashamed to use the word white?" Based in Wolfe's hometown of Callahan, Florida, by 2000 the grassroots organization—which was officially called NAAWP, National Inc., in order to distinguish it from Duke's group—claimed to have 52 chapters across the United States, with overseas outposts in Canada and South Africa. Much of its activity really took place online, however, through an electronic newsletter that identified instances of interracial crime and sought to document examples of discrimination against whites with respect to employment, education, and government service.

As for Duke himself, after spending much of the 1990s unsuccessfully pursuing high political office, in January 2000 he created a new organization called the National Organization for European American

Rights, although within a year NOFEAR had become EURO—or the European-American Unity and Rights Organization—following a copyright infringement claim by a clothing company called No Fear Inc. Like Wolfe's group, Duke regarded both NOFEAR and EURO as civil rights organizations that would preserve "the heritage and way of life of European Americans" in the United States and combat the "pernicious racial discrimination" that was taking place against whites in all areas of American life, including "in college admissions, in scholarship programs, in hiring for major companies, in promotions in major companies, and also in the public sphere, such as police departments, fire departments, city government, the federal government, [and] the United States Post Office." In particular, Duke railed against the "misguided" values of multiculturalism and the high levels of non-white immigration that were rapidly transforming the United States, he said, from a "European-descended society to a Third World society."

As well as building up his organization within the United States—NOFEAR claimed to have 26 American chapters by the beginning of 2001—Duke also sought to create alliances with other similarly minded groups in Europe, especially Russia, France, and Germany. All these efforts were cut short in December 2002, however, when he pleaded guilty to mail fraud and tax evasion and was sentenced to 15 months in federal prison. He was released in May 2004 and spent increasing amounts of time overseas before trying to re-establish his public profile in the United States, with the rise of the Tea Party and then again with Donald Trump.

The most successful and influential of the new white nationalists was Samuel Jared Taylor. Erudite and cosmopolitan, he would become, in the words of George Hawley, "a revered figure" on the alt-right. Taylor was the son of missionaries. He was born in Kobe, Japan, in 1951, and lived there until he was 16. He graduated from Yale University in 1973 and went on to receive a master's degree in international economics from the Paris Institute of Political Studies. (Taylor was fluent in both French and Japanese.) On his return to the States, Taylor became the West Coast editor of PC magazine and published his first book, *Shadows of the Rising Sun: A Critical View of the Japanese Miracle*, in 1983. Under the auspices of the New Century Foundation, he began the magazine *American Renaissance* in November 1990, describing it as a "literate, undeceived, journal of race, immigration and the decline of civility." As Carol Swain has noted, in short order it would become the "leading journal of contemporary white nationalism"—although Taylor preferred the term "racial realist" to describe his politics and beliefs. In 1992 Taylor's second book, *Paved with Good Intentions: The Failure of Race Relations in Contemporary America*, was released, and in 1994 the first annual, academic-style American Renaissance conference took place. Five years later, Taylor's booklet *The Color of Crime*, purporting to show that Blacks were more prone to commit crime than whites, appeared.

Affirmative action programs, multiculturalism, and the nation's dangerously "liberal" immigration policies all attracted Taylor's ire. Whites in the United States were being "displaced," he contended; the very "survival of my people" was at stake, he said. Taylor rooted his ideas in what he regarded as the "essential biological differences" between whites and Blacks and deployed a raft of pseudoscientific "evidence," including reams of charts, graphs, and authoritative sounding statistics, to make his case. But his basic position was laid bare in an October 2005 article about the supposed "lessons" to be learned following the impact of Hurricane Katrina on the Gulf Coast that August, in which 1,200 people were killed, $125 billion in damage was caused, and 50,000 people, most of them African Americans, had been forced to take shelter in appalling conditions inside the New Orleans Superdome and Convention Center. The "story of Hurricane Katrina does have a moral for anyone not deliberately blind," Taylor wrote. "The races are different. Blacks and whites are different. When blacks are left entirely to their own devices, Western civilization—any kind of civilization—disappears. And in a crisis, civilization disappears overnight."

David Duke's EURO organization also tried to exploit the hurricane in a series of articles on its website with titles such as "White Genocide in New Orleans," "Did New Orleans Blacks Resort to Cannibalism?" and "Welcome—To the America of the Future!" "Hurricane Katrina has blown away with her fierce winds and raging floods, the lies of multiculturalism, the lies of egalitarianism," Duke wrote. "She has exposed the underlying dangers to our people that is growing like a slow-moving Tsunami across the European-American world. My God, may our people . . . awaken in time!"

Taylor pioneered a seemingly sophisticated, highbrow, and educated style of racism that would become an important strand of both the white nationalist and the alt-right movements in the United States. Interestingly, unlike many other racists, he was not overtly anti-Semitic, regarding Jews—or at least European Jews—as a legitimate part of the "white race." Other "academic racists" such as Michael Hart, a Princeton-trained astrophysicist, and Michael Levin, a philosopher at the City University of New York, were themselves Jewish. Hart delivered a paper at the 1996 American Renaissance conference arguing for the separation of the United States along racial lines, while Levin was the author of *Why Race Matters: Race Differences and What They Mean* (1998), which contended that innate biological differences between whites and Blacks explained the "difficulty blacks have in competing in a white world." (Levin's position was similar to another highly controversial, if best-selling, book of this period: Charles Murray and Richard Herrnstein's *The Bell Curve* [1994], which argued that the variable socioeconomic performance of different ethnic groups was directly linked to genetics and heredity.) For the most part, however, anti-Semitism remained just as important to white nationalists as it had always been to white supremacists, and it would become a central part of the ideology of the alt-right too.

During the 1990s, for example, another "academic racist," Kevin MacDonald, a professor of psychology at California State University, Long Beach (CSULB), published three books on the so-called "Jewish Question." Taken together, *A People That Shall Dwell Alone: Judaism as a Group Evolutionary Strategy* (1994), *Separation and its Discontents: Toward an Evolutionary Theory of Anti-Semitism* (1998) and *The Culture of Critique: An Evolutionary Analysis of Jewish Involvement in Twentieth-Century Intellectual and Social Movements* (1998) made the argument that anti-Semitism was actually a logical reaction to the historical practices of Jewish people, rather than being the product of irrational hatred and prejudice. In MacDonald's view, a strong in-group preference in combination with Jews' elevated IQs meant they had often been able to outcompete "other races" for wealth and resources. He went on to suggest that having secured positions of influence in Western societies, Jewish people then deliberately promoted policies such as race mixing, immigration, and feminism as a way of undermining those societies and strengthening their own positions within them. To counter such activities, MacDonald called for special taxes to be placed on Jews, as well as restrictions in hiring and college admission practices.

Despite extensive protests, MacDonald remained on the faculty at CSULB until his retirement in 2014, at which point, as David Neiwert notes, he "began to devote himself full-time to promoting the white-nationalist movement." He did so largely through his association with the online site *The Occidental Quarterly*, one of the in-house organs of the emerging alt-right. Less academically inclined "new" white nationalists such as David Duke and his former colleague Don Black also continued to embrace anti-Semitism. The destructive and pernicious influence of Jews around the world was the overriding theme of Duke's 1998 auto-biography, *My Awakening: A Path to Racial Understanding*, as well as his 2001 tome *Jewish Supremacism: My Awakening to the Jewish Question*, for example. It was also fundamental to Black's *Stormfront* website, which was established in March 1995, the first major white supremacist/white nationalist forum to find a home on the Web.

Black had learned his computer skills in federal prison, while serving three years for his part in the botched invasion of the Caribbean island of Dominica in 1981 (see chapter 3). *Stormfront* was run out of his home in West Palm Beach, Florida, and its message boards, forums, and postings were extremely effective in building an online community of racists and anti-Semites, foreshadowing—and eventually becoming part of—the alt-right's own Internet community. Black also adopted the language of white nationalism. In an interview with Russell Nieli in April 2000, he explained why he thought the term "white supremacist" was an "inaccurate description of most of the people that are part of our movement." As Black saw it:

> white supremacy implies a system, such as we had throughout most of this country through the fifties and early sixties, in which there was legally enforced segregation and in which whites were in a position of dominance . . . but today the people who are attracted to the white nationalist movement want separation. . . . We are separatists. We believe that we as white people, as European Americans, have the right to pursue our destiny without interference from other races. And we feel that other races have that right as well—the right to develop a nation with a government which reflects their interest and their values without domination or any other interference from whites. We believe that segregation certainly didn't work, and the only long-term solution to racial conflict is separation.

Stormfront's motto was "White Pride Worldwide," and as part of its attempt to seem more reasonable and palatable, in 2008 it banned the use of all Nazi and Klan symbols from its website, along with the use of crude racial epithets such as "nigger." By 2015, it had almost 300,000 members, up from 5,000 in 2002.

Another online enterprise that would become a prominent part of the alt-right was the anti-immigrant VDare.com—more commonly referred to simply as VDare. It was formed in 1999 by Peter Brimelow, a former senior editor at *Forbes* magazine, and was named for Virginia Dare, said to be the first English child born in the New World, in 1587. The British-born Brimelow had been an enthusiastic booster for Taylor's *Paved with Good Intentions*, and in 1995 he wrote his own book—published by Random House—called *Alien Nation: Common Sense About America's Immigration Disaster*, which argued that the United States had always been a "white nation" and that it should do its utmost to remain that way—by taking back control of its porous borders, cutting off subsidies to illegal immigrants, and perhaps even placing a moratorium on immigration altogether. The Immigration and Nationality Act of 1965—which eliminated the system of national quotas that had been in place since 1924 and established a more liberal immigration policy based on reuniting families and attracting more skilled labor to the United States—was identified by Brimelow as the particular source of the nation's problems in this respect, a point echoed by almost every other prominent white nationalist, together with significant elements of both the alt-right and the alt-lite. Although expressed with his own particular conspiratorial emphasis, Kevin MacDonald summed up the white nationalist concern about the act in *The Culture of Critique*, when he wrote: "The organized Jewish community was the most important force in enacting the 1965 law which *changed the ethnic balance of the country, ensuring that Whites will be a minority in the U.S. well before 2050*" (emphasis added). This "fear" is addressed more fully later in the chapter.

Anti-immigrant sentiment was also evident on the U.S. southern border in the early years of the twenty-first century, driven in large part by a significant increase in the number of undocumented immigrants arriving in the country from Mexico, where the North American Free Trade Agreement (NAFTA) had had a devastating—if largely predictable—effect on the prospects of many unskilled workers, especially in the agricultural sector. By 2000 there were approximately 8.6 million "illegal" immigrants from Mexico in the country, up from 3.5 million in 1990—at its peak, in 2007, there were 12.2 million; the number of unauthorized immigrants from other nations stood at 5.3 million. In an echo of David Duke's "Klan Border Watch" project of 1977, a number of vigilante-style "border patrol" groups soon sprang into action. One of the first was Glenn Spencer's American Patrol organization, which began its operations in 1995. Spencer was a retired California businessman who believed a secret *reconquista* was under way to return the Southwest of the United States to Mexico. In 2002, two Arizona ranchers, Jack Foote and Casey Nethercott, created Ranch Rescue; and in 2004 Chris Simcox, a Tombstone shootout reenactor, and Jim Gilchrist, a Vietnam veteran, established the Minuteman Project. By 2006 the Minutemen claimed to have as many as 12,000 members across 34 states, in a range of groups with names such as the American Border Patrol, the Mountain Minutemen, and Minutemen American Defense.

Finally, a number of neo-Confederate groups fed into the emerging white nationalist movement, helping to set the scene for the rise of the alt-right as well. The most long-standing was the Council of Conservative Citizens (CCC), which had grown directly out of the anti-segregation Citizens' Councils movement of the 1950s and 1960s. Others include the League of the South, the Sons of Confederate Veterans, the Heritage Protection Association, and the Southern Party. Initially, these groups claimed to be interested only in the "preservation" of Confederate memorials and the Confederate flag, as well as the protection of the distinctively Southern "way of life"—to be about "heritage not hate." But as Leonard Zeskind, among others, has documented, it wasn't long before their deep-seated racism came to the fore. Jared Taylor was welcomed to the editorial board of the CCC's tabloid newspaper, the *Citizens' Informer*, for example, and the organization also keenly promoted his *Color of Crime* booklet. Repeating the Biblical arguments of centuries gone by, an article on the Council of Conservative Citizens' website in 2001 claimed that "God is the author of racism," that "God is the one who divided mankind into different types," and that "Mixing the races is rebelliousness against God."

In Taylor's view, the reason "why the Confederacy is under such violent attack is that it is a symbol not only of the white culture that the ethnic saboteurs wish to destroy, but it is also seen . . . as a symbol of a white culture that refuses to apologize." "What better way to attack white America than to insult the last remnant of a proud white America?" he asked. Michael Hill, president of the League of the South, took a similar view. "The Confederate battle flag, along with our other cultural icons, is not merely an historical banner that represents the South," he declared in the summer of 2000. "It is a shorthand symbol of our very ethnic identity as a distinct people—Southerners." The Council of Conservative Citizens came under increased scrutiny in 1999 when it was revealed that the Mississippi Republican majority leader Senator Trent Lott had addressed the group at least five times, and that Georgia Republican Congressman Bob Barr had given the keynote address at its 1998 annual convention. A resolution condemning the organization for promulgating "white supremacy and anti-Semitism" was even introduced in the House of Representatives, although it went nowhere. Yet according to an investigation by the Southern Poverty Law Center (SPLC), numerous Southern lawmakers were still willing to associate themselves with the group, with 38 federal, state, and local elected officials attending CCA events between 2000 and 2004.

The appearance of these new white nationalist groups was not just a consequence of the impact the Oklahoma City bombing had had on the racist right in the United States. It was also because a significant vacuum had opened up in the leadership of the movement. Willis Carto's Liberty Lobby had gone out of business in 2001. William Pierce died in 2002, leaving the National Alliance essentially rudderless. Richard Butler, patriarch of the Aryan Nations, died in 2004, aged 86. And Matthew Hale, leader of the World Church of the Creator, was serving 40 years in prison for soliciting an undercover informant of the FBI to murder a federal judge. In addition, the Internet was transforming the extremist political landscape as much as it was transforming other aspects of society and the economy, a process that became even more pronounced when new social media platforms such as Facebook, Twitter, and Instagram came online. The younger activists of the alt-right would prove especially adept at the exploitation of these new technologies.

Yet during the two administrations of George W. Bush (2001–2009), white nationalists made little headway with their mainstreaming plans. To a considerable extent, this was because the "war on terror" unleashed by the terrorist attacks of al-Qaeda on September 11, 2001, dominated almost everything in American politics, both domestically and internationally, as "radical Islam" became the nation's new number one enemy. To be sure, widespread anti-Muslim sentiment and Islamophobia were readily folded into the white nationalist worldview, and the activities of the anti-immigrant border vigilantes were also spurred on by the hunt for foreign "invaders," but it took the election of Barack Obama in 2008 to really energize the American racist right, propelling it closer and closer to the political center.

"My bet is that whether Obama wins or loses in November, millions of European Americans will inevitably react with new awareness of their heritage and the need for them to defend and advance it," predicted David Duke in an essay on his website in June 2008 titled "A Black Flag for White America." Similarly, Don Black took the view that "white people, for a long time, have thought of our government as being for us and Obama is the best possible evidence that we've lost that." "This is scaring a lot of people," he went on, "and it's bringing them over to our side." Concern about the potential threats to Obama were such that he was assigned a Secret Service protection detail in May 2007, nine months before the Democratic primaries had even begun, the earliest the Secret Service had ever issued a security detail to a presidential candidate. And once in office, the threats, insults, and racist innuendoes kept pouring forth—and not just from those publicly committed to the cause of white supremacy.

Conservative politicians and pundits often referred to Obama using his middle name Hussein in order to accentuate his "foreignness." He was depicted frequently in pictures and on placards as an African witch doctor, as the terrorist Osama bin Laden, with a Hitler mustache, or as Heath Ledger's Joker from the film *The Dark Knight* (2008). The Fox News personality Glenn Beck contended that Obama had a "deep-seated hatred for white people," while the conservative talk radio host Rush Limbaugh regularly played a song called "Barack the Magic Negro" on his show—it was set to the tune of "Puff the Magic Dragon"—and claimed that the president wanted Americans to get Ebola as some kind of "payback" for slavery. Then there was the racist birther conspiracy theory. This was the "theory"—which was propagated by numerous right-wing figures, most notably by Donald Trump (discussed further below)—that Obama was not actually a U.S. citizen: that he was born in Kenya, or maybe Indonesia, and was therefore ineligible to be the president. "I don't remember any other president who was challenged about where he was born despite having a birth certificate," Obama responded in his usual cool manner. (The Obama campaign had posted a copy of Obama's short-form Hawaiian birth certificate on its website shortly after the controversy began in 2008, but it had not laid the conspiratorial speculation to rest, so in the run-up to the 2012 election his long-form birth certificate was also released.)

Both Beck and Limbaugh were also fervent advocates of the Tea Party movement that started to organize itself in opposition to the Obama administration in early 2009 and had a distinct racial element to it. The movement was composed of hundreds of grassroots groups such as the Jefferson Area Tea Party Patriots of Virginia; the Southwest Metro Tea Party of Chanhassen, Minnesota; and the Pink Slip Patriots of Tempe, Arizona. It was supported by wealthy right-wing lobbying organizations such as FreedomWorks—led by the former Republican House majority leader Dick Armey—and Charles and David Koch's Americans for Prosperity organization. Several would-be national coordinating groups also emerged, including Tea Party Patriots, Tea Party Nation, Tea Party Express, and ResistNet, and the whole movement had the backing of the right-wing mediasphere, Fox News most of all.

Gauging the size of the movement is difficult, but it was clearly considerable, as was its political impact—estimates of the number of Tea Party activists range from 160,000 to 350,000, but opinion poll data suggested that as many as 20 percent of Americans, or some 45 million people, regarded themselves as "supporters." Not only did the Tea Party hold hundreds of raucous rallies around the country throughout 2009 and 2010, but it also succeeded in getting 42 Tea Party-aligned candidates elected to Congress in the 2010 midterm elections, helping the Republican Party to regain control of the House of Representatives in the process. The newly installed governors of Wisconsin, Florida, and Ohio—Scott Walker, Rick Scott, and John Kasich—were also Tea Party advocates.

Members of the Tea Party denied that they were motivated by racism. Tea Partiers were vehemently opposed to Obama only because of the massive economic stimulus package he and the Democrats had introduced in order to deal with the "great recession" that had begun during the Bush presidency in the aftermath of the financial crisis in 2007–2008, they said. (Ironically, in many respects the Obama administration was simply continuing with policies initiated during the supposedly conservative and "free market" Bush administration. It was Bush who had begun the "bailout" of the banking and auto industries, spending $717.4 billion in the process, for example.) They were simply against "big government" and "socialism" and wanted lower levels of taxation, fewer bureaucratic regulations, and a smaller welfare state. The evidence suggested otherwise, however. Research conducted by scholars at the University of Washington in 2010 revealed that Tea Party supporters were less favorably disposed toward African Americans and Hispanics than most Americans, and a CBS/*New York Times* poll conducted the same year found that 52 percent of Tea Partiers believed that "too much had been made of the problems facing black people" in America, compared to 28 percent of non-Tea Party respondents. Subsequent investigations merely confirmed the trend. As the political scientist Ashley Jardina notes in *White Identity Politics* (2019), "racial resentment emerges repeatedly as a powerful predictor of Tea Party opinion."

In their 2013 book *Change They Can't Believe In: The Tea Party and Reactionary Politics in America*, Christopher Parker and Matthew Barreto concluded that support for the movement was being driven by people who believed that the "country they love [is] slipping away, threatened by the rapidly changing face of what they believe is the 'real' America: a heterosexual, Christian, middle-class, (mostly) male, *white country*" (emphasis added). In their sloganeering desire to "take the country back," Tea Party supporters really want to "turn the clock back," Parker and Barreto write: "They hope to return to a point in American life before Barack Obama held the highest office in the land, before a Latina [Sonia Sotomayor] was elevated to the Supreme Court, and when powerful members of Congress were all heterosexual (at least publicly)." The political space opened up the Tea Party movement and its allies in Congress—the racial resentments stoked and the "dog whistles" so skillfully deployed—would all be exploited by white nationalists and the alt-right in the years that followed, while Donald Trump's desire to "Make America Great Again" could easily be read as a rehash of the Tea Party's desire to "take the country back," a not-so-subtle call to make America "white" again.

"The Tea Party people are incredible people," Trump told a campaign rally in Nashville in 2016, as he both tried to elicit their support and demonstrate his connection to the movement. "These are people who work hard and love the country, and they get beat up all the time by the media. . . . I love the Tea Party."

Far from ushering in a post-racial America, as many had hoped, the Obama years actually witnessed a growing racial polarization. The appearance of the Black Lives Matter movement in July 2013, following the acquittal of George Zimmerman for the killing of the African-American teenager Trayvon Martin, and the subsequent deaths of Michael Brown and Eric Garner at the hands of the police in Ferguson, Missouri, and New York City, only seemed to deepen the divide. (Controversy over the movement would erupt again during the Trump administration, following the killing of George Floyd in Minneapolis in May 2020.) There was also a notable increase in the number of Patriot and militia groups in operation. By 2012, the Southern Poverty Law Center had identified 1,360 such groups, up from 149 in 2008, a growth of over 800 percent. New militia-style groups such as the Oath Keepers and the Three Percenters also emerged.

The Oath Keepers were formed in March 2009 by Stewart Rhodes, a former Army paratrooper and Yale Law School graduate, who had also worked as a congressional staffer for Texas Republican congressman Ron Paul. The organization was aimed at retired and currently serving military officers, police officers, and first responders—although others could become "associate members"—and was dedicated, it said, to the protection of the U.S. Constitution and the defense of American citizens from impending government "tyranny." Among the list of ten orders that its members promised not to obey were: "1. . . . any order to disarm the American people"; "4. . . . orders to impose martial law or a 'state of emergency' on a state"; "5. . . . any orders to invade and subjugate any state that asserts its sovereignty"; and "7. . . . any order to force American citizens into any form of detention camps under any pretext." By 2014, Rhodes claimed that the group had 35,000 members in all 50 states, although seasoned observers put the figure closer to 5,000. The Oath Keepers denied that they were racist, but as Sam Jackson notes, the organization "repeatedly made vocal statements attacking so-called illegal immigrants" and also provided "de facto security for neo-Confederate and alt-right groups." A similar organization called the Constitutional Sheriffs and Peace Officers Association was formed by a former Arizona sheriff named Richard Mack in 2011.

The Three Percenters—or Threepers as they are also known—grew out of a blog called the Sipsey Street Irregulars, run by a longtime member of the Patriot movement, Mike Vanderboegh, in 2008. It was named for the supposed number of Americans who had fought against the British during the Revolutionary War, although the actual number of American combatants is difficult to determine and was probably closer to 15 percent. Initially, as the Anti-Defamation League pointed out, Vanderboegh's concept functioned largely as "a way to simplify, popularize and spread the ideology and beliefs of the militia movement," but over time people began to explicitly identify themselves as Three Percenters, and groups with names such as the Washington State Three Percenters and the 3% of Idaho began to appear. (Because anyone can claim to be one, it is impossible to know just how many Threepers there actually are.) The Three Percenter logo—the Roman numeral III surrounded by thirteen stars—also became popular, both online and in the real world—on flags, T-shirts, and buttons, for example—and heavily armed members of the group began appearing regularly at Tea Party events, at Trump rallies, and at anti-Black Lives Matter protests.

In April 2009 the Extremism and Radicalism Branch of the Department of Homeland Security's Homeland Environment Threat Analysis Division issued a reported titled "Rightwing Extremism: Current Economic and Political Climate Fueling Resurgence in Radicalization and Recruitment." It warned that the election of Obama in combination with the stock market crash and resulting economic recession was likely to result in a significant growth in the number of extreme right-wing groups—including white supremacists—in the United States, as well as an increase in associated acts of violence. In the context of the ongoing wars in Iraq and Afghanistan, it further warned that "rightwing extremists will attempt to recruit and radicalize returning veterans in order to exploit their skills and knowledge derived from military training and combat." The report's analysis was historically grounded, and its predictions proved to be correct, but when it was leaked to the press it caused a storm of controversy. Republican members of Congress demanded that the report be retracted, the American Legion asked for an official apology on behalf of all veterans, while right-wing media pundits and Tea Partiers claimed that the good name of "conservatism" itself was under attack.

After initially defending the report's accuracy, the Homeland Security Secretary Janet Napolitano caved in to the political pressure. Not only did she apologize for any "offense" that had been caused to the nation's veterans, but the unit responsible for the report was shut down. The training of law enforcement personnel on the threat posed by right-wing extremists in the United States was also halted. It was precisely at this time that the alt-right started to come into existence.

The term originated in November 2008 at a lecture for the H. L. Mencken Club by Paul Gottfried, a professor of humanities at Elizabeth College in Pennsylvania. Gottfried was a paleoconservative, which is to say, he saw himself as a "traditional" and nationalistic conservative. He was sharply critical of "establishment" conservatism, neoconservatism, multiculturalism, and immigration, and wanted to create what he called an "an independent intellectual right." Gottfried's talk was titled "The Decline and Rise of the Alternative Right," and it was a protégé of Gottfried's, Richard Spencer, who gave the alternative right its shorter "alt-right" name. At the time, Spencer was the editor of an obscure right-wing journal called *Taki's Magazine*. He was born in Boston in 1978 and grew up in Texas. He was educated at the University of Virginia and at the University of Chicago, but dropped out of a PhD program in modern European intellectual history at Duke University in 2007. With funding from Peter Brimelow's VDare Foundation, in 2009 Spencer started his own website called *Alternative Right*. Two years later he became president of the white nationalist National Policy Institute, helping to turn it into the leading think tank of the emerging alt-right movement; its annual conference also became an important gathering place for the alt-right, as did Jared Taylor's American Renaissance conferences. In December 2013 Spencer shut down *Alternative Right* to create a new online journal called *Radix*, by which point he had also moved his operations to Whitefish, Montana, in the Pacific Northwest.

In addition to Gottfried, another significant influence on Spencer— as well as on other, more intellectually inclined members of the alt-right, such as those associated with VDare, *Occidental Dissent*, *Occidental Quarterly*, and Identity Evropa—was a political movement known as the European New Right. The European New Right originated in 1968 under the leadership of the French political philosopher Alain de Benoist and his expansively named Group for the Research and Study of European Civilization (GRECE). By the early 2000s, de Benoist and GRECE's pursuit of an "authentically European" but "non-egalitarian" identity had given birth to a wider "identitarianism" movement that had spread to Italy, Germany, and several other European countries, as well as to the United States. Spencer initially referred to himself as an "identitarian," for example, arguing that all of his political beliefs were built on his identity as a white man of European descent.

Although expressed in slightly more sophisticated terms, the concept of "identarianism" was hardly much different from Duke, or Taylor, or the 1960s Klan's insistence on the importance of their "white identity," and the same is true of some of the alt-right's other key ideas, many of which were clearly deeply rooted in already well-established white supremacist beliefs. For example, many alt-righters advocate the idea of "human biodiversity," often abbreviated as HBD, to "explain" why Blacks are less intelligent, or more prone to crime, violence, and other "inherent behaviors" than whites, which is simply the long-discredited notion of biological determinism in more contemporary garb. The movement has also revived the idea of a separate, territorial homeland for whites: a "white ethnostate." And just as the Aryan Nations and The Order regarded the Pacific Northwest as the best location for this new, all-white society, so too do the alt-right embrace the "Great White Northwest." It is true, however, that other locations have also been proposed. As Alexandra Minna Stern has documented, these include Maine, Vermont, and New Hampshire, which together would become known as "New Albion"; "Ozarkia," made up of most of Arkansas and Missouri; "Gulflandia," stretching from Brownsville, Texas, to the Florida Atlantic Coast; and Alaska, which would simply be renamed "New Europa."

The alt-right's dedication to the creation of a white ethnostate flows directly from its beliefs about human biodiversity and identitarianism, since if the races are fundamentally biologically different, it is only "natural," its advocates insist, that people should wish to live and work among their own. As Greg Johnson, editor in chief of Counter-Currents Publishing, the principal publishing house of the alt-right, put it in his 2015 book *Truth, Justice, and a Nice White Country*, the "central rationale for ethnonationalism is that it is the political philosophy that best allows different races and nations to live in accordance with their own identities." In the view of the alt-right, what differentiates its position from that of earlier generations of white supremacists is that it has no desire to dominate or oppress other races and is only seeking to enact ethnocentric arrangements that will be of benefit to *all* racial and ethnic groups.

Yet even if one accepts this supposedly altruistic rationale—which, to a considerable extent, seems to be little more than the attempted re-animation of the "separate but equal" doctrine of *Plessy v. Ferguson*—it is also the case that much of the alt-right's motivation in this regard comes from a profound sense of defeat and displacement. Just like their white nationalist predecessors, alt-right advocates fear that immigration, inter-marriage, multiculturalism, and a low white birth rate are rapidly turning the United States into a "non-white" nation. Like those who came before them, they point to the passage of the 1965 Immigration Act as the beginning of the end of "white America," and they regularly cite official U.S. Census data that indicate that whites are likely to be a minority in the country by 2050, if not sooner, to support their case. Intentionally provocative phrases such as "The Great Replacement" and "White Genocide" are frequently deployed to describe these dreaded developments. "As long as whites continue to avoid and deny their own racial identity, at a time when almost every other racial and ethnic category is rediscovering and asserting its own, whites will have no chance to resist their dispossession," argues Spencer. Johnson contends that if "present trends are not reversed, whites will disappear as a distinct race."

One area where the alt-right has forged a somewhat new path compared to previous generations of American white supremacists is in its stress on the importance of culture and ideas to the achievement of its goals—an emphasis on the broad sphere of "metapolitics," as many in the movement call it. This too is a product of the influence of the European New Right, which itself adapted the idea from the Marxist political philosopher Antonio Gramsci. As articulated in his famous *Prison Notebooks* (1926), Gramsci's position, simply put, was that political change followed cultural and social change, and that those who wanted to bring about major alterations in a society's makeup would first need to shift that society's intellectual and cultural landscape. Spencer expressed this idea clearly enough at a press conference in 2016. "I don't think the best way of understanding the alt-right is strictly in terms of policy," he said. "I think metapolitics is more important than politics. I think big ideas are more important than politics." Recognizing this helps to explain why the alt-right's initial focus was on the development of new journals, new websites, and new media outlets, rather than any new kind of political organization. It would take time to shift the culture, alt-righters argued, and they didn't want to get too far ahead of themselves. They believed they needed to insert their ideas into the political mainstream slowly, carefully extending the notion of what was deemed to be "acceptable" in public discourse—expanding the Overton Window, as they put it—and gradually converting more and more people to their cause.

The Overton Window is a concept that was invented by Joseph P. Overton, an executive at the Mackinac Center for Public Policy in Michigan, during the 1990s, to refer to the range of public policy of ideas that are considered to be politically acceptable at any given time. Language in general is important to alt-righters, it is important to note, and it is used both as a weapon and as a means of generating solidarity and cohesiveness within the movement. Among the many new words and phrases either created or popularized by the alt-right, for example, are "cuckservative," usually used to attack other right-wingers for being too moderate or too willing to compromise; "normie," a derogative term for someone who doesn't understand the alt-right or "Internet culture" in general; "snowflake," perhaps derived from Chuck Palahniuk's 1996 novel *Fight Club*, and used to denote an easily offended person; and "kek," which is a term used to both indicate laughter and also an alt-right "deity."

The key metaphor employed by the alt-right in this respect is the idea of the "red pill," or "red pilling," which the movement appropriated from the 1999 film *The Matrix*, starring Keanu Reeves. In the movie Reeves plays a futuristic freedom fighter named Neo who is battling an oppressive and seemingly all-encompassing simulated reality that has enslaved most of humanity. Neo's mentor, Morpheus, played by Laurence Fishburne, reveals the truth to Neo and then offers him the choice between a red pill and a blue pill. The blue pill will return Neo to his previously unaware and enslaved state, but the red pill will allow him to go on seeing the "reality" of his existence and enable him to continue his fight against a system that has both imprisoned and diminished him. Neo, of course, takes the red pill. For members of the alt-right the underlying "truth" that has been hidden from most Americans is the imminent destruction of the white race. But "red pilling" also functions as a way for them to more gradually "wake" their fellow citizens to what is going on around them by exposing them to such lesser "ills" as the supposed inequities of political correctness, affirmative action, feminism, or immigration in the hope that once "awakened" those citizens will then embrace the broader beliefs and aims of the racist right.

In contrast to the highbrow aspirations of Spencer, Johnson, and their associates, beginning in 2011 the ideas of the alt-right also started to take root in the decidedly lower brow reaches of the Internet, in forums such as 4chan, Reddit, and Twitter, where memes, trolling, and "shitposting" were very much the order of the day. Initially, the primary outlet for this aspect of the alt-right was a discussion board on 4chan called "Politically Incorrect," more usually shortened to "/pol/." One of the most important features of 4chan—as well as its successor 8chan—is that it is an open venue, and most of its postings are anonymous. In addition, discussion threads are designed to disappear quickly—within days, or even hours—which further encourages contentious and transgressive postings. As a result, a culture of "anything goes" humor and semi-protective irony quickly became the norm, one in which deeply offensive postings are often dismissed as being mere "jokes" (a strategy that supporters of Donald Trump would deploy to defend some of his more outrageous and offensive statements as well). Because of this, judging both the size and the seriousness of this aspect of the alt-right is extremely difficult. As the journalist Mike Wendling writes: "Their fondness for jokes and pranks, pushing boundaries and twisting language, mean that it's often not possible to tell whether . . . the anons slinging racial and gay slurs on 4chan actually hold extreme beliefs, or think shouting 'nigger' and 'faggot' is funny, or are just trying to shock or offend for effect."

Nonetheless, it is also the case that alt-right activists tried to exploit and utilize these anonymous online foot soldiers while also adopting and imitating their provocative and "playful" tactics. Country music star Taylor Swift was promoted as a striking example of "Aryan beauty" and as a closet white nationalist who was herself secretly "red pilling" America, for example (although this particular effort floundered somewhat in 2018, when Swift endorsed several progressive causes and actively encouraged her fans to vote for Democrats in that year's midterm elections). Recent *Star Wars* films such as *Rogue One* (2016) and *The Last Jedi* (2017) have been attacked for featuring too many non-white and female characters, and the same tactic was also used against the female reboot of the film *Ghostbusters* in 2016, with particular vitriol being directed against the African-American actress Leslie Jones. All of these efforts fit comfortably with the alt-right's emphasis on the importance of shifting the culture and metapolitics, reflecting its attempts to both smuggle its ideas into the public arena and also "normalize" its racism. The campaign against the *Star Wars* films was largely conducted through an online "front group" called Down with Disney's Treatment of Franchises and its Fanboys, for example.

In 2016 the alt-right website *The Right Stuff* posted an article explicitly extolling the benefits of trolling. "You should assume that you will never manage to convince your ideological enemies of the merit of your position," it explained:

> Rather, the purpose of trolling is to convince people reading your comments of the merit of your position. On many different web forums, lurkers outnumber posters by 10 to 1. The purpose of trolling raids is to convince these anonymous people, not the person you disagree with. As such, you can win hearts and minds even when met with universal opposition.

The Right Stuff was founded in 2012 by someone using the pseudonym "Mike Enoch." It was committed to "reinvigorating dialogue among a disparate and edgy right-wing," it said, adding: "We're white and we're not sorry." It was also deeply anti-Semitic. In 2014 *The Right Stuff* began hosting a podcast called the "Daily Shoah," which deployed an audio "echo effect" whenever a Jewish-sounding name was mentioned. By the summer of 2016 this had developed into a widely deployed alt-right meme, whereby names or phrases associated with Jewish people were regularly presented with three sets of parentheses like this: (((Amy Schummer))), (((Carl Bernstein))), or (((banker))). As one of *The Right Stuff*'s editors explained, the intention of this ploy was to "expose" the supposedly immense hidden power of Jews in the United States. "The inner parenthesis represents the Jews' subversion of the home [and] destruction of the family through mass-media degeneracy," journalists Anthony Smith and Cooper Fleishman were informed. "The next [parenthesis] represents the destruction of the nation through mass immigration and the outer [parenthesis] represents international Jewry and world Zionism." In January 2017 it was revealed that "Mike Enoch" was actually a New York website developer named Mike Peinovich, and that his wife was Jewish. Yet after a short burst of initial controversy, Peinovich continued on with the propagation of his racist politics largely unaffected.

Another area of the Internet, the so-called "manosphere," also inter-connected with the alt-right during this period. The manosphere—also referred to as the "men's Internet"—is a diffuse and often ugly arena in which a range of "men's rights" activists operate in the usual dizzying array of blogs, discussion boards, social media accounts, and websites. They range from groups sincerely advocating for the rights of fathers after divorce, to so-called Pick Up Artists offering "expert advice" for men seeking to have sex with as many women as possible, to Incels—or the involuntary celibate—to adherents of Men Going Their Own Way, who aim to live their lives with as little female contact as possible, to open advocates of rape and violence. Underpinning much of the manosphere is a deep-seated misogyny and a belief that feminism represents a fun-damental threat to the rights of men in American society. Interestingly, though, this too is an irony-rich subculture, in which many of the mostly young white men who inhabit it actively celebrate their "loser" or "beta" status in contrast to the more successful and admirable "alpha males" they see around them.

Members of the alt-right and the manosphere first came together in 2013 during "Gamergate," an extensive and largely manufactured con-troversy about supposed antiwhite bias, untoward feminist influence, and poor journalistic standards in the video game industry. But perhaps the most successful of the "men's rights" groups are the Proud Boys, which was formed in September 2016 by the Canadian Gavin McInnes, one of the founders of Vice Media. Determinedly anti-feminist, anti-leftist, and anti-Muslim, the group's members proudly describe themselves as "Western chauvinists" who "refuse to apologize for creating the modern world" and who also reject "white guilt." The group, which has approxi-mately 6,000 members but many more thousands of followers on social media, also adopts many of the jokey, ironic, and transgressively perfor-mative aspects of the chans—its name, for example, is taken from a song from *Aladdin* (1998) called "Proud of Your Boy." McInnes denies that the Proud Boys are part of the alt-right, characterizing it instead—albeit with his tongue firmly in his cheek—as the "greatest fraternal organization in the world"—a kind of twenty-first century "Elks Lodge"—but the Southern Poverty Law Center considers it to be a hate group, arguing that if it cannot be considered to be a fully fledged member of the alt-right, then it is certainly a central component of the broader alt-lite. The SPLC points to the group's presence at the Unite the Right rally in Charlottesville, as well as its creation of a "tactical defense arm" called the Fraternal Order of Alt-Knights in early 2017, to support this designation, while also noting that McInnes contributed essays to both VDare and American Renaissance before forming the group.

Not surprisingly, the role of women within the alt-right is extremely limited. As Stern writes in her book *Proud Boys and the White Ethnostate; How the Alt-Right is Warping the American Imagination* (2019):

> Almost to a person, the alt-right is a world for men, by men, and of men—and straight white men. Women do not lead organizations or speak at nationalist gatherings. . . . They do not write the books or signature essays that constitute the canon of the alt-right, and with few exceptions, no female authors are distributed by nationalist presses. Alt-right intellectual production is the bailiwick of white men writing from a decidedly masculinist perspective, no matter the topic at hand.

Indeed, the role of women within the movement is restricted largely to those that they have always played within the white supremacist right: as wives, mothers, and the guardians of "traditional" family and moral values. After all, as Stern also points out, only if white women agree to produce more white babies will it be possible for the alt-right to avert the catastrophe of "white genocide."

If women are not prominent within the world of the alt-right, the same cannot be said for neo-Nazis. In fact, along with the "academics" and the "intellectuals," the "channers" and the "trolls," neo-Nazis and other avowed and unapologetic white supremacists form a third key wing of the movement.

The most well-known alt-right neo-Nazi website is Andrew Anglin's *The Daily Stormer*, which went online in July 2013, shortly after Anglin had shuttered his previous site *Total Fascism*. It is named for Julius

Streicher's infamous Nazi propaganda newspaper *Der Stürmer* and regularly publishes articles with titles such as "All Intelligent People in History Disliked the Jews," "Black Murdered White Girl He Was Pimping Out," and "Blacks Loved Slavery and Regretted its End." With the assistance of Andrew Auernheimer—a computer hacker better known as "weev"—Anglin also regularly deployed his "Stormer Troll Army" to conduct the online harassment of his "enemies." These have included Taylor Dumpson, the first African-American woman to serve as student government president at the University of Washington; Tanya Gersh, a Jewish real estate agent from Whitefish, Montana, who had fallen into dispute with Richard Spencer's mother; and comedian and political commentator Dean Obeidallah, a Muslim, whom Anglin accused of being behind the terrorist attack at an Ariana Grande concert in Manchester, England, in May 2017. (Obeidallah was awarded $4.1 million for the defamatory claim in June 2019.)

Other white supremacist and neo-Nazi groups that have associated themselves with the alt-right include Matthew Heimbach's Traditional Workers Party, Vanguard News Network—the last remnant of William Pierce's National Alliance—several Klan groups, Vanguard America, the self-proclaimed "face of American fascism," and even, at some points, Don Black's *Stormfront*, as well as many individual racists and neo-Nazis with no group affiliation at all. As George Hawley has pointed out, in part this was simply a consequence of the term "alt-right" becoming increasingly well-known and more visible, especially after it was picked up by the mainstream media. In effect it became a fashionable term that white supremacists of varying stripes wished to identify with and exploit for their own purposes—"a catch-all term" for the new racist right, as Hawley puts it.

Clearly, then, the alt-right is a somewhat amorphous movement, one that can be very difficult to pin down, particularly since most of its actions take place online and are often conducted anonymously or through pseudonyms and pen names. The activities of the so-called "alt-lite" only adds to the complexity. As noted at the beginning of the chapter, the term is used to describe people or groups who share some of the concerns of the alt-right on subjects such as immigration, feminism, or the "evils" of political correctness but who do not explicitly advocate white nationalism or the creation of a white ethnostate, although they are often regarded as providing a "gateway" to the alt-right. Included among the ranks of the alt-lite are the *InfoWars* conspiracy theorist Alex Jones, fellow conspiracy theorist Jack Posobiec, right-wing media commentator Ann Coulter, the misogynistic blogger and filmmaker Mike Cernovich, and the previously mentioned Proud Boys. But perhaps its most influential members have been the far-right news outlet *Breitbart News Network* and its onetime columnist Milo Yiannopoulos.

Breitbart was founded in 2007 by Andrew Breitbart, who had previously been involved with both *The Drudge Report* and *The Huffington Post*. His own site was staunchly conservative. It attacked liberals and other advocates of "big government" and regularly ran material that was both anti-Muslim and racially provocative. An enthusiastic supporter of the Tea Party movement, Breitbart also believed in the value of metapolitics. ("Politics is downstream from culture," he liked to say.) Breitbart died from a heart attack in 2012, aged 43; and Stephen Bannon, a former Goldman Sachs investment banker, right-wing documentary film producer, and self-described "economic nationalist," took over as the network's executive chairman. It was Bannon who pushed *Breitbart* more firmly in a white nationalist direction, going so far as to call it the "go-to platform of the alt-right" in an interview in 2016.

This dubious accolade had not been obtained through any direct promotion of white supremacy or "racial separatism," it should be noted— and it was a claim that in any event could never be verified, and seemed designed mostly to call attention to itself, as well as to attract more traffic to the *Breitbart* site. Instead, it was because under Bannon's direction *Breitbart* published countless sensationalist, alt-right friendly, click-baiting stories with headlines such as "Hoist It High and Proud: The Confederate Flag Proclaims A Glorious Heritage," "Political Correctness Protects Muslim Rape Culture," "Would You Rather Your Child Had Feminism or Cancer?" and "Race Murder in Virginia: Black Reporter Suspected of Executing White Colleagues—on Live Television!" *Breitbart* was especially hostile to the Black Lives Matter movement and featured numerous stories about the dangers of immigration and Islamic terrorism. In addition, in 2014, Bannon hired Milo Yiannopoulos to be the site's senior technology editor, and it was Yiannopoulos, as the journalist David Neiwert points out, who became *"Breitbart's* primary connection to the alt-right."

Born in 1984, Yiannopoulos was originally from the United Kingdom. Flamboyantly gay and Catholic, he was an expert troller, defiantly—and "jokingly"—opposed to feminists, Muslims, and SJWs, or Social Justice Warriors. In 2016, for example, he undertook a "Dangerous Faggot Tour" of college campuses in the name, he said, of "free speech." Yiannopoulos first rose to prominence during the Gamergate controversy, and in March 2016 he and his colleague Allum Bokhari wrote a highly sympathetic account of the alt-right for *Breitbart* called "An Establishment Conservative's Guide to the Alt-Right." The centerpiece of the article was an attempt to distance the movement from what Yiannopoulos and Bokhari called "the 1488ers," which is to say, anti-Semites, white supremacists, and "other members of the *Stormfront* set." ("1488" is a white supremacist code representing David Lane's "fourteen words" and "Heil Hitler"—because H is the eighth letter of the alphabet.) The authors did not deny the presence of the 1488ers within the alt-right— that would have been impossible—but they did try to minimize both their numbers and their importance. "Every ideology has them," Yiannopoulos and Bokhari explained:

> Humourless ideologues who have no lives beyond their political crusade, and live for the destruction of the great. They can be found on *Stormfront* and other sites, not just joking about the race war, but eagerly planning it. They are known as "Stormfags" by the rest of the internet.
>
> Based on our research we believe this stands in stark contrast with the rest of the alt-right, who focus more on building communities and lifestyles based around their values than plotting violent revolution.
>
> 1488ers are the equivalent of the Black Lives Matter supporters who call for the deaths of policemen, or feminists who unironically want to #KillAllMen. Of course, the difference is that while the media pretend the latter are either non-existent, or a tiny extremist minority, they consider 1488ers to constitute the whole of the alt-right.
>
> Those looking for Nazis under the bed can rest assured that they do exist. On the other hand, there's just not very many of them, no-one really likes them, and they're unlikely to achieve anything significant in the alt-right.

Five months later, Andrew Anglin of the *Daily Stormer* wrote his own article in response, in which he attacked Yiannopoulos and Bokhari's essay as a "contrived and largely nonsensical" history of the movement. It was called "A Normie's Guide to the Alt-Right," and it put anti-Semitism, white supremacy, and "scientific racism" firmly back at the center of the "white struggle." "The core concept of the movement, upon which all else is based," Anglin wrote, "is that Whites are undergoing an extermination, via mass immigration into White countries which was enabled by a corrosive liberal ideology of White self-hatred, and that the Jews are at the center of this agenda." In somewhat ominous terms, Anglin also firmly embraced the highly fluid composition of the alt-right. "The movement is, at this point, entirely leaderless," he argued. "The people involved in contributing to and/or consuming the content are on different Alt-Right sites and forums, many are on Twitter, reddit, 4chan, etc. There are minor 'leaders,' people who others listen to, but because there is yet to be an officially codified doctrine, no actual leader exists. *The mob is the movement*" (emphasis added).

All of this online agitation could have significant repercussions in the real world, however. On June 17, 2015, Dylann Roof, a 21-year-old white supremacist, shot and murdered nine African-American worshippers during a Bible study meeting at the Emanuel African Methodist Episcopal Church in Charleston, South Carolina. Roof claimed to have been "awakened" to the white supremacist cause by the Trayvon Martin case, but he had been radicalized through the Internet, first by visits to the website of the Council of Conservative Citizens and then on *Daily Stormer*, where he posted under the name "AryanBlood1488." He was hoping to start a race war. Found guilty of all the charges against him, he was given the death penalty in January 2017.

Another extremist radicalized online was Robert Bowers, who regularly posted anti-immigrant and anti-Jewish conspiracy theories on the social media site Gab, another platform widely used by the racist right. Convinced that Jews were "committing a genocide to his people," on October 27, 2018, Bowers killed eleven and injured seven others in an attack on the Tree of Life synagogue in Pittsburgh. Another proponent of "The Great Replacement" theory was Brenton Tarrant, a 28-year-old Australian citizen, who on March 15, 2019, killed 51 people and injured 49 others in attacks on two mosques in Christchurch, New Zealand. Inspired by Tarrant's actions, on August 3, 2019, Patrick Crusius, aged 21, walked into a Walmart store in El Paso, Texas, armed with an

AK-47-style assault rifle, and opened fire. He killed 22 people and injured 27 others. Shortly before the attack Crusius had posted a 2,300-word manifesto titled "The Inconvenient Truth" on an 8chan message board, explaining that he was deeply concerned about the "Hispanic invasion of Texas," "open borders," and the "cultural and ethnic replacement" of whites. Like Dylann Roof, Crusius expressed his hope that his actions would help to spark a race war in the United States.

In many respects, the precursor to these contemporary "lone wolf" terrorist attacks was Norwegian Anders Behring Breivik's killing of 77 people in July 2011. Breivik struck at two targets, first bombing a government building in Oslo and then going on a shooting rampage at a summer camp for young members of the Norwegian Labour Party on the island of Utøya. Breivik's "manifesto" *2083: A European Declaration of Independence* has been praised by Richard Spencer among other members of the alt-right.

Donald Trump announced his candidacy for the presidency from the lobby of Trump Tower in New York City on June 16, 2015. All the competing elements of the alt-right soon swung their support toward him. They did so for a range of reasons. Some of the alt-right did it just for "fun": for the "lulz" and for "kek" in chan speak. As Dale Beran writes in his book *It Came from Something Awful: How a Toxic Troll Army Accidently Memed Donald Trump into Office* (2019), "it turned out that the politics of offensive publicity stunts aligned in an uncanny way with the vast group of netizens waiting for someone who spoke to their lived experience of racist jokes, screen performances, and garbage ads." Much of Trump's appeal in this respect, Beran went on, was a consequence of "his strange talent for emitting both the bullying signals of an alpha male and an insecure, loser beta, who, no matter how vigorously he scrubbed, could not shed his status as an outsider whose desperation to be accepted among the elite prevented it from ever happening. . . . Boorish, brash, and ill-mannered, [Trump] was, to his fans' delight, an insult to everyone." In these terms, Trump was ironically hailed as a "God Emperor," or depicted as the alt-right's adopted cartoon mascot, Pepe the Frog.

Other alt-righters quickly recognized that Trump could also be an effective "agent of chaos," a mainstream figure with significant potential to aid the alt-right's entire political and ideological agenda. As Greg Johnson put it in an article on "The Year in White Nationalism" in

Counter-Currents in December 2015: "Like an icebreaker, Trump has plowed through the frozen crust of the artificial political consensus, smashing it to bits, and releasing the turbulent populist currents beneath. It is our job to crowd into the breach, widen it, and turn every outcome in our direction." Brad Griffin on the blog *Occidental Dissent*, simply called Trump "the rock that White America finally threw through the glass window of the status quo." Peter Brimelow referred to the Republican Party presidential candidate as a "wrecking ball."

Then there was Trump's apparent racism. The alt-right did not get behind Trump because they thought he was a committed white supremacist, it is important to emphasize—he was not advocating for the creation of a white ethnostate. But they did see him as someone whose views on race and on immigration were not totally removed from their own either. After all, his signature campaign 2016 issue was the building of "a great big beautiful wall" on the southern border, and his opening campaign address had directly addressed the issue of "illegal" immigration, famously, if somewhat incoherently, suggesting: "When Mexico sends its people, these aren't the best and the finest. They are not sending you. . . . They're sending people that have lots of problems, and they're bringing those problems with us [*sic*]. They're bringing drugs. They're bringing crime. They're rapists. And some, I assume, are good people." In addition, both of Trump's campaign slogans—"Make America Great Again" and "America First"—seemed at the very least alt-right "friendly."

Richard Spencer's views on the matter were effectively conveyed in an article in *Radix Journal* in September 2015 called "Our Big, Fat, Beautiful Dog Whistle." Trump was "expressing the deeply symbolic nature of the immigration issue," Spencer explained. This did not mean that immigration was "not a real issue with palpable and often immediate effects," Spencer wrote, but rather that "when we talk about immigration, we're really talking about something else," which in Spencer's view, of course was "White displacement by Hispanics and other non-Whites." In other words, the Great Replacement. However, perhaps the best summary of the alt-right's position on Trump prior to the 2016 election was provided by Matthew Heimbach on his Traditional Youth Network website. Like most of the rest of the alt-right—and many other Americans— Heimbach did not expect Trump to win the presidency, nor did he see

him as a fully committed white nationalist, but he did see considerable
benefits to his candidacy, writing:

> While Trump is neither a Traditionalist nor a White nationalist, he
> is a threat to the economic and social powers of the international Jew.
> For this reason alone, as long as Trump stands strong on deportation
> and immigration enforcement we should support his candidacy insofar
> as we can use it to push more hardcore positions on immigration and
> Identity. Donald Trump is not the savior of Whites in America, he is
> however a booming salvo across the bow of the Left and Jewish power
> to tell them that White America is awakening and we are tired of busi-
> ness as usual.

Donald Trump was born in Queens, New York, in 1946, the son of a
successful local property developer, Frederick "Fred" C. Trump. After
college at Fordham University and the University of Pennsylvania's
Wharton School—where he majored in real estate—Donald went into
the family business, expanding the company's operations into Manhattan, beginning in the late 1970s. A skilled promoter and salesman who
attached the Trump name to various properties and businesses, he suffered a series of reversals during the 1990s with the bankruptcies of several Trump casinos, as well as the famed Plaza Hotel in New York. He
rebounded however, and by 2000 *Forbes* estimated his net worth to be
$1.7 billion, although Trump himself claimed the figure was $5 billion.
(Despite this, two more company bankruptcies took place in the 2000s:
Trump Hotels and Casino Resorts in 2004 and Trump Entertainment
Resorts in 2009.) In 2004 Trump also became a television star as part of
a new "reality TV show" called *The Apprentice*, where contestants com-
peted for a chance to win a one-year $250,000 job with the Trump Orga-
nization. The show and its spinoff, *The Celebrity Apprentice*, would run
for 14 seasons.

Trump had flirted with a run for the presidency in 1988 and again in
2000, both times with the assistance of former Nixon political operative
and self-confessed "dirty trickster" Roger Stone. But each "campaign"
had seemed little more than an extended publicity stunt, and many
people suspected the same of his 2016 bid as well. After all, Trump was
hardly a dyed-in-the-wool Republican, his official party registration having shifted regularly between the GOP and the Democratic Party in the
preceding years. Somewhat more consistent had been his racial positions,

however, both in politics and in business, a fact that undoubtedly contributed to his appeal among the alt-right as well. And as with the property developing, this too was something that seemed to run in the family. As noted in chapter 1, Fred Trump had been arrested at a Memorial Day parade organized by the Ku Klux Klan in Queens in 1927, although whether as a participant or an observer remained unclear. He also had a reputation for discriminating against African Americans as a landlord. During the 1950s, the noted folk singer Woody Guthrie, who lived in a Trump-owned apartment in Brooklyn, had even rewritten his famous "I Ain't Got No Home" ballad to attack "Old Man Trump" and his "Beach Haven" property "where no black ones come to roam." And in 1973 both Fred and Donald Trump were sued by the federal government for discriminating against African-American tenants in contravention of the Fair Housing Act of 1968.

One of Donald Trump's earliest political interventions had also involved racial issues—the case of the so-called "Central Park five" in 1989, when he had taken out full-page ads in four New York newspapers to call for the death penalty for the five Black and brown youths accused of the brutal rape of a white investment banker named Trisha Meili. Even when the five men were cleared by DNA evidence in 2002, Trump refused to back down, and he called New York's 2014 payment of $41 million to the men in settlement of their wrongful imprisonment lawsuit "a disgrace," insisting that the five did "not exactly have the pasts of angels" and were still likely guilty. Then there was his position as a leader of the birther movement. Trump only finally abandoned the racist conspiracy theory in September 2016. "President Obama was born in the United States, period. Now, we all want to get back to making America strong and great again," he stated during a campaign event in Washington, D.C. Even as he did so, though, he blamed his Democratic opponent Hillary Clinton for starting the controversy while somehow trying to claim credit for "finishing" it.

At the annual White House Correspondent's Dinner in April 2011, a few days after the White House had released Obama's long form birth certificate, the president ridiculed Trump for his promotion of birtherism as Trump sat uncomfortably in the audience. "I know he's taken some flack lately. But no one is happier, no one is prouder to put this birth certificate matter to rest than The Donald. And that's because he can finally get back to focusing on the issues that matter—like, did we fake the moon landing? What really happened in Roswell? And where are Biggie and Tupac?" Obama joked. Trump was humiliated, and many observers have suggested that this was the point at which he decided to run for the presidency himself, in order that he might get "revenge" on Obama.

On August 17, 2016, Trump further cemented his association with the alt-right when he appointed Steve Bannon to be the chief executive officer of his campaign. During this time he also regularly retweeted alt-right material on his Twitter feed, including an image of the star of David next to Hillary Clinton's head, complete with dollar bills cascading down from it, and a posting from someone known only as "WhiteGenocideTM." In addition, Trump had been a guest on Alex Jones' *InfoWars* show, where he praised Jones for his "amazing" reputation and promised not to let him down. Sensing an opportunity, Clinton went on the attack. "A man with a long history of racial discrimination, who traffics in dark conspiracy theories drawn from the pages of supermarket tabloids and the far, dark reaches of the Internet, should never run our government," she declared in a speech in in Reno, Nevada, on August 25. "This is not conservatism as we have known it. This is not Republicanism as we have known it," she went on, calling out Trump and the alt-right in the starkest terms:

> These are race-baiting ideas, anti-Muslim and anti-woman—all key tenets making up an emerging racist ideology known as the alt-right. . . .
> The de facto merger between Breitbart and the Trump campaign represents a landmark achievement for the alt-right. A fringe element has effectively taken over the Republican Party. . . .
> Of course, there has always been a paranoid fringe in our politics, a lot of it rising from racial resentment. But it's never had the nominee of a major party stoking it, encouraging it, and giving it a national megaphone. Until now.

The problem with Clinton's speech, however, was that it considerably exaggerated the importance of the alt-right, both within the country and within the Trump campaign, elevating it to a status—and providing it with a level of unity and coherence—that it did not really warrant. Traffic to alt-right websites increased dramatically in the aftermath of Clinton's address, and the media amplified the story even further.

Alt-righters themselves were delighted with all the new attention they received. Almost overnight they had come much closer to achieving their goal of becoming a mainstream political force. As Richard Spencer put it to a reporter: "The alt-right as a moniker of resistance is here to stay. Hillary just ensured that. . . . I never thought this would happen so quickly." Nor was Trump in any way chagrined by his opponent's critique. Just three weeks after Clinton's Reno speech he retweeted an image of himself as Pepe the Frog, complete with the message "You Can't Stump the Trump." As Mike Wendling notes, "The channers nearly exploded with joy."

When the seemingly unthinkable happened and Trump won the election, albeit by a small margin, and having lost the popular vote—by 62.9 million votes to Clinton's 65.8 million—the alt-right was overjoyed, even attempting to take credit for the result. While this was impossible to determine—although the size of Trump's victory in the key states of Pennsylvania, Wisconsin, and Michigan was a little more than 80,000 votes combined—numerous studies, including Alan Abramowitz's *The Great Realignment: Race, Party Transformation, and the Rise of Donald Trump* (2018), Rory McVeigh and Kevin Estep's *The Politics of Losing: Trump, the Klan, and the Mainstreaming of Resentment* (2019), and Ashley Jardina's *White Identity Politics* (2019), did establish that white racial resentment, in broader terms, played a key role in Trump's support. And once in office Trump demonstrated time and again that racial issues, immigration, and nationalism would be central to his administration's governing approach. Although the actual building of "the wall" with Mexico proved to be more difficult in practice than it had on the campaign trail, Trump's endorsement of it never wavered, a "travel ban" for predominantly Muslim nations was put in place, and a "zero tolerance" policy for "illegal" immigrants was announced, among other initial measures, for example.

Emboldened by this apparently supportive climate, in the summer of 2017 numerous alt-right, white nationalist, militia, and neo-Nazi groups gathered in Charlottesville, Virginia, for a "Unite the Right" rally. Two of the key organizers of the rally were Richard Spencer and Jason Kessler, a leading member of the Proud Boys, although he was later expelled from the group. Among those in attendance were members of Identity Evropa, Vanguard America, the Three Percenters, the Traditional

Workers Party, the League of the South, the New York Light Foot Militia, the Confederate Knights of the Ku Klux Klan, American Guard, the Loyal White Knights of the Ku Klux Klan, and assorted alt-right online figures such as The Right Stuff founder Mike Enoch, *Radical Agenda* host Christopher Cantwell, and *The Daily Stormer* contributors Robert Ray and Gabriel Sohier Chaput. Among those scheduled to speak at the event were Spencer, Cantwell, Enoch, Michael Heimbach, and David Duke. Ostensibly, the rally was supposed to be a protest against the planned removal of a statue of the Confederate general Robert E. Lee from a local park, but it was really intended as a demonstration of the newfound strength of the racist right, as well yet another attempt to bring its many disparate strands together.

On the evening of August 11, about 200 marchers, most of them young men and many of them carrying flaming tiki torches, descended on the campus of the University of Virginia, chanting white supremacist slogans such as "Blood and Soil!," "Jews will not replace us!," and "White lives matter!" They were met by a small group of counterprotestors, and a brief brawl ensued. The following day about 500 alt-right demonstrators and over 1,000 counterprotestors were involved in a series of increasingly violent confrontations around the city. The violence was such that the governor of Virginia Terry McAuliffe declared a state of emergency and the entire "Unite the Right" rally was canceled. Shortly thereafter, at about 1:45 in the afternoon a 20-year-old neo-Nazi, James Alex Fields Jr., who had earlier been seen marching with Vanguard America protestors—although the group denied that Fields was an actual member organization—drove his Dodge Challenger sports car into a crowd of anti-racism demonstrators. Heather Heyer, a 32-year-old paralegal, was killed, and dozens more were injured. In December 2018, Fields was found guilty of first-degree murder and sentenced to life in prison. Numerous charges against other alt-right perpetrators were also filed.

Reaction to the events at Charlottesville was swift, with political and religious leaders from across the country forcefully denouncing the white supremacist march and the violence that had ensued. Not so President Trump, however. Speaking from his Bedminster golf course in New Jersey on August 12, he criticized the "hatred, bigotry, and violence . . . *on many sides*" (emphasis added). Two days later, under pressure to say something more forceful about what had happened, he declared that racism was "evil" and that "those who use violence in its name are criminals and thugs, including the KKK, neo-Nazis, white supremacists, and other hate groups that are repugnant to everything we hold dear as Americans." The following day, however, in a combative and ill-tempered news conference at Trump Tower in New York, the president reversed course again, suggesting that there were "very fine people on both sides" and attacking the media for not treating all of the Unite the Right rally's participants fairly. "Not all of those people were neo-Nazis, believe me," he said, "not all of those people were white supremacists by any stretch." In response, David Duke thanked Trump for his "honesty" and for his "courage to tell the truth," while Richard Spencer said that he was "really proud" of the president because Trump had "bucked the narrative of alt-right violence" with his "fair and down to earth" comments.

In truth, however, Charlottesville was a major reversal for the alt-right. The ugly racist chants. The helmets, the shields, the baseball bats. The street brawls and the horrific murder of Heather Heyer all significantly undermined the attempt it had been making to "normalize" its message. In addition, the recriminations that followed clearly revealed, in the words of journalist Vegas Tenold, that "the Unite the Right groups were never truly united in anything but being white and angry." Spencer issued a statement expressing his regret for Heyer's death and was immediately denounced as a coward and a turncoat. Jason Kessler in contrast tweeted out an article from *The Daily Stormer* claiming that Heyer had been a communist, seeming to suggest that she had deserved to be killed. "The great travesty of Charlottesville was the iconography that was used to promote the event, and a lot of the flyers that came out," lamented Paul Kersey, a prominent writer for both *American Renaissance* and VDare, whose real name was actually Michael J. Thompson. "There was no coherent message."

Steve Bannon was forced out of the Trump administration in the aftermath of the events at Charlottesville, although another prominent adviser with ties to the white nationalist right, Stephen Miller, remained in place. Miller, a senior policy advisor for Trump, was believed to be the architect of the administration's hard-line immigration policies, as well as one of his principal speechwriters. He was a classmate of Richard Spencer at Duke University and worked for the Minnesota Tea Party Republican Congresswoman and conspiracy theorist Michelle Bachmann before becoming the communications director for Alabama Republican Senator Jeff Sessions. In November 2019 it was revealed that while he was working for Sessions—who would go on to become Trump's attorney general—Miller had been in regular contact with colleagues at *Breitbart News*, promoting white nationalist websites such as VDare and *American Renaissance*.

Trump himself also continued to offer succor to racists in various ways. In January 2018, during a meeting with lawmakers in the Oval Office, he reportedly stated that he wanted fewer immigrants from "shithole countries" in Africa and more from places like Norway. As the November 2018 midterm elections approached, he attacked the presence of a "caravan" of some 4,000 migrants from Central America who were traveling to the United States to claim asylum, calling the caravan an "invasion" and dispatching 5,800 troops to "harden the border." In July of 2019 he told four recently elected progressive congresswomen of color—Democratic Representatives Alexandria Ocasio Cortez of New York, Ilhan Omar of Minnesota, Rashida Tlaib of Michigan, and Ayanna Pressley of Massachusetts—that they should "go back" to the places "from which they came," leading the House to pass a formal resolution condemning the president for his "racist comments" (the vote was 240 to 187, with four Republicans supporting it). And in 2020, amid the ravages of the COVID-19 pandemic, the massive economic downturn that resulted from it, and the widespread Black Lives Matter protests that followed the killing of George Floyd by the police in Minneapolis, Minnesota, he made the shrill dog whistle of "law and order" the centerpiece of his reelection campaign.

Black Lives Matter protestors were dismissed as "anarchists, agitators, and looters." The movement itself was said to represent "hate," and on May 29, 2020, Trump tweeted a phrase associated with the notoriously racist Miami police chief Walter Headley from 1967 that "when the looting starts, the shooting starts." He defended Confederate monuments and the Confederate flag as "beautiful" symbols of "our heritage" and refused to countenance the renaming of U.S. military bases that had been named after Confederate generals. He also retweeted videos of his supporters shouting "white power!" at a Florida retirement community and others attacking Black Lives Matter protestors with paintballs and pepper spray in Portland, Oregon. When a 17-year-old militia member named Kyle

Rittenhouse killed two protestors and injured another in Kenosha, Wisconsin, in August 2020, Trump refused to condemn him. "No one will be safe in [Joe] Biden's America," he declared on the steps of the White House during the Republican National Convention, while also asserting "very modestly that I have done more for the African-American community than any president since Abraham Lincoln." Nor did he, or Attorney General William Barr, condemn attacks on the Michigan State Capitol building by white supremacists and other armed groups in opposition to the extension of "stay-at-home" orders during the COVID-19 crisis, nor even a plot to kidnap the state's governor, Democrat Gretchen Whitmer, by 13 members and associates of a militia group, the Wolverine Watchmen, in October 2020.

During the Democratic Party primaries, both Massachusetts Senator Elizabeth Warren and Vermont Senator Bernie Sanders explicitly accused Trump of being a white supremacist. The eventual winner, former vice president Joe Biden, did not go quite that far, although he did accuse Trump of fanning "the flames of white supremacy," and then, in July 2020, said he believed that Trump was America's "first" racist president. "The way he deals with people based on the color of their skin, their national origin, where they're from, is absolutely sickening," Biden said. "No sitting president has ever done this. . . . We've had racists, and they've existed. They've tried to get elected president. He's the first one that has." Asked during the first presidential debate, in September 2020, to condemn white supremacists, Trump initially prevaricated. He was then prompted by both Biden and the moderator, Fox News host Chris Wallace, to explicitly denounce the Proud Boys. He couldn't bring himself to do it. Instead Trump told the group "to stand back and stand by."

Trump lost the 2020 presidential election—by 74,223,744 votes to Biden's 81,283,485, and by 232 to 306 in the Electoral College—but the forces and attitudes he helped to unleash and sustain during his four tumultuous years in office are not likely to simply disappear with a new presidency. As this chapter has shown, white supremacists have been hard at work trying to advance and normalize their agenda for the past 20 years, rebranding themselves first as white nationalists and then as the alt-right. They have been aided in this quest by major demographic and technological changes: a significant projected decline in the number of

Americans identifying as white by 2050 and the rise of the Internet, most of all. Accurate figures are difficult to come by, but George Hawley has estimated that about 6 percent of Americans can be said to either identify with, or be sympathetic to, the white nationalist political cause—about 11 million out of a total white population of 200 million. This is hardly an insignificant number. Although many of the groups and organizations examined here remain relatively small—or exist almost entirely online—the potential for growth remains huge.

Conclusion

ON JUNE 10, 2020, PRESIDENT TRUMP announced that his first campaign rally since the coronavirus outbreak that had forced most of the country into an extensive shutdown three months earlier would take place in Tulsa, Oklahoma, on June 19. Both the date and the location were highly significant. "Juneteenth," as it is known, is an annual holiday commemorating the end of slavery in the United States. On June 19, 1865, Union Army General Gordon Granger had arrived in Galveston, Texas, to inform enslaved African Americans of their freedom, two months after Robert E. Lee's surrender at Appomattox, and more than two and half years since Abraham Lincoln had issued the Emancipation Proclamation on January 1, 1863. And in 1921 Tulsa was the site of one of the worst race massacres in American history, when white mobs attacked Black citizens and their businesses for 18 hours on May 31 and June 1. The prosperous business district of Greenwood, often referred to as "Black Wall Street," was effectively burned to the ground, over 1,000 homes were destroyed, and perhaps as many as 300 people were killed (the official death toll was 36, but historians have long cast doubt on the official figures). Trump's decision to hold his rally in Tulsa on June 19 was widely condemned, with many seeing it as just one more example of the president's willingness to engage in racist dog-whistling. Senator Kamala Harris of California, the soon-to-be vice president, went much further in her criticism, however. "This isn't just a wink to white supremacists," she said. "He's throwing them a welcome-home party."

The previous year the cable network HBO had broadcast Damon Lindelof's *Watchmen*, a reimagining of Alan Moore and Dave Gibbons's highly influential comic book series from the 1980s about hooded vigilantes and superheroes set in an alternative America in which the United States won the Vietnam War and Watergate never happened. White supremacy and racism were the central themes of Lindelof's new version of the story. Not only was the series set in Tulsa in 2019, but it opened with a graphic depiction of the 1921 massacre and featured characters such as Sister Night—played by the African-American actress Regina King—battling a racist terrorist group called the Seventh Kavalry, a kind of updated Ku Klux Klan. As well as giving renewed attention to the Tulsa massacre—which had often been forgotten, or dismissed in the almost 100 years since it had taken place—overall, *Watchmen* was a powerful reminder of William Faulkner's famous dictum in *Requiem for a Nun* (1951) that "The past is never dead. It's not even past." (*Watchmen* was not the only notable television show to tackle issues of racism and white supremacy during this time. Others include David Simon and Ed Burns's *The Plot Against America*, Misha Green's *Lovecraft Country*, and John Logan's *Penny Dreadful: City of Los Angeles*.)

Barack Obama invoked Faulkner's phrase—although misquoting it slightly—as part of a speech on American race relations that he delivered in Philadelphia on March 18, 2008, during his first presidential campaign. He was describing the structural racism that has plagued American life from its inception. "So many of the disparities that exist between the African-American community and the larger American community today can be traced directly to inequalities passed on from an earlier generation that suffered under the brutal legacy of slavery and Jim Crow," he said, and he urged Americans to remind themselves of "how we arrived at this point." Obama was right, of course, such historical reckoning is absolutely vital, not just to understanding the past, but also to moving on from it, to rectifying its mistakes, and improving things in the present— to continuing "on the path of a more perfect union," as the future president would have it. "In the white community, the path to a more perfect union means acknowledging that what ails the African-American community does not just exist in the minds of black people," Obama went on:

> that the legacy of discrimination—and current incidents of discrimination, while less overt than in the past—are real and must be addressed. Not just with words, but with deeds—by investing in our schools and our communities; by enforcing our civil rights laws and ensuring fairness in our criminal justice system; by providing this generation with ladders of opportunity that were unavailable for previous generations. It requires all Americans to realize that your dreams do not have to come at the expense of my dreams; that investing in the health, welfare, and education of black and brown and white children will ultimately help all of America prosper.

In the end, then, what is called for is nothing more, and nothing less, than what all the world's great religions demand—that we do unto others as we would have them do unto us. Let us be our brother's keeper, Scripture tells us. Let us be our sister's keeper. Let us find that common stake we all have in one another, and let our politics reflect that spirit as well.

The address took place at the National Constitution Center in Philadelphia. It was occasioned, in part, over a controversy about sermons that had been made by the Reverend Jeremiah Wright, whose church Obama attended in Chicago, that were highly critical of the history of the United States. Obama quoted Faulkner as writing, "The past isn't dead and buried. In fact, it isn't even past."

As this book has demonstrated—and as Obama himself well knew—overcoming this past, getting beyond what Obama called the racial politics of "division, and conflict, and cynicism" would not be easy. From the second Ku Klux Klan to the contemporary alt-right, white supremacists have been an almost constant feature of American life and American politics for the past 100 years. To be sure, many of these groups have been relatively small, with only a few thousand members—and sometimes less—but during the 1920s with the Klan, and again during the 1950s and early 1960s with the Citizens' Council movement, large swaths of the American population were either attracted to, or were supportive of, proudly racist organizations that were determined to keep Blacks as second-class citizens. And the rise of the Tea Party movement, the emergence of the alt-right, and the presidency of Donald Trump have further demonstrated that there is no insuperable barrier preventing racism and white supremacy from becoming a major political force in the United States once again.

What's more, even relatively small groups—and even lone individuals like Dylann Roof or J. B. Stoner—can still inflict tremendous damage on local communities and on the body politic of the United States. The actions of the Oklahoma City bomber Timothy McVeigh and his accomplices are clear evidence of that.

In general terms, three competing tendencies have existed within the world of the white supremacist right since the mid-1960s, when the success of the civil rights movement made overt racism much less acceptable in American public life. The first, initiated by the likes of Willis Carto and David Duke, and subsequently propagated by figures including Pete Peters, Jared Taylor, and Richard Spencer, has sought to renormalize white supremacy, making it once again an integral part of the political mainstream, as it was in the 1950s and 1920s (and for much of America's history before that, as well). This approach emphasizes the importance of ideas and propaganda, as it seeks to build bridges to Americans outside the white power movement on issues such as immigration, affirmative action, religious freedom, and gun rights. As part of this strategy, white supremacists have regularly rebranded themselves as "racialists," "white separatists," "white nationalists," and, most recently, as members of the "alternative-" or "alt-right."

In contrast, the second approach has been much more confrontational and revolutionary. Associated most closely with the thinking of William Pierce, Louis Beam, and Robert Miles, white supremacists of this ilk—those in The Order, the Aryan Republican Army, the Covenant, the Sword, and the Arm of the Lord, and various Klan and neo-Nazi groups—have embraced violence and even race war as a means of bringing about their goals. The third tendency has been more defeatist, emphasizing a withdrawal from the main currents of American society into separatist and survivalist compounds such as that of the Aryan Nations in Idaho, Elohim City in Oklahoma, and the Christian-Patriots Defense League in Illinois—a tendency that is also reflected in the decision of individual families like the Weavers to move to remote locations such as Ruby Ridge in the Selkirk Mountains, of course.

Initiatives like the "Northwest Territorial Imperative" might be said to reflect this latter tendency too, but the idea of creating a new territorial homeland for whites within the United States is one that has been advocated by both avowedly revolutionary groups like The Order and the would-be mainstreamers of the alt-right. In truth, there is considerable overlap and much common ground to be found among all three elements of the American racist right. Indeed, despite the vast range of differing groups that have appeared on the racist scene since the revival of the Klan in 1915—from Silver Shirts and members of the Black Legion, through Citizen Councillors, American Nazis, National Socialists, Posse members, Christian Identity adherents, militia members, and so on—there has been a remarkable continuity in the ideas and rationalizations that have been used to justify their prejudices: religious justifications;

CONCLUSION 213

biological justifications; concerns about "purity," crime, and immigration; and a recurring fear about the imminent displacement of whites—economically, politically, or demographically—from their supposedly preordained position at the top of American society. Recall, for example, the views of Citizens' Council leader Louis W. Hollis, who argued in 1965 that the United States should be "ruled by the white man until the end of time." He could have been speaking for all the white supremacists examined in this book.

The role of women within the white supremacist right has also been consistent. While some women from Elizabeth Tyler and Nell Battle Lewis to Sandra Bergeron and Lana Lokteff—who, along with her husband, Henrik Palmgren, runs the alt-right media company Red Ice—have obtained prominent positions within the movement, for the most part women have been largely consigned to their "traditional" roles as mothers, daughters, wives, and helpers, or have otherwise been celebrated for being widows of "martyrs" like Gordon Kahl and Bob Mathews. The white supremacist right remains an overwhelming masculinist movement, with all that entails.

Over many years—from the attempt to arrange a Nazi-Klan alliance during the 1970s, through the "gathering of Christian men" at Estes Park, Colorado, in 1992, and on to the Unite the Right rally in Charlottesville in 2017—there has also been a persistent effort to unify the disparate elements of the American racist right, but none has yet been successful. The movement as a whole remains fractured, contested, and highly volatile. It is a world in which internecine conflicts erupt with regular frequency, as different groups and different leaders compete for influence, members, and power, or seek to promote one set of strategies or tactics over another.

How to respond to such a situation? How should the government, the media, or anti-racist groups deal with the threat posed by these white supremacists? How should ordinary American citizens?

Answering such questions is not easy. As this book has shown, important issues of freedom of speech and freedom of association are raised by the activities of white supremacist and other racist groups. Many of the most high-profile prosecutions of movement members, from the Greensboro trial in 1979 to the Fort Smith sedition trial of 1988, have been unsuccessful. The government has also regularly overstepped its bounds, whether through the use of COINTELPRO operations against the Klan during the 1960s or the entrapment of Randy Weaver in 1989. At other times, the government has largely ignored or downplayed the threat posed by white supremacists in the United States. Indeed, a whistle-blower complaint filed by Brian Murphy, former head of the Department of Homeland Security's (DHS) intelligence division, in September 2020, accused his superiors of actively blocking the publication of a threat assessment that identified white supremacy as one of the most pressing dangers facing the United States because of how it would "reflect upon President Trump."

When DHS published a similar report in 2009, it was greeted with howls of protests from right-wing politicians and military veterans' groups, but righteous indignation and rigid partisanship are no excuse for ignorance. The threat posed by white supremacists in the United States is real, and so too—as seen repeatedly throughout this book—is the movement's targeting of the military and the police as ready sources of recruits and "expertise." Of course, only a small percentage of active-duty or former military and law enforcement personnel actually join white supremacist groups, but their presence is significant nonetheless, and there needs to be a clear strategy to deal with it. This was recognized by Dick Durbin (D-IL) when he introduced the Domestic Terrorism Prevention Act in the Senate in 2019. Among the bill's provisions was a clear requirement that the FBI regularly investigate and collect data on white supremacist and neo-Nazi infiltration of American law enforcement and the armed services.

On the other hand, there is also a danger of overexaggerating the size, significance, and appeal of white supremacist groups; of granting them too much attention, when such attention is just what they desire in order to grow and expand their influence. For example, extensive press exposés and a major congressional investigation into the Klan in 1921 led only to a significant increase in its membership, and Hillary Clinton's very public denunciation of the alt-right during the 2016 presidential election arguably elevated its importance far beyond that which it actually deserved. In our current information age, where the power of the Internet is central to the activities of mainstream and extremist political groups alike, this raises a major dilemma for social media companies such as Facebook and Twitter, which are increasingly asked to monitor or police the material that is being posted on their platforms.

In the mid-1960s, amending the "quarantine policy" that had been used successfully against Depression-era demagogues like Gerald L. K. Smith and Gerald Winrod, Rabbi Solomon Andhil Fineberg proposed a strategy of "dynamic silence" for dealing with George Lincoln Rockwell and his American Nazi Party, as he encouraged activists like those in the Jewish War Veterans to refrain from responding directly and with force to the Commander's various provocations. Subsequent generations of anti-racist activists like those in the John Brown Anti-Klan Committee, the Montana Human Rights Network, or the contemporary—and extremely amorphous—"Antifa" movement have had to wrestle with similar issues. Violent confrontations like those against Tom Metzger's California Knights of the Ku Klux Klan in the 1980s, or the pitched battles that took place in the streets of Charlottesville in 2017 have frequently been the result. Meanwhile, organizations such as the Anti-Defamation League and the Southern Poverty Law Center have pursued white supremacist organizations through the court system, often succeeding in putting them out of business altogether.

Is the answer to the threat posed by white supremacists in the United States more government monitoring, more extensive law enforcement, more street-level activism, and more speech, or is it less speech, greater repression, and increased restrictions on political activity—the kind of hate speech laws that exist in Canada or Germany, for example? These matters are unlikely to be resolved in the near future, not just because they are difficult, but because they raise fundamental questions about the nature of American society, its identity, and its history. White supremacy—in various forms—has been a major feature of that history for the past 100 years and more, and it is not going to disappear quickly, or without a fight. The rage that has driven white supremacists in the United States since the rebirth of the Klan in 1915 burns fiercely on.

Notes on Sources

INTRODUCTION

George Hawley's views on the theoretical differences between white supremacists and white nationalists are expressed in his book *Right-Wing Critics of American Conservatism* (Lawrence: University Press of Kansas, 2016). On this issue, see also Betty A. Dobratz and Stephanie L. Shanks-Meile's *"White Power, White Pride!": The White Separatist Movement in the United States* (New York: Twayne, 1997). For excellent introductions to the issues of structural racism and the social construction of race in the United States, readers should begin with Nell Irvin Painter's *The History of White People* (New York: W. W. Norton, 2010), and Carol Anderson's *White Rage: The Unspoken Truth of Our Racial Divide* (New York: Bloomsbury, 2016). Philippa Strum's *When the Nazis Came to Skokie: Freedom for Speech We Hate* (Lawrence: University Press of Kansas, 1999) examines the circumstances and results of the National Socialist Party of America's efforts to march in the village of Skokie in detail; and Clive Webb has an illuminating chapter on freedom of speech issues and white supremacy in *Rabble Rousers: The American Far Right in the Civil Rights Era* (Athens: University of Georgia Press, 2010). Both the Anti-Defamation League and the Southern Poverty Law Center run websites with essential resources on the history and current practices of the white supremacist right in the United States. They can be found at www.adl.org and www.splcenter.org, respectively

CHAPTER 1: THE BURNING CROSS

There are numerous books on the Ku Klux Klan. The best overviews are Wyn Craig Wade's *The Fiery Cross: The Ku Klux Klan in America* (New York: Simon & Schuster, 1987); David M. Chalmers *Hooded Americanism: The History of the Ku Klux Klan*, 3rd ed. (Durham, NC: Duke

University Press, 1987); David H. Bennett's *The Party of Fear: The American Far Right from Nativism to the Militia Movement* rev. ed. (New York: Vintage, 1995), 199–237; Rory McVeigh's *The Rise of the Ku Klux Klan: Right-Wing Movements and National Politics* (Minneapolis: University of Minnesota Press, 2009); and Linda Gordon's *The Second Coming of the KKK: The Ku Klux Klan of the 1920s and the American Political Tradition* (New York: Liveright Publishing Corporation, 2017).

More detailed analysis of particular aspects of the Klan is available in Charles C. Alexander's "Kleages and Cash: The Ku Klux Klan As a Business Organization, 1915–1930," *Business History Revue*, 39 (September 1965): 348–67; Kenneth T. Jackson's *The Ku Klux Klan in the City, 1915–1930* (New York: Oxford University Press, 1967); Robert Alan Goldberg's *Hooded Empire: The Ku Klux Klan in Colorado* (Urbana: University of Illinois Press, 1981); Kathleen M. Blee's *Women of the Klan: Racism and Gender in the 1920s* (Berkeley: University of California Press, 1991); the essays in Shawn Lay's edited collection *The Invisible Empire in the West: Toward a New Historical Interpretation of the Ku Klux Klan of the 1920s* (Urbana: University of Illinois Press, 1992); Nancy MacLean's *Behind the Mask of Chivalry: The Making of the Second Ku Klux Klan* (New York: Oxford University Press, 1994), which focuses on Athens, Georgia; Chris Rhomberg's "White Nativism and Urban Politics: The 1920s Ku Klux Klan in Oakland, California," *Journal of American Ethnic History*, 17, no. 2 (Winter 1998): 39–55; and Felix Harcourt's *Ku Klux Kulture: America and the Klan in the 1920s* (Chicago: University of Chicago Press, 2017).

Charles O. Jackson's "William J. Simmons: A Career in Ku Kluxism," *The Georgia Historical Quarterly*, 50, no. 4 (December 1966): 351–65 is still worth reading for its succinct biographical account of the revived Klan's first Imperial Wizard. There is no biography of his successor, Hiram Wesley Evans, but readers wanting more on David Stephenson should consult M. William Lutholtz's *Grand Dragon: D. C. Stephenson and the Ku Klux Klan in Indiana* (West Lafayette, IN: Purdue University Press, 1991). Maxim Simcovitch's "The Impact of Griffith's *Birth of a Nation* on the Modern Ku Klux Klan," *Journal of Popular Film*, 1, no. 1 (1972): 45–54, demonstrates the long-lasting appeal of Griffith's film for the racist right in the United States, while Tom Rice provides a fascinating account of the Klan's own brief foray into the film industry in "'The True

Story of the Ku Klux Klan': Defining the Klan through Film," *Journal of American Studies* 42, no. 3 (December 2008): 471–88. The larger history of the Immigration Act of 1924 and the eugenics movement of the 1920s is covered in Daniel Okrent's *The Guarded Gate: Bigotry, Eugenics, and the Law That Kept Two Generations of Jews, Italians and Other European Immigrants Out of America* (New York: Scribner, 2019). Finally, Rory McVeigh and Kevin Estep offer a revealing comparison between the second Klan and the appeal of Donald Trump in *The Politics of Losing: Trump, the Klan, and the Mainstreaming of Resentment* (New York: Columbia University Press, 2019).

Scott Beekman's *William Dudley Pelley: A Life in Right-Wing Extremism and the Occult* (Syracuse, NY: Syracuse University Press, 2005) is an excellent study of the self-styled American führer, but Suzanne G. Ledeboer's "The Man Who Would Be Hitler: William Dudley Pelley and the Silver Legion," *California History*, 65, no. 2 (June 1986): 126–36 and Eckard V. Toy Jr.'s "Silver Shirts in the Northwest: Politics, Prophecies, and Personalities in the 1930s," *Pacific Northwest Quarterly* (October 1989): 139–46, are also invaluable. On the Black Legion and other "fascists" of the 1930s, see both Peter H. Amann's "Vigilante Fascism: The Black Legion as an American Hybrid," *Comparative Studies in Society and History* 25, no. 3 (July 1983): 490–524, and his additional article "A 'Dog in the Nighttime' Problem: American Fascism in the 1930s," *History Teacher*, 19, no. 4 (August 1986): 559–84, as well as Seymour Martin Lipset and Earl Raab's "The 1930's: Extremism of the Depression" in *The Politics of Unreason: Right-Wing Extremism in America, 1790– 1977*, 2nd ed. (Chicago: University of Chicago Press, 1978), and Leland V. Bell's "The Failure of Nazism in America: The German American Bund, 1936–1941," *Political Science Quarterly*, 15, no. 4 (December 1970): 585–599. The early chapters of Leo P. Ribuffo's *The Old Christian Right: The Far Right from the Great Depression to the Cold War* (Philadelphia: Temple University Press, 1983) are also essential.

CHAPTER 2: FIGHTING CIVIL RIGHTS

The best account of the Citizens' Council movement remains Neil R. McMillen's superb study *Citizens' Councils: Organized Resistance to the*

Second Reconstruction, 1954–64 (Urbana: University of Illinois Press, 1971, 1994). The movement is also considered in great detail in Numan V. Bartley's *The Rise of Massive Resistance: Race and Politics in the South During the 1950s* (Baton Rouge: Louisiana State University Press, 1969). Other important works on the various elements of the South's "massive resistance" to the *Brown* decision and the civil rights movement include Francis M. Wilhoit's *The Politics of Massive Resistance* (New York: George Braziller, 1973); George Lewis's *The White South and the Red Menace: Segregationists, Anticommunism, and Massive Resistance, 1945– 1965* (Gainesville: University Press of Florida, 2004) and *Massive Resistance: The White Response to the Civil Rights Movement* (London: Hodder Arnold, 2006); the collected essays in Clive Webb's *Massive Resistance: Southern Opposition to the Second Reconstruction* (New York: Oxford University Press, 2005); and Anders Walker's *The Ghosts of Jim Crow: How Southern Moderates Used Brown v Board of Education to Stall Civil Rights* (New York: Oxford University Press, 2009). Elizabeth Gillespie McRae offers a deeper analysis of the role played by women in *Mothers of Massive Resistance: White Women and the Politics of White Supremacy* (New York: Oxford University Press, 2018), which covers the longer period from the 1920s to the 1970s. On the importance of the Southern Manifesto, see John Kyle Day's *The Southern Manifesto: Massive Resistance and the Fight to Preserve Segregation* (Jackson: University Press of Mississippi, 2014).

More detail on the *Brown v. Board of Education* decision and its impact on the United States can be found in J. Harvie Wilkinson III's *From Brown to Bakke: The Supreme Court and School Integration, 1954–1978* (New York: Oxford University Press, 1979); Michael J. Klarman's *From Jim Crow to Civil Rights: The Supreme Court and the Struggle for Racial Equality* (New York: Oxford University Press, 2006); and also his hugely influential article "How *Brown* Changed Race Relations: The Backlash Thesis," *Journal of American History* vol. 81, no. 1 (June 1994): 81–118. Detailed and compelling studies of the school desegregation fight are available in Matthew D. Lassiter and Andrew B. Lewis's *The Moderates Dilemma: Massive Resistance to School Desegregation in Virginia* (Charlottesville: University of Virginia Press, 1998); Karen Anderson's *Little Rock: Race and Resistance at Central High School* (Princeton, NJ: Princeton University Press, 2013); and Matthew F. Delmont's *Why Busing*

Failed: Race, Media, and the National Resistance to School Desegregation (Berkeley: University of California Press, 2016).

Those interested in the attitudes, interests, and history of the South more broadly should consult C. Vann Woodward's *The Strange Career of Jim Crow* (New York: Oxford University Press, 1955, 2003); Leon F. Litwack's *Trouble in Mind: Black Southerners in the Age of Jim Crow* (New York: Vintage, 1999); James C. Cobb's *The Most Southern Place on Earth: The Mississippi Delta and the Roots of Regional Identity* (New York: Oxford University Press, 1992); Jason Sokol's *There Goes My Everything: White Southerners in the Age of Civil Rights, 1945–1975* (New York: Alfred A. Knopf, 2006); and Matthew Lassiter's *The Silent Majority: Suburban Politics in the Sunbelt South* (Princeton, NJ: Princeton University Press, 2006). W. J Cash's classic *The Mind of the South* (New York: Alfred A. Knopf, 1941) also remains indispensable.

The activities of the "third Klan" are well covered in Wyn Craig Wade's *The Fiery Cross: The Ku Klux Klan in America* (New York: Simon & Schuster, 1987) and David M. Chalmers's *Hooded Americanism: The History of the Ku Klux Klan*, 3rd ed. (Durham, NC: Duke University Press, 1987), together with Chalmer's subsequent book—which actually examines a much wider range of white supremacist groups—*Backfire: How the Ku Klux Klan Helped the Civil Rights Movement* (Lanham, MD: Rowman & Littlefield, 2003). Both Wade and Chalmers consider the careers of extremists such as John Kasper, Asa Carter, and J. B. Stoner, but the best account of their activities, as well as those of other figures such as Bryant Bowles, John Crommelin, Pedro del Valle, and Edwin Walker, is Clive Webb's excellent *Rabble Rousers: The American Far Right in the Civil Rights Era* (Athens: University of Georgia Press, 2010). John George and Laird Wilcox's *American Extremists: Militias, Supremacists, Klansmen, Communists and Others* (Amherst, NY: Prometheus Books, 1996) is also extremely useful, as are the contemporaneous accounts contained in *The Segregationists* (New York: Appleton-Century-Crofts, 1962) by James Graham Cook and *The Farther Shores of Politics: The American Political Fringe Today*, 2nd ed. (New York: Clarion, 1968) by George Thayer. On the life and career of George Lincoln Rockwell, see Frederick Simonelli's *American Fuehrer: George Lincoln Rockwell and the American Nazi Party* (Urbana: University of Illinois Press, 1999) and William H. Schmaltz's *Hate: George Lincoln Rockwell and the American Nazi Party* (Washington,

DC: Brassey's, 2000), as well as Rockwell's own account, *This Time the World* (Arlington, VA: Parliament House, 1963).

There are a number of books on the FBI's COINTELPRO campaign against the Klan and other white supremacist groups, including Frank J. Donner's *The Age of Surveillance: The Aims and Methods of America's Political Intelligence System* (New York: Alfred A. Knopf, 1980); Kenneth O'Reilly's *"Race Matters": The FBI's Secret File on Black America, 1960–1972* (New York: Free Press, 1989); Michael Newton's *The FBI and the Ku Klux Klan: A Critical History* (Jefferson, NC: McFarland, 2009); and Jay Feldman's *Manufacturing Hysteria: A History of Scapegoating, Surveillance, and Secrecy in Modern America* (New York, Pantheon Books, 2011). The most comprehensive, though, is David Cunningham's *There's Something Happening Here: The New Left, the Klan and FBI Counterintelligence* (Berkeley: University of California Press, 2004). More on Gary Thomas Rowe, as well as the broader implications of the FBI's informer system, can be found in Gary May's *The Informant: The FBI, the Ku Klux Klan and the Murder of Viola Liuzzo* (New Haven, CT: Yale University Press, 2011).

The complex figure of George Wallace is captured most fully in Dan T. Carter's *The Politics of Rage: George Wallace, the Origins of the New Conservatism and the Transformation of American Politics* (Baton Rouge: Louisiana State University Press, 1996), but Stephen Lesher's *George Wallace: An American Populist* (Reading, PA: Addison-Wesley Publishing Co., 1994) is also useful. The four essays in Carter's *From George Wallace to Newt Gingrich, Race in the Conservative Counterrevolution, 1963–1994* (Baton Rouge: Louisiana State University Press, 1996) should also be considered. The importance of racial issues to the development of modern American politics and the rise of conservatism in the United States are addressed in various works including Thomas Edsell and Mary Edsell's *Chain Reaction: The Impact of Race, Rights and Taxes on American Politics* (New York: W. W. Norton, 1992); Rick Perlstein's *Before the Storm: Barry Goldwater and the Unmaking of the American Consensus* (New York: Hill & Wang, 2001); Joseph E. Lowndes's *From the New Deal to the New Right: Race and the Southern Origins of Modern Conservatism* (New Haven, CT: Yale University Press, 2009); and my own *Enemies of the States: The Radical Right in America from FDR to Trump*, rev. ed. (Lanham, MD: Rowman & Littlefield, 2020). Ian Haney-López explores the history of "dog-whistle politics" in *Dog Whistle Politics: How Coded Racial Appeals Have Reinvented Racism and Wrecked the Middle Class* (New York: Oxford University Press, 2015); and the broader significance of the 1968 election is addressed in Michael Cohen's *American Maelstrom: The 1968 Election and the Politics of Division* (New York: Oxford University Press, 2016).

Not surprisingly, the historiography on the civil rights movement is enormous. Perhaps the best single-volume history is Adam Fairclough's *Better Day Coming: Blacks and Equality, 1890–2000* (London: Penguin, 2001). Other invaluable works include Gilbert Jonas's *Freedom's Sword: The NAACP and the Struggle Against Racism in America, 1909–1969* (New York: Routledge, 2005); John Dittmer's *Local People: The Struggle for Civil Rights in Mississippi* (Urbana: University of Illinois Press, 1994); David Garrow's *Bearing the Cross: Martin Luther King, Jr. and the Southern Christian Leadership Conference* (New York: W. Morrow, 1986); and Clayborne Carson's *In Struggle: SNCC and the Black Awakening of the 1960s* (Cambridge, MA: Harvard University Press, 1981, 1995). The fullest account of the key period between 1954 and 1968 is Taylor Branch's magisterial three-volume series: *Parting the Waters: America in the King Years, 1954–63* (New York: Simon & Schuster, 1988); *Pillar of Fire: America in the King Years, 1963–65* (New York: Simon & Schuster, 1998); and *At Canaan's Edge: America in the King Years, 1965-68* (New York: Simon & Schuster, 2006). Finally, Mary L. Dudziak's *Cold War Civil Rights: Race and the Image of American Democracy* (Princeton, NJ: Princeton University Press, 2000) provides a penetrating analysis of the interconnections between the Cold War and the civil rights struggle.

CHAPTER 3: THE "NEW" KLAN

There are a number of very good books on David Duke and his "new" Klan. The best remains Tyler Bridges's *The Rise of David Duke* (Jackson: University of Mississippi Press, 1984), but readers should also consult Michael Zatarian's *David Duke: Evolution of a Klansman* (New York: Pelican, 1990), together with the various essays collected in Douglas D. Rose's *The Emergence of David Duke and the Politics of Race* (Chapel Hill: University of North Carolina Press, 1992), and John C. Kuzenski's *David*

Duke and the Politics of Race in the South (Nashville, TN: Vanderbilt University Press, 1995).

Duke, the Klan, its "Nazification," as well as the broader white supremacist movement of the 1970s and 1980s are also covered extensively in Wyn Craig Wade's *The Fiery Cross: The Ku Klux Klan in America* (New York: Simon & Schuster, 1987); James Ridgeway's *Blood in the Face: The Ku Klux Klan, Aryan Nations, Nazi Skinheads, and the Rise of a New White Culture* (New York: Thunder Mouth Press, 1990); John George and Laird Wilcox's *American Extremists: Militias, Supremacists, Klansmen, Communists and Others* (Amherst, NY: Prometheus Books, 1996); Betty A. Dobratz and Stephanie L. Shanks-Meile's *"White Power, White Pride!": The White Separatist Movement in the United States* (New York: Twayne, 1997); Jeffrey Kaplan's edited collection, *Encyclopedia of White Power: A Sourcebook on the Radical Racist Right* (Walnut Creek, CA: Altamira Press, 2000); Martin Durham's *White Rage: The Extreme Right and American Politics* (London: Routledge, 2007); and Leonard Zeskind's *Blood and Politics: The History of the White Nationalist Movement from the Margins to the Mainstream* (New York: Farrar, Straus & Giroux, 2009). The journalist Philip Finch also provides an interesting contemporary study in *God, Guts, and Guns: A Close Look at the Radical Right* (New York: Seaview/Putnam, 1983).

Extensive interviews with various racist leaders including David Duke, Don Black, and William Pierce can be found in Carol M. Swain and Russ Nieli's *Contemporary Voices of White Nationalism in America* (Cambridge, MA: Cambridge University Press, 2003). Lyman Tower Sargent provides a useful collection of primary source material derived from several Klans, the American Nazi Party, the National States' Rights Party, the National Alliance, WAR, and the National Association for the Advancement of White People in *Extremism in America: A Reader* (New York: New York University Press, 1995). And Raphael S. Ezekiel offers a fascinating psychological study of various white supremacists in *The Racist Mind: Portraits of American Neo-Nazis and Klansmen* (New York: Viking, 1995).

Kathleen Belew's *Bring The War Home: The White Power Movement and Paramilitary America* (Cambridge, MA: Harvard University Press, 2018) is a compelling and detailed history of the "militarization" of the racist right from the 1970s to the 1990s, focusing especially on the impact of the Vietnam War. Readers wanting more on this area should consider James William Gibson's *Warrior Dreams: Violence and Manhood in Post-Vietnam America* (New York: Hill & Wang, 1994).

The fullest account of the Greensboro Massacre can be found in Elizabeth Wheaton's *Codename Greenkil: The 1979 Greensboro Killings* (Atlanta: University of Georgia Press, 1987)—"Greenkil" being the name the FBI assigned to investigate that had been ordered by President Jimmy Carter. Michael Newton's *The FBI and the KKK: A Critical History* (Jefferson, NC: McFarland, 2005) also offers a good analysis of the events. Signe Waller's *Love and Revolution: A Political History, A People's History of the Greensboro Massacre, Its Setting and Its Aftermath* (Lanham, MD: Rowman & Littlefield, 2002) and Sally Avery Bermanzohn's *Through Survivors' Eyes: From the Sixties to the Greensboro Massacre* (Nashville, TN: Vanderbilt University Press, 2011) are also important.

Detailed inside accounts of the anti-Klan movement are available in Bill Stanton's *Klanwatch: Bringing the Klan to Justice* (New York: Grove Weidenfeld, 1990) and Morris Dees's *A Season of Justice: The Life and Times of Civil Rights Lawyer Morris Dees* (New York: Scribner, 1991). Hilary Moore and James Tracy's *No Fascist USA!: The John Brown Anti-Klan Committee and Lessons for Today's Movements* (San Francisco: City Light Books, 2020) is a powerful history of the JBAKC and its legacy.

George Michael's *Willis Carto and the American Far Right* (Gainesville: University of Florida Press, 2008) is a fascinating account of the man and his many associates and activities. For more on the broader history of Holocaust denial, see Michael Shermer and Alex Grobman's *Denying History: Who Says the Holocaust Never Happened and Why Do they Say it?* (Berkeley: University of California Press, 2002). For more on Francis Yockey, see Kevin Coogan's *Dreamer of the Day: Francis Parker Yockey and the Postwar Fascist International* (New York: Autonomedia, 1999). The white supremacist novels of William Pierce are discussed in detail in Eugene V. Gallagher's "God and Country: Revolution as a Religious Imperative on the Radical Right," *Terrorism and Political Violence* 9, no. 3 (1997): 63–79; and George Michael's "The Revolutionary Model of Dr. William L. Pierce," *Terrorism and Political Violence* 15, no. 3 (2003): 62–80. Zeskind's *Blood and Politics* is also worth consulting for its illuminating chapters on both Carto and Pierce.

Elinor Langer provides a comprehensive examination of the killing of Mulugeta Seraw, Tom Metzger, and WAR in *A Hundred Little Hitlers: The Death of a Black Man, the Trial of a White Racist, and the Rise of the Neo-Nazi Movement in America* (New York: Picador, 2004). See also Morris Dees and Steve Fiffer's *Hate on Trial: The Case Against America's Most Dangerous Neo-Nazi* (New York: Villard Books, 1993). For more on the music of the white power movement, readers should seek out Jonathan Pieslak's *Radicalism & Music: An Introduction to the Music Cultures of al'Qa'ida, Racist Skinheads, Christian Affiliated Radicals and Eco-Animal Rights Militants* (Middleton, CT: Wesleyan University Press, 2015). On the skinhead movement more broadly, see Mark Hamm's *American Skinheads: The Criminology and Control of Hate Crime* (Westport, CT: Praeger, 1993); and Robert Forbes and Eddie Stampton's *The White Nationalist Skinhead Movement: UK & USA, 1979–1993* (Los Angeles: Feral House, 2015).

Finally, for those interested in the broader context of the 1980s, Ronald Reagan, and the New Right, a good place to start is with Doug Rossinow's *The Reagan Era: A History of the 1980s* (New York: Columbia University Press, 2017), Jules Tygiel's *Ronald Reagan and the Triumph of American Conservation*, 2nd ed. (New York: Pearson Longman, 2006), and John S. Saloma's *Ominous Politics: The New Conservative Labyrinth* (New York: Hill & Wang, 1984). Manning Marable's views on the Reagan era are expressed in *How Capitalism Underdeveloped Black America: Problems in Race, Political Economy, and Society* (Cambridge, MA: South End Press, 2000).

CHAPTER 4: RELIGION AND REVOLUTION

The most comprehensive account of William Pottter Gale and the Posse Comitatus movement is Daniel Levitas's *The Terrorist Next Door: The Militia Movement and the Radical Right* (New York: Thomas Dunne Books, 2002), which also expertly covers groups such as the Covenant, the Sword, and the Arm of the Lord, and The Order, along with key figures such as Henry Lamont Beach, James Wickstrom, and Gordon Kahl. More specific detail on Kahl's life and politics is provided in James Corcoran's *Bitter Harvest: The Birth of Paramilitary Terrorism in the Heartland,* rev. ed. (New York: Penguin Books, 1995), and Capstan Turner and A. J. Lowery's *There Was a Man: The Saga of Gordon Kahl* (Nashville, TN: Sozo, 1985). On the farm crisis of the 1980s, see Joel Dyer's *Harvest of Rage: Why Oklahoma City is Only the Beginning* (Boulder, CO: Westview Press, 1997), and Neil Harl's *The Farm Debt Crisis of the 1980s* (Ames: Iowa State University Press, 1990). Readers with an interest in the larger historical context behind these events should consult Catherine McNicol Stock's *Rural Radicals: From Bacon's Rebellion to the Oklahoma City Bombing* (New York: Penguin, 1996), and Lawrence Goodwyn's *The Populist Moment: A Short History of the Agrarian Revolt in America* (New York: Oxford University Press, 1978).

The best overview of Identity Christianity is provided by Michael Barkun in *Religion and the Racist Right: The Origins of the Christian Identity Movement* (Chapel Hill: North Carolina University Press, 1994), but Jeffrey Kaplan's *Radical Religion in America: Millenarian Movements from the Far Right to the Children of Noah* (Syracuse, NY: Syracuse University Press, 2000), and James A. Aho's *The Politics of Righteousness: Idaho Christian Patriotism* (Seattle: University of Washington Press, 1990) are also highly recommended. Fascinating discussions of Odinism, Nazism, and other extreme right-wing religious beliefs can be found in Mattias Gardell's *Gods of the Blood: The Pagan Revival and White Separatism* (Durham, NC: Duke University Press, 2003), and Nicholas Goodrick-Clarke's *The Black Sun: Aryan Cults, Esoteric Nazism and the Politics of Identity* (New York: New York University Press, 2002). George Michael's *Theology of Hate: A History of the World Church of the Creator* (Gainesville: University Press of Florida, 2009) covers much important ground in this area too, while Mark Jurgensmyer provides an illuminating transnational perspective in *Terror in the Mind of God: The Global Rise of Religious Violence* (Berkeley: University of California Press, 2000). Glen Jeansonne's biography of *Gerald L. K. Smith: Minister of Hate* (Baton Rouge: University of Louisiana Press, 1997) is important to consider, and Matthew Avery Sutton's *American Apocalypse: A History of Modern Evangelicalism* (Cambridge, MA: Belknap Press, 2014) offers a broader study of millennialism and apocalyptic thinking in more mainstream American theologies.

James Coates's *Armed and Dangerous: The Rise of the Survivalist Right*, rev. ed. (New York: Hill & Wang, 1995) provides an informative and highly readable account of various groups including the Covenant, the Sword, and the Arm of the Lord, the Christian-Patriot Defense League, the Posse, and The Order. Leonard Zeskind goes deeper in his analysis in *Blood and Politics: The History of the White Nationalist Movement from the Margins to the Mainstream* (New York: Farrar, Straus & Giroux: 2009), and addresses the importance of key thinkers such as William Pierce, Louis Beam, and Robert Miles in detail. Richard Butler, the Aryan Nations, and white supremacists' urgent desire for a "white homeland" are all closely examined in Evalyn A. Schlatter's *Aryan Cowboys: White Supremacists and the Search for a New Frontier* (Austin: University of Texas Press, 2006). Also important to consult are Martin Durham's *White Rage: The Extreme Right and American Politics* (London: Routledge, 2007); Howard Bushard, John R. Craig, and Myra Barnes's *Soldiers of God: White Supremacists and Their Holy War for America* (New York: Kensington Books, 1998); James Ridgeway's *Blood in the Face: The Ku Klux Klan, Aryan Nations, Nazi Skinheads, and the Rise of a New White Culture* (New York: Thunder Mountain Press, 1990); and Betty A. Dobratz and Stephanie L. Shanks-Meile, *"White Power, White Pride!": The White Separatist Movement in the United States* (London: Twayne, 1997). On the importance of computer networks and the Internet to white supremacists in the United States, see Jesse Daniels, *Cyber Racism: White Supremacy Online and the New Attack on Civil Rights* (Lanham, MD: Rowman & Littlefield, 2009). Interesting primary source material from Aryan Nations, the Covenant, the Sword, and the Arm of the Lord, the Church of Israel, the Posse Comitatus, and the Christian Defense League can be found in Lyman Tower Sargent's wide-ranging edited collection, *Extremism in America: A Reader* (New York: New York University Press, 1995).

Useful discussion of the broader social, political, economic, and cultural climate of this period is provided in Richard G. Mitchell Jr.'s *Dancing at Armageddon: Survivalism and Chaos in Modern Times* (Chicago: University of Chicago Press, 2002); James William Gibson's *Warrior Dreams: Violence and Manhood in Post-Vietnam America* (New York: Hill & Wang, 1994); Susan Jeffords's *The Remasculinization of America: Gender and the Vietnam War* (Bloomington: Indiana University Press, 1989); Jefferson Cowie's *Stayin' Alive: The 1970s and the Last Days of the Working Class* (New York: New Press, 2010); and Jules Tygiel's *Ronald Reagan and the Triumph of Conservatism* 2nd ed. (New York: Pearson, 2006). Harry J.

Jones Jr.'s *The Minutemen* (Garden City, NY: Doubleday, 1968), and my own *The World of the John Birch Society: Conspiracy, Conservatism, and the Cold War* (Nashville, TN: Vanderbilt University Press, 2014) address two of the most significant anti-communist groups of the 1960s, both of which had a significant impact on subsequent far-right groups.

The activities of The Order are well covered in many of the books already mentioned, but the group receives its most comprehensive examination in Kevin Flynn and Gary Gerhardt's *The Silent Brotherhood: Inside America's Racist Underground* (New York: Free Press, 1989). The "revolutionary turn" of the American white power movement is superbly examined by Kathleen Belew in *Bring the War Home: The White Power Movement and Paramilitary America* (Cambridge, MA: Harvard University Press, 2018). Belew also addresses the important role played by women in the movement, as does Martin Durham in chapter 6 of *White Rage*. For a more detailed consideration of this topic, see Kathleen M. Blee, *Inside Organized Racism: Women in the Hate Movement* (Berkeley: University of California Press, 2002); Jesse Daniels, *White Lies: Race, Class, Gender, and Sexuality in White Supremacist Discourse* (New York: Routledge, 1997), and the essays in Abby L. Ferber's *White Man Falling: Race, Gender and White Supremacy* (Lanham, MD: Rowman & Littlefield, 1998).

CHAPTER 5: TERROR IN THE HEARTLAND

Jess Walter provides the most detailed and compelling account of the Weaver family and the "siege" at Ruby Ridge in *Ruby Ridge: The Truth and Tragedy of the Randy Weaver Family* (New York: Regan Books, rev. ed., 2002). Other useful accounts can be found in Alan W. Bock's *Ambush at Ruby Ridge: How Government Agents Set Randy Weaver Up and Took His Family Down* (Irvine, CA: Dickens Press, 1995); and James Aho's *This Thing of Darkness: A Sociology of the Enemy* (Seattle: University of Washington Press, 1994). Sara Weaver provides her own version of events in *The Federal Siege at Ruby Ridge* (Marion, MT: Ruby Ridge, Inc., 1998).

The significance of the Estes Park gathering is examined in Leonard Zeskind's *Blood and Politics: The History of the White Nationalist Movement from the Margins to the Mainstream* (New York: Farrar, Straus &

Giroux, 2009); Kathleen Belew's *Bring the War Home: The White Power Movement and Paramilitary America* (Cambridge, MA: Harvard University Press, 2018); and Kenneth S. Stern's *A Force Upon the Plain: The American Militia Movement and the Politics of Hate* (Norman: University of Oklahoma Press, 1997). Ann Burlein provides a fascinating study of both Pete Peters's Scriptures for America and James Dobson's Focus on the Family in *Lift High the Cross: Where White Supremacy and the Christian Right Converge* (Durham, NC: Duke University Press, 2002). For more on the Christian Right of this period, see Sara Diamond's *Spiritual Warfare: The Politics of the Christian Right* (Boston: South End Press, 1999).

There are numerous studies of events at Waco. Dick J. Reavis provides a good overview in *The Ashes of Waco: An Investigation* (New York: Simon & Schuster, 1995), as do James Tarbor and Eugene Gallagher in *Why Waco?: Cults and the Battle for Religious Freedom in America* (Berkeley: University of California Press, 1995). But the differing perspectives provided in the essay collections *Armageddon in Waco: Critical Perspectives on the Branch Davidian Conflict* (Chicago: University of Chicago Press, 1995), edited by Stuart Wright, and *From the Ashes: Making Sense of Waco* (Lanham, MD: Rowman & Littlefield, 1994), edited by James R. Lewis, are also invaluable. For a detailed insider account, see David Thibodeau and Leon Whiteson's *A Place Called Waco: A Survivor's Story* (New York: Public Affairs, 1999). For more on the "militarization" of American law enforcement during the 1990s, see David B. Kopel and Paul H. Blackman's *No More Wacos: What's Wrong with Federal Law Enforcement and How to Fix It* (Amherst, NY: Prometheus Books, 1997); and Peter B. Kraska's *Militarizing the American Criminal Justice System: The Changing Roles of the Armed Forces and the Police* (Boston: Northeastern University Press, 2001).

There is also an extensive literature on the militia movement. In addition to Stern's aforementioned *A Force Upon the Plain*, the most informative and interesting works on the subject include Morris Dees and James Corcoran's *Gathering Storm: America's Militia Threat* (New York: Harper Perennial, 1996); Richard Abanes's *American Militias: Rebellion, Racism and Religion* (Downers Grove, IL: InterVarsity Press, 1996); Robert L. Snow's *Terrorists Among Us: The Militia Threat* (Cambridge, MA: Perseus, 2002); JoEllen McNergney Vinyard's *Right in Michigan's*

Grassroots: From the KKK to the Michigan Militia (Ann Arbor: University of Michigan Press, 2011); Steven Chermak's *Searching for a Demon: The Media Construction on the Militia Movement* (Boston: Northeastern University Press, 2002); and Daniel Levitas's *The Terrorist Next Door: The Militia Movement and the Radical Right* (New York: Thomas Dunne Books, 2002). The best collection of primary source material of the militias is my own *Homegrown Revolutionaries: An American Militia Reader* (Norwich, UK: Arthur Miller Centre for American Studies, University of East Anglia, 1999). For a detailed examination of how militia groups sought to present themselves as American "patriots," as well as their use—and abuse—of American history, readers should consult my book *American Extremism: History, Politics and the Militia Movement* (London: Routledge, 2004), and Robert H. Churchill's *To Shake Their Guns in the Tyrant's Face: Libertarian Political Violence and the Origins of the Militia Movement* (Ann Arbor: University of Michigan Press, 2009). Larry Pratt's views on citizen militias can be found in *Armed People Victorious* (Springfield, VA: Gun Owners of America, 1990), as well as the edited collection *Safeguarding Liberty: The Constitution and Citizen Militias* (Franklin, TN: Legacy Communications, 1995), for which he provided the introduction, "Firearms: The People's Liberty Teeth."

Penetrating examinations of both the militias and the broader Patriot movement can also be found in Carolyn Gallaher's *On the Fault Line: Race, Class and the American Patriot Movement* (Lanham, MD: Rowman & Littlefield, 2002); Martin Durham's *The Christian Right, the Far Right and the Boundaries of American Conservatism* (Manchester, UK: University of Manchester Press, 2000); and Chip Berlet and Matthew N. Lyons's *Right-Wing Populism in America: Too Close for Comfort* (New York: The Guildford Press, 2000). In addition, Evelyn A. Schlatter and David A. Niewert provide compelling studies of these movements in the Pacific Northwest in their respective works, *Aryan Cowboys: White Supremacists and the Search for a New Frontier* (Austin: University of Texas Press, 2006) and *In God's Country: The Patriot Movement and the Pacific Northwest* (Pullman: Washington State University Press, 1999). Jane Kramer offers a fascinating account of John Pitner, the head of the Washington State Militia, in *Lone Patriot: The Short Career of an American Militiaman* (New York: Vintage, 2002).

Lou Michael and Dan Herbeck's biography of Timothy McVeigh, *American Terrorist: Timothy McVeigh and the Oklahoma City Bombing* (New York: Regan Books, 2001) is compelling and richly detailed. The books I found to be most useful in coming to terms with both the history and the various conspiracy theories surrounding the Oklahoma City bombing were Mark Hamm's *Apocalypse in Oklahoma: Waco and Ruby Ridge Revenged* (Boston: Northeastern University Press, 1997) and *In Bad Company: America's Terrorist Underground* (Boston: Northeastern University Press, 2002); Stephen Jones and Peter Israel's *Others Unknown: The Oklahoma City Bombing Case and Conspiracy* (New York: Public Affairs, 1998); Stuart Wright's *Patriots, Politics, and the Oklahoma City Bombing* (New York: Cambridge University Press, 2007); and Andrew Gumble and Roger Charles' *Oklahoma City: What the Investigation Missed—and Why It Still Matters* (New York: William Morrow, 2012). On the long-term impact of the bombing on American society, see Edward T. Linenthal's *The Unfinished Bombing: Oklahoma City in American Memory* (Oxford, UK: Oxford University Press, 2001).

Kerry Noble is a former leading member of the Covenant, the Sword, and the Arm of the Lord, who has renounced his racist beliefs. In 1998 he wrote *Tabernacle of Hate: Why They Bombed Oklahoma City* (Prescott, ON, Canada: Voyageur Publishing). A substantially revised edition, *Tabernacle of Hate: Seduction into Right-Wing Extremism* (Syracuse, NY: Syracuse University Press) was published in 2011. Both are important to consider. For an "insider view" of Elohim City, see Somer Shook, Wesley Delano, and Robert W. Balch's article "Elohim City: A Participant-Observer Study of a Christian Identity Compound," *Novo Religio: The Journal of Alternate and Emergent Religions* 2, no. 2 (April 1999): 245–65. And, for more on "lone wolf" terrorism, readers should consult George Michael's *Lone Wolf Terror and the Rise of Leaderless Resistance* (Nashville, TN: Vanderbilt University Press, 2012); and Mark Hamm and Ramón Spaaij's *The Age of Lone Wolf Terrorism* (New York: Columbia University Press, 2017).

CHAPTER 6: FACING THE PRESIDENT

The fullest account of the new, white nationalist movement in the United States at the beginning of the twenty-first century is Carol M. Swain's *The New White Nationalism in America: Its Challenge to Integration* (New York: Cambridge University Press, 2002). See also the detailed interviews with Jared Taylor, Reno Wolfe, Don Black, and David Duke in *Contemporary Voices of White Nationalism in America* (New York: Cambridge University Press, 2002) edited by Swain and Russ Nieli. Leonard Zeskind's discussion of white nationalism, the neo-Confederate movement, and the impact of 9/11 on white supremacy in *Blood and Politics: The History of the White Nationalist Movement from the Margins to the Mainstream* (New York: Farrar, Straus & Giroux, 2009) is also important, as is George Hawley's chapter on white nationalism in *Right-Wing Critics of American Conservatism* (Lawrence: University Press of Kansas, 2016). Vegas Tenold and Seyward Darby bring the story up to date in their respective books *Everything You Love Will Burn: Inside the Rebirth of White Nationalism in America* (New York: Nation Books, 2018) and *Sisters in Hate: American Women on the Front Lines of White Nationalism* (New York: Little, Brown, 2020).

Two fascinating accounts of young men finding their way out of the contemporary world of white supremacy can be found in Christian Picciolini's *White American Youth: My Descent into America's Most Violent Hate Movement and How I Got Out* (New York: Hachette Books, 2007); and Eli Saslow's *Rising Out of Hatred: The Awakening of a Former White Nationalist* (New York: Anchor Books, 2019), which concerns Don Black's son, Derek Black. Michael Kimmel provides a scholarly examination of this process in *Healing from Hate: How Young Men Get Into—And Out Of—Violent Extremism* (Oakland: University of California Press, 2018). Kimmel's earlier book, *Angry White Men: American Masculinity at the End of an Era* (New York: Nation Books, 2013), also contains useful insights.

Harel Shapra examines the border vigilantes of The Minutemen and other anti-immigrant organizations in *Waiting for José: The Minutemen's Pursuit of America* (Princeton, NJ: Princeton University Press, 2017), as do Justin Akers Chacón and Mike Davis in *No One is Illegal: Fighting Racism and State Violence on the U.S.-Mexico Border*, rev. ed. (Chicago:

Haymarket Books, 2018). For a broader, historical perspective, readers should consult Greg Grandin's *The End of the Myth: From Frontier to the Border Wall in the Mind of America* (New York: Metropolitan Books, 2019) and Erika Lee's *America for Americans: A History of Xenophobia in the United States* (New York: Basic Books, 2019). On the revival of the militias during this period, see Sam Jackson's *Oath Keepers: Patriotism and the Edge of Violence in a Right-Wing Antigovernment Group* (New York: Columbia University Press, 2020). The collected essays in J. Michael Martinez ed., *Confederate Symbols in the Contemporary South* (Gainesville: University Press of Florida, 2000) are also valuable.

For more on the Tea Party movement, see Kate Zernike's *Boiling Mad: Inside Tea Party America* (New York: Times Books, 2010); Will Bunch's *The Backlash: Right-Wing Radicals, High-Def Hucksters, and Paranoid Politics in the Age of Obama* (New York: HarperCollins, 2010); Ronald P. Formisano's *The Tea Party: A Brief History* (Baltimore, MD: Johns Hopkins University Press, 2013); Theda Skocpol and Vanessa Williamson's *The Tea Party and the Remaking of Republican Conservatism* (New York: Oxford University Press, 2013); and Christopher S. Parker and Matt A. Barreto's *Change They Can't Believe In: The Tea Party and Reactionary Politics in America* (Princeton, NJ: Princeton University Press, 2014).

There is a burgeoning literature on the alt-right. The best current accounts of the movement can be found in George Hawley's *Making Sense of the Alt-Right* (New York: Columbia University Press, 2017); David Neiwert's *Alt-America: The Rise of the Radical Right in the Age of Trump* (New York: Verso, 2017); Mike Wendling's *Alt-Right: From 4chan to the White House* (Halifax, Canada: Fernwood Publishing, 2018); and especially Alexandra Minna Stern's *Proud Boys and the White Ethnostate: How the Alt-Right is Warping the American Imagination* (Boston: Beacon Press, 2019). In addition, Angela Nagle and Dale Beran provide excellent guides to the complex and often bewildering world of the chans and the wider online environment of the alt-right in their books *Kill All Normies: Online Culture Wars from 4chan and Tumblr to Trump and the Alt-Right* (Winchester, UK: Zero Books, 2017), and *It Came from Something Awful: How a Toxic Troll Army Accidentally Memed Donald Trump into Office* (New York: All Points Books, 2019). Detailed consideration of the wider men's rights movement is available in Laura Bates' *The Men Who Hate Women: From Incels to Pick Up Artists, the Truth About Extreme Misog-*

yny and How it Affects Us All (London: Simon & Schuster, 2020). The collected essays in Mark Sedgwick's *Key Thinkers of the Radical Right: Behind the New Threat to Liberal Democracy* (New York: Oxford University Press, 2019), in which various scholars examine the thought and ideas of Alain de Benoist, Jared Taylor, Paul Gottfried, Richard Spencer, and Greg Johnson, among others, is also vital to consult. A wider, global perspective on the current "fourth wave" of radical right activity taking place around the world is provided by Cas Mudde in *The Far Right Today* (Cambridge, UK: Polity Press, 2019); and Amy S. Kaufman and Paul B. Sturtevant offer an intriguing analysis of how white supremacists and other extremists misuse and distort the past in *The Devil's Historians: How Modern Extremists Abuse the Medieval Past* (Toronto, Canada: University of Toronto Press, 2020).

For more on the Trump presidency, readers should consider Bob Woodward's *Fear: Trump in the White House* (New York: Simon & Schuster, 2018), together with its follow-up *Rage* (New York: Simon & Schuster, 2020); as well as Philip Rucker and Carol Leoning's *A Very Stable Genius: Donald J. Trump's Testing of America* (New York: Penguin Press, 2020); and James Poniewozik's *Audience of One: Donald Trump, Television and the Fracturing of America* (New York: W. W. Norton & Co., 2019). A longer historical perspective can be found in my own book *Enemies of the State: The Radical Right in America from FDR to Trump*, rev. ed. (Lanham, MD: Rowman & Littlefield, 2020). Masha Gessen's *Surviving Autocracy* (New York: Riverhead Books, 2020) is also useful to examine, as are Joshua Green's *Devil's Bargain: Steve Bannon, Donald Trump, and the Storming of the Presidency* (New York: Penguin Press, 2017); Jean Guerrero's *Hatemonger: Stephen Miller, Donald Trump and the White Nationalist Agenda* (New York: William Morrow, 2020); and Julie Hirschfield Davis and Michael D. Shear's *Border Wars: Inside Trump's Assault on Immigration* (New York: Simon & Schuster, 2019).

In addition, my account of both the alt-right and the Trump administration has relied on the vital reporting that has been carried out by publications such as the *New York Times*, the *Washington Post*, the *New Yorker*, *The Guardian*, *The New York Review of Books*, *The Atlantic*, *Harper's*, *Mother Jones*, and the *Nation*, as well as the invaluable work of the Southern Poverty Law Center and the Anti-Defamation League.

Finally, on the importance of race to Trump's 2016 election victory and in American society more broadly, see Alan Abramowitz's *The Great Realignment: Race, Party Transformation, and the Rise of Donald Trump* (New Haven, CT: Yale University Press, 2018); Rory McVeigh and Kevin Estep's *The Politics of Losing: Trump, the Klan, and the Mainstreaming of Resentment* (New York: Columbia University Press, 2019); Ashley Jardina's *White Identity Politics* (Cambridge, UK: Cambridge University Press, 2019); and Carol Anderson's *White Rage: The Unspoken Truth of Our Racial Divide* rev. ed. (New York: Bloomsbury, 2017).

CONCLUSION

Detailed accounts of the Tulsa massacre can be found in Tim Madigan's *The Burning: The Tulsa Race Massacre of 1921* (New York: St. Martins Griffin, 2003), and Alfred L. Brophy's *Reconstructing the Dreamland: The Tulsa Riot of 1921, Race, Reparations, and Reconciliation* (New York: Oxford University Press, 2003). Interested readers should certainly view David Lindoff's brilliant version of *Watchmen* (2019), and consult Alan Moore and Dave Gibbon's earlier comics, which have been collected together in *Watchmen* (New York: D.C. Comics, 1987). In August 2020, a former FBI agent named Michael German produced a report for the Brennan Center for Justice at the New York University Law School, "Hidden in Plain Sight: Racism, White Supremacy, and Far-Right Militancy in Law Enforcement." It can be found at www .brennancenter.org/our-work/research-reports/hidden-plain-sight-racism -white-supremacy-and-far-right-militancy-law.

Index

by, 80; distinct elements in
Klan revival of, 71; electoral
endeavors of, 98, 99; "Freedom
Rides North" address of, 77;
on Hurricane Katrina, 175; on
immigration, 77–78; Jefferson
Parish and, 98; KKKK leadership
and transformation of, 73–74;
"Klan Border Watch" initiative
of, 77, 100, 179; Klan membership
list sale of, 82; Klan resignation
of, 82; Klan revival success of,
78, 99–100; on Klan women, 75;
Kunstler lecture protest of, 73;
leadership style criticism of, 80;
mail fraud and tax evasion sentence
of, 174; media exploitation of, 76;
Molotov cocktails possession of,
73; NAAWP and, 173; as National
Socialist Liberation Front member,
72–73; "Nazification of the Klan"
and, 72, 80, 88, 100; Nazism and
racism research of, 72; neo-Nazi
past downplay of, 78; NOFEAR
and EURO creation of, 171,
173–74, 175; nonviolent political
action belief of, 133–34; on Obama,
181; Pierce, W., influence on, 79;
political office pursuit of, 76; on
Posse Comitatus, 109; publicity
events staging of, 76; rhetorical
skills honing of, 73; Rockwell as
hero of, 73; Shelton article on, 80;
United Kingdom tour of, 80–81;
variation order against, 81; white
identity and, 187; on white rights,
75–76; white supremacy interest of,
72; White Youth Alliance of, 73;
Wilkinson dispute with, 81

Eastland, James O., 41, 42
Edwards, Eldon Lee, 51
Effinger, Virgil H., 31–32

Eisenhower, Dwight D., 37, 50, 103–4
Ellison, James, 101, 115, 120, 130,
165, 167; Fort Smith sedition trial
and, 131; on Kahl, G., 116; on
Oklahoma bombing plan, 168
Elohim City, 6, 118, 159, 212; ARA
in, 165; Ellison and Snell in, 165;
Howe as ATF informant in, 166–
67; McVeigh, T., connections to,
166; Millar establishing of, 164–65;
Oklahoma City bombing planning
at, 167–68
Equal Employment Opportunities
Commission, 65
Essays of a Klansmen (Beam), 122
Estep, Kevin, 21–22
Estes Park, Colorado, 170, 213; armed
citizen militias creation idea in,
135, 144; far right activists meeting
at, 6; leaderless resistance idea in,
135, 144; leaders modification in,
146; participants at, 143; Peters
summit convening in, 143; Temple
and Lyons strategy at, 145; white
power movement unity attempt in,
143
European-American Unity and
Rights Organization (EURO), 174,
175
Evans, Hiram Wesley, 9, 27, 28; on
America, 26; early life of, 18; Klan
changes of, 18–19; Klan properties
sale of, 33; Ku Klux Klan
characterization of, 20; Ku Klux
Klan leadership change of, 17–18;
on new immigrants, 24; vocational
Klanishness of, 19

farm crisis, 5, 102, 107–8
Farmers Liberation Army, 109, 111
Faul, Scott, 111–12
FBI. *See* Federal Bureau of
Investigation

About the Author

D. J. Mulloy is chair and professor of history at Wilfrid Laurier University, where he specializes in the study of post-1945 U.S. history. He is the author of *American Extremism: History, Politics and the Militia Movement* (2004), *The World of the John Birch Society: Conspiracy, Conservatism and the Cold War* (2014), and *Enemies of the State: The Radical Right in America from FDR to Trump* (2018, 2020).